The Second World War

and th

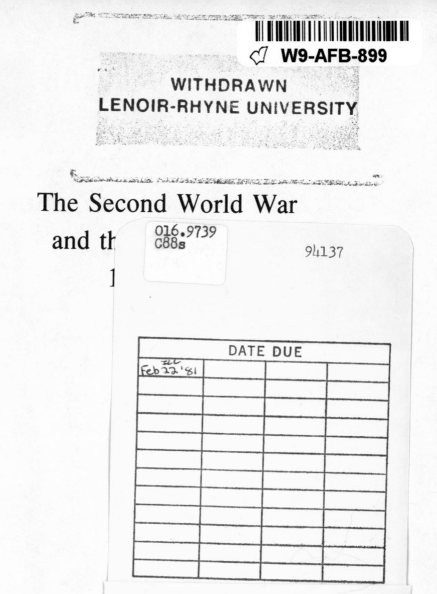

DATE DUE			
Feb 22 '81			

GOLDENTREE BIBLIOGRAPHIES
In American History
under the series editorship of
Arthur S. Link

The Second World War
and the Atomic Age,
1940-1973

compiled by

E. David Cronon
University of Wisconsin—Madison

Theodore Rosenof

AHM Publishing Corporation
Northbrook, Illinois 60062

Copyright © 1975

AHM PUBLISHING CORPORATION

All rights reserved

ISBN: 0-88295-538-1

Library of Congress Card Number: 74-28589

016.9739
C88s
94137
aug 1975

PRINTED IN THE UNITED STATES OF AMERICA
765

Contents

CONTENTS

Editor's Foreword

Goldentree Bibliographies in American History are designed to provide students, teachers, and librarians with ready and reliable guides to the literature of American history in all its remarkable scope and variety. Volumes in the series cover comprehensively the major periods in American history, while additional volumes are devoted to all important subjects.

Goldentree Bibliographies attempt to steer a middle course between the brief list of references provided in the average textbook and the long bibliography in which significant items are often lost in the sheer number of titles listed. Each bibliography is, therefore, selective, with the sole criterion for choice being the significance—and not the age—of any particular work. The result is bibliographies of all works, including journal articles and doctoral dissertations, that are still useful, without bias in favor of any particular historiographical school.

Each compiler is a scholar long associated, both in research and teaching, with the period or subject of his volume. All compilers have not only striven to accomplish the objective of this series but have also cheerfully adhered to a general style and format. However, each compiler has been free to define his field, make his own selections, and work out internal organization as the unique demands of his period or subject have seemed to dictate.

The single great objective of *Goldentree Bibliographies in American History* will have been achieved if these volumes help researchers and students to find their way to the significant literature of American history.

Arthur S. Link

Preface

We must acknowledge at the outset that this is a highly selective bibliography, for it would be impossible to include in any manageable form the entire body of historical writing about this or any other period of American history. The fact that we are dealing here with the very recent past complicates this basic dilemma. On many topics the historical record is as yet far from open or complete, and definitive scholarly work is more a long-range hope than a present reality. Accordingly, one of our major problems has been to decide which of the many popular or journalistic accounts of recent developments are sufficiently valuable to include in this bibliography. Limitations of space have obliged us to discard four or five such titles for every one retained. We have tried to include most significant books, articles, doctoral dissertations, memoirs, and collections of printed documents pertaining to the history of the United States between 1940 and 1973. No doubt other scholars will question some of our choices, and we invite their suggestions for additions to future editions of this bibliography.

We hope that the topical organization of this volume, combined with appropriate cross-references, will facilitate its use. Readers should remember, however, that any topical arrangement involves some essentially arbitrary groupings. It may therefore be necessary to consult several sections of the bibliography in order to locate all of the references desired. To cite but one example, references to the Yalta Conference may be found in sections III, C, Diplomacy of the Second World War; III, D, Europe, Russia, and the Cold War; and, more generally, V, C, Civil Liberties and McCarthyism. In a few cases where the titles are obscure we have added a brief descriptive entry.

Finally, we trust that this bibliography will serve as a helpful guide to our nation's recent past, and that readers will learn as much from using it as we did in compiling it.

E. David Cronon
Theodore Rosenof

Abbreviations

Aero Hist	Aerospace Historian
Af Hist Stud	African Historical Studies
Ag Hist	Agricultural History
Airpower Hist	Airpower Historian
Ala Hist Q	Alabama Historical Quarterly
Ala Rev	Alabama Review
Am Econ Rev	American Economic Review
Am Her	American Heritage
Am Hist Rev	American Historical Review
Am J Econ Socio	American Journal of Economics and Sociology
Am J Psychia	American Journal of Psychiatry
Am J Soc	American Journal of Sociology
Am Jew Arch	American Jewish Archives
Am Jew Hist Q	American Jewish Historical Quarterly
Am Nep	American Neptune
Am Pol Sci Rev	American Political Science Review
Am Q	American Quarterly
Am Stud	American Studies
Ann Am Acad Pol Soc Sci	Annals of the American Academy of Political and Social Science
Ann Assoc Am Geog	Annals of the Association of American Geographers
Ann Wyo	Annals of Wyoming
Ant Rev	Antioch Review
Ariz West	Arizona and the West
Ark Hist Q	Arkansas Historical Quarterly
Art Am	Art in America
Art J	Art Journal
Aust J Pol Hist	Australian Journal of Politics and History
Bapt Hist Her	Baptist History and Heritage
Brit J Soc	British Journal of Sociology
Bull Hist Med	Bulletin of the History of Medicine
Bus Hist Rev	Business History Review
Calif Hist Soc Q	California Historical Society Quarterly
Cath Hist Rev	Catholic Historical Review
Church Hist	Church History
Chron Okla	Chronicles of Oklahoma
Com Stud Soc Hist	Comparative Studies in Society and History

ABBREVIATIONS

Conn Rev	Connecticut Review
Dalhousie R	Dalhousie Review
Duquesne R	Duquesne Review
E Tenn Hist Soc Pub	East Tennessee Historical Society Publications
E Tex Hist J	East Texas Historical Journal
Fil C Hist Q	Filson Club Historical Quarterly
Fla Hist Q	Florida Historical Quarterly
For Aff	Foreign Affairs
Ga Hist Q	Georgia Historical Quarterly
Geo Wash Law Rev	George Washington Law Review
His-Am Hist Rev	Hispanic-American Historical Review
Hist	Historian
Hist Edu Q	History of Education Quarterly
Hist N H	Historical New Hampshire
Hist Pol Econ	History of Political Economy
Ind Mag Hist	Indiana Magazine of History
Indust Lab Rel Rev	Industrial and Labor Relations Review
Int Aff	International Affairs
Int J	International Journal
Int Mig Rev	International Migration Review
Int Rev Soc Hist	International Review of Social History
Inter-Am Eco Aff	Inter-American Economic Affairs
Jew Soc Stud	Jewish Social Studies
J Am Folk	Journal of American Folklore
J Am Hist	Journal of American History
J Am Stud	Journal of American Studies
J Ariz Hist	Journal of Arizona History
J Asian Stud	Journal of Asian Studies
J Black Stud	Journal of Black Studies
J Ch State	Journal of Church and State
J Con Res	Journal of Conflict Resolution
J Contemp Hist	Journal of Contemporary History
J Econ Hist	Journal of Economic History
J Geog	Journal of Geography
J Hist Behav Sci	Journal of the History of Behavioral Sciences
J Hist Ideas	Journal of the History of Ideas
J Human Rel	Journal of Human Relations
J Ill State Hist Soc	Journal of the Illinois State Historical Society
J Inter-Am Stud W Aff	Journal of Inter-American Studies and World Affairs
J Interdis Hist	Journal of Interdisciplinary History
J Miss Hist	Journal of Mississippi History
J Neg Edu	Journal of Negro Education
J Neg Hist	Journal of Negro History
J Pol	Journal of Politics
J Pop Cult	Journal of Popular Culture
J Pop Film	Journal of Popular Film
J Presby Hist	Journal of Presbyterian History
J S Hist	Journal of Southern History

ABBREVIATIONS

J San Diego Hist	Journal of San Diego History
J Soc Hist	Journal of Social History
J Soc Issues	Journal of Social Issues
J Space Rock	Journal of Spacecraft and Rockets
Jour M	Journalism Monographs
Jour Q	Journalism Quarterly
Kan Hist Q	Kansas Historical Quarterly
La Hist	Louisiana History
Lab Hist	Labor History
M W J Pol Sci	Midwest Journal of Political Science
Md Hist	Maryland Historian
Mich Acad	Michigan Academician
Mich Hist	Michigan History
Mid Am	Mid-America
Mid W Q	Midwest Quarterly
Midcon Am Stud J	Midcontinent American Studies Journal
Mil Aff	Military Affairs
Minn Hist	Minnesota History
Miss Val Hist Rev	Mississippi Valley Historical Review
Mo Hist Rev	Missouri Historical Review
Mont Mag W Hist	Montana Magazine of Western History
N C Hist Rev	North Carolina Historical Review
N D Hist	North Dakota History
N Y Hist	New York History
N Eng Q	New England Quarterly
Neb Hist	Nebraska History
New Mex Q	New Mexico Quarterly
Ohio Hist	Ohio History
Pa Hist	Pennsylvania History
Pac Aff	Pacific Affairs
Pac Hist Rev	Pacific Historical Review
Pac N W Q	Pacific Northwest Quarterly
Pers Am Hist	Perspectives in American History
Pol Am Stud	Polish American Studies
Pol Sci Q	Political Science Quarterly
Pol Soc	Politics and Society
Pop Mus Soc	Popular Music and Society
Proc Acad Pol Sci	Proceedings of the Academy of Political Science
Proc Am Philos Soc	Proceedings of the American Philosophical Society
Proc Mass Hist Soc	Proceedings of the Massachusetts Historical Society
Prol	Prologue
Pub Opin Q	Public Opinion Quarterly
Pub Pol	Public Policy
Q Rev Econ Bus	Quarterly Review of Economics and Business
Record	The Record
Reg Ky Hist Soc	Register of the Kentucky Historical Society

ABBREVIATIONS

Rev Pol	Review of Politics
Rocky Mt Law Rev	Rocky Mountain Law Review
Rocky Mt Soc Sci J	Rocky Mountain Social Science Journal
S Atl Q	South Atlantic Quarterly
S Calif Q	Southern California Quarterly
S Eco J	Southern Economic Journal
S W Hist Q	Southwestern Historical Quarterly
S W Soc Sci Q	Southwestern Social Science Quarterly
S W Stud	Southwestern Studies
School Rev	School Review
Sci Soc	Science and Society
Soc Forces	Social Forces
Soc Res	Social Research
Soc Sci	Social Science
Soc Sci Q	Social Science Quarterly
Soc Stud	Social Studies
South Q	Southern Quarterly
Sus Univ Stud	Susquehanna University Studies
Tech Cult	Technology and Culture
Tenn Hist Q	Tennessee Historical Quarterly
U S N Inst Proc	United States Naval Institute Proceedings
Utah Hist Q	Utah Historical Quarterly
Va Mag Hist Biog	Virginia Magazine of History and Biography
Va Q Rev	Virginia Quarterly Review
Vt Hist	Vermont History
W Aff Q	World Affairs Quarterly
W Econ J	Western Economic Journal
W Pol Q	Western Political Quarterly
West Va Hist	West Virginia History
Wis Mag Hist	Wisconsin Magazine of History
World Pol	World Politics
Yale Law J	Yale Law Journal
Yale Rev	Yale Review

NOTE: *The publisher and compiler invite suggestions for additions to future editions of the bibliography. Entries marked by a dagger (†) are available in paperback editions at the time this goes to press.*

I. Bibliographical Guides and Reference Works

1 BASLER, Roy P., *et al.,* eds. *A Guide to the Study of the United States of America: Representative Books Reflecting the Development of American Life and Thought.* Washington, 1960.

2 *Biographical Directory of the American Congress, 1774–1971.* Washington, 1971.

3 BLANCHARD, Carroll H., Jr., ed. *Korean War Bibliography and Maps of Korea.* Albany, N.Y., 1964.

4 BOEHM, Eric, ed. *America: History and Life: A Guide to Periodical Literature.* Santa Barbara, Cal., 1964–

5 COHEN, Hennig, ed. *Articles in American Studies, 1954–1968.* 2 Vols. Ann Arbor, Mich., 1972.

6 CROWN, James Tracy. *The Kennedy Literature: A Bibliographical Essay on John F. Kennedy.* New York, 1968.

7 *Current Biography.* New York, 1940–

8 *Dissertation Abstracts.* Ann Arbor, Mich., 1940–

9 FREIDEL, Frank, ed. *Harvard Guide to American History.* 2 Vols. Cambridge, Mass., 1974.

10 GRANTHAM, Dewey W., Jr. "The Twentieth Century South." *Writing Southern History: Essays in Historiography in Honor of Fletcher M. Green.* Eds. Arthur S. Link and Rembert W. Patrick. Baton Rouge, La., 1965.†

11 GRANTHAM, Dewey W., Jr. *The United States since 1945.* Washington, 1968.

12 HOPKINS, J. G. E., and Wayne ANDREWS, eds. *Dictionary of American History.* Vol. VI (Supplement One). New York, 1961.

13 KUEHL, Warren F., ed. *Dissertations in History: An Index to Dissertations Completed in History Departments of United States and Canadian Universities, 1873–1960.* Lexington, Ky., 1965.

14 KUEHL, Warren F., ed. *Dissertations in History: An Index to Dissertations Completed in History Departments of United States and Canadian Universities, 1961–1970.* Lexington, Ky., 1972.

15 LOVETT, Robert W., ed. *American Economic and Business History Information Sources.* Detroit, Mich., 1971.

16 MCPHERSON, James M., *et al. Blacks in America: Bibliographical Essays.* Garden City, N.Y., 1971.†

17 MASON, Elizabeth B., and Louis M. STARR, eds. *The Oral History Collection of Columbia University.* New York, 1973.

18 MILLER, Elizabeth W., and Mary L. FISHER, eds. *The Negro in America: A Bibliography.* Cambridge, Mass., 1970.†

19 MORGAN, Richard P., ed. *American History and Culture.* Mentor, Ohio, 1974–

20 MORRIS, Richard B., ed. *Encyclopedia of American History.* New York, 1970.

21 MORTON, Louis, ed. *Writings on World War II.* Washington, 1967.

22 NEUFIELD, Maurice F., ed. *A Representative Bibliography of American Labor History.* Ithaca, N.Y., 1964.

23 *The New York Times Index.* New York, 1941–

24 *Readers' Guide to Periodical Literature.* New York, 1940–

25 SEIDMAN, Joel, *et al.*, eds. *Communism in the United States: A Bibliography.* Ithaca, N.Y., 1969.

26 SOBEL, Robert, ed. *Biographical Directory of the United States Executive Branch: 1774–1971.* Westport, Conn., 1971.

27 *Social Sciences and Humanities Index* (Formerly *International Index*). New York, 1940–

28 STAPLETON, Margaret L., ed. *The Truman and Eisenhower Years, 1945–1960: A Selective Bibliography.* Metuchen, N.J., 1973.

29 STEWART, William J., ed. *The Era of Franklin D. Roosevelt: A Selected Bibliography of Periodical, Essay, and Dissertation Literature, 1945–1971.* Hyde Park, N.Y., 1974.

30 *Writings on American History.* Washington, 1952–

31 WRONE, David R. "The Assassination of John Fitzgerald Kennedy: An Annotated Bibliography." *Wis Mag Hist,* LVI (1972), 21–36.

II. General Studies

A. Period Surveys and Interpretive Accounts

32 AGAR, Herbert. *The Price of Power: America since 1945.* Chicago, 1957.†

33 AMBROSE, Stephen E., ed. *Institutions in Modern America: Innovation in Structure and Process.* Baltimore, 1967.

34 BARCK, Oscar T., Jr. *A History of the United States since 1945.* New York, 1965.

35 BERNSTEIN, Barton J. "America in War and Peace: The Test of Liberalism." *Towards a New Past: Dissenting Essays in American History.* Ed. Barton J. Bernstein. New York, 1968.†

36 BROGAN, Denis W. *The Era of Franklin D. Roosevelt: A Chronicle of the New Deal and Global War.* New Haven, Conn., 1950.

37 BROOKS, John. "A Clean Break with the Past." *Am Her,* XXI (August 1970), 4–7, 68–75.

38 BROOKS, John. *The Great Leap: The Last Twenty-Five Years in America.* New York, 1966.†

39 BUCHANAN, A. Russell. *The United States and World War II.* 2 Vols. New York, 1964.†

40 BURNER, David, *et al. A Giant's Strength: America in the 1960s.* New York, 1971.†

41 DEGLER, Carl N. *Affluence and Anxiety: 1945–Present.* Glenview, Ill., 1968.[†]

42 *Fortune* Editors, and Russell W. DAVENPORT. *U.S.A., The Permanent Revolution.* New York, 1951.

43 GOLDMAN, Eric F. *Rendezvous with Destiny: A History of Modern American Reform.* New York, 1956.[†]

44 GOLDMAN, Eric F. *The Crucial Decade—and After: America, 1945–1960.* New York, 1960.[†]

45 HEATH, Jim F. "Domestic America during World War II: Research Opportunities for Historians." *J Am Hist,* LVIII (1971), 384–414.

46 KIRKENDALL, Richard S. *The Global Power: The United States since 1941.* Boston, 1973.[†]

47 LASKI, Harold J. *The American Democracy: A Commentary and An Interpretation.* New York, 1948.

48 LERNER, Max. *America as a Civilization: Life and Thought in the United States Today.* New York, 1957.[†]

49 LEUCHTENBURG, William E. *A Troubled Feast: American Society since 1945.* Boston, 1973.[†]

50 LINK, Arthur S., and William B. CATTON. *American Epoch.* Vols. 2 & 3. New York, 1974.[†]

51 MOWRY, George E. *The Urban Nation 1920–1960.* New York, 1965.[†]

52 O'NEILL, William L. *Coming Apart: An Informal History of America in the 1960's.* Chicago, 1971.[†]

53 PERKINS, Dexter. *The New Age of Franklin Roosevelt, 1932–1945.* Chicago, 1957.[†]

54 PERRETT, Geoffrey. *Days of Sadness, Years of Triumph: The American People, 1939–1945.* New York, 1973.[†]

55 POLENBERG, Richard. *War and Society: The United States, 1941–1945.* Philadelphia, 1972.[†]

56 ROSTOW, W. W. *The Diffusion of Power: An Essay in Recent History.* New York, 1972.

57 SHANNON, David A. *Twentieth Century America.* Vol. 3. Chicago, 1974.[†]

58 TUGWELL, Rexford G. *A Chronicle of Jeopardy, 1945–1955.* Chicago, 1955.

59 WEBER, Ronald E., ed. *America in Change: Reflections on the 60's and 70's.* Notre Dame, Ind. 1972.[†]

60 WOODWARD, C. Vann, ed. *The Comparative Approach to American History.* New York, 1968.[†]

61 ZINN, Howard. *Postwar America: 1945–1971.* Indianapolis, Ind., 1973.[†]

B. National Administrations

62 ADAMS, Sherman. *Firsthand Report: The Story of the Eisenhower Administration.* New York, 1961.

63 ALBERTSON, Dean, ed. *Eisenhower as President.* New York, 1963.[†]

64 BAKER, Leonard. *The Johnson Eclipse: A President's Vice Presidency.* New York, 1966.

65 BELL, Jack. *The Johnson Treatment: How Lyndon B. Johnson Took Over the Presidency and Made It His Own.* New York, 1965.

66 BERNSTEIN, Barton J., ed. *Politics and Policies of the Truman Administration.* Chicago, 1970.[†]

67 BERNSTEIN, Barton J., and Allen J. MATUSOW, eds. *The Truman Administration: A Documentary History.* New York, 1966.[†]

68 BLUM, John Morton, ed. *The Price of Vision: The Diary of Henry A. Wallace, 1942–1946.* Boston, 1973.

69 BRANYAN, Robert L., and Lawrence H. LARSEN, eds. *The Eisenhower Administration, 1953–1961: A Documentary History.* 2 Vols. New York, 1971.

70 BURNS, James MacGregor. *Roosevelt: The Soldier of Freedom.* New York, 1970.[†]

71 CARLETON, William G. "Kennedy in History: An Early Appraisal." *Ant Rev,* XXIV (1964), 277–299.

72 CHILDS, Marquis. *Eisenhower: Captive Hero.* New York, 1958.

73 CHRISTIAN, George. *LBJ—The President Steps Down: A Personal Memoir of the Transfer of Power.* New York, 1970.

74 COCHRAN, Bert. *Harry Truman and the Crisis Presidency.* New York, 1973.

75 CROWN, James Tracy, and George P. PENTY. *Kennedy in Power.* New York, 1961.

76 DANIELS, Jonathan. *The Man of Independence.* Philadelphia, 1950.

77 DONALD, Aïda Di Pace, ed. *John F. Kennedy and the New Frontier.* New York, 1966.[†]

78 DONOVAN, Robert J. *Eisenhower: The Inside Story.* New York, 1956.

79 EISENHOWER, Dwight D. *The White House Years.* 2 Vols. Garden City, N.Y., 1963–1965.

80 EVANS, Rowland, and Robert D. NOVAK. *Lyndon B. Johnson: The Exercise of Power.* New York, 1966.

81 EVANS, Rowland, and Robert D. NOVAK. *Nixon in the White House: The Frustration of Power.* New York, 1971.[†]

82 FAIRLIE, Henry. *The Kennedy Promise: The Politics of Expectation.* Garden City, N.Y., 1973.

83 FRIER, David A. *Conflict of Interest in the Eisenhower Administration.* Ames, Iowa, 1969.

84 FULLER, Helen. *Year of Trial: Kennedy's Crucial Decisions.* New York, 1962.

85 GOLDMAN, Eric F. *The Tragedy of Lyndon Johnson.* New York, 1968.[†]

86 HARTMANN, Susan M. *Truman and the 80th Congress.* Columbia, Mo., 1971.

87 HARWOOD, Richard, and Haynes JOHNSON. *Lyndon.* New York, 1973.

88 HASSETT, William D. *Off the Record with F. D. R., 1942–1945.* New Brunswick, N.J., 1958.

89 HENDERSON, Charles P., Jr. *The Nixon Theology.* New York, 1972.

GENERAL STUDIES

90 HUGHES, Emmet John. *The Ordeal of Power: A Political Memoir of the Eisenhower Years.* New York, 1963.

91 ICKES, Harold L. *The Secret Diary of Harold L. Ickes: The Lowering Clouds, 1939–1941.* New York, 1954.

92 JOHNSON, Lady Bird. *A White House Diary.* New York, 1970.[†]

93 JOHNSON, Lyndon Baines. *The Vantage Point: Perspectives of the Presidency, 1963–1969.* New York, 1971.[†]

94 JOHNSON, Walter. *1600 Pennsylvania Avenue: Presidents and the People, 1929–1959.* Boston, 1960.[†]

95 KIRKENDALL, Richard S., ed. *The Truman Period as a Research Field.* Columbia, Mo., 1967.

96 KIRKENDALL, Richard S., ed. *The Truman Period as a Research Field: A Reappraisal, 1972.* Columbia, Mo., 1974.

97 KOENIG, Louis W., ed. *The Truman Administration: Its Principles and Practice.* New York, 1956.

98 LARSON, Arthur. *Eisenhower: The President Nobody Knew.* New York, 1968.[†]

99 LASH, Joseph P. *Eleanor: The Years Alone.* New York, 1972.[†]

100 LASH, Joseph P. *Eleanor and Franklin.* New York, 1971.[†]

101 LINCOLN, Evelyn. *Kennedy and Johnson.* New York, 1968.

102 LINCOLN, Evelyn. *My Twelve Years with John F. Kennedy.* New York, 1965.

103 MANCHESTER, William. *Portrait of a President: John F. Kennedy in Profile.* Boston, 1962.[†]

104 MILLER, Merle. *Plain Speaking: An Oral Biography of Harry S. Truman.* New York, 1974.[†]

105 NEUSTADT, Richard E. "Congress and the Fair Deal: A Legislative Balance Sheet." *Pub Pol,* V (1954), 349–381.

106 NEUSTADT, Richard E. "Kennedy in the Presidency: A Premature Appraisal." *Pol Sci Q,* LXXIX (1964), 321–334.

107 NIXON, Richard M. *Six Crises.* Garden City, N.Y., 1962. Autobiographical episodes.

108 PARMET, Herbert S. *Eisenhower and the American Crusades.* New York, 1972.

109 PERKINS, Frances. *The Roosevelt I Knew.* New York, 1946.[†]

110 PHILLIPS, Cabell. *The Truman Presidency: The History of a Triumphant Succession.* New York, 1966.[†]

111 *Public Papers of the Presidents of the United States.* Washington, 1961.

112 PUSEY, Merlo. *Eisenhower the President.* New York, 1956—.

113 REICHARD, Gary Warren. "The Reaffirmation of Republicanism: Dwight Eisenhower and the Eighty-Third Congress." Doctoral dissertation, Cornell University, 1971.

114 RIEMER, Neal. "Kennedy's Grand Democratic Design." *Rev Pol,* XXVII (1965), 3–16.

115 ROBINSON, Edgar Eugene. *The Roosevelt Leadership 1933–1945.* Philadelphia, 1955.

116 ROOSEVELT, Eleanor. *This I Remember*. New York, 1949.

117 ROOSEVELT, Elliott, ed. *F. D. R. His Personal Letters, 1928–1945*. Vol. 2. New York, 1950.

118 ROSENMAN, Samuel I., comp. *The Public Papers and Addresses of Franklin D. Roosevelt*. [1940–45] 5 Vols. New York, 1941–1950.

119 ROSENMAN, Samuel. *Working with Roosevelt*. New York, 1952.

120 SALINGER, Pierre. *With Kennedy*. Garden City, N.Y., 1966.†

121 SCHLESINGER, Arthur M., Jr. *A Thousand Days: John F. Kennedy in the White House*. Boston, 1965.†

122 SHERWOOD, Robert E. *Roosevelt and Hopkins: An Intimate History*. New York, 1948.

123 SIDEY, Hugh. *A Very Personal Presidency: Lyndon Johnson in the White House*. New York, 1968.

124 SIDEY, Hugh. *John F. Kennedy, President*. New York, 1964.

125 SORENSEN, Theodore C. *Kennedy*. New York, 1965.†

126 STEINBERG, Alfred. *The Man from Missouri: The Life and Times of Harry S. Truman*. New York, 1962.

127 STEINBERG, Alfred. *Sam Johnson's Boy: A Close-up of the President from Texas*. New York, 1968.

128 THEOHARIS, Athan. "The Truman Presidency: Trial and Error." *Wis Mag Hist*, LV (1971), 49–58.

129 TOLL, William. "Policy under the Great Society: Reflections on the Sources of Policy and of Violence." *J Human Rel*, XVIII (1970), 849–874.

130 TRUMAN, Harry S. *Memoirs by Harry S. Truman*. 2 Vols. Garden City, N.Y., 1955–1956.

131 TRUMAN, Margaret. *Harry S. Truman*. New York, 1973.†

132 TUGWELL, Rexford G. *The Democratic Roosevelt: A Biography of Franklin D. Roosevelt*. Garden City, N.Y., 1957.†

133 WICKER, Tom. *JFK and LBJ: The Influence of Personality in Politics*. New York, 1968.†

C. Regional, State, and Local History

134 BECK, Warren A., and David A. WILLIAMS. *California: A History of the Golden State*. Garden City, N.Y., 1972.

135 CAVNES, Max Parvin. *The Hoosier Community at War*. Bloomington, Ind., 1961.

136 CLARK, Thomas D. *The Emerging South*. New York, 1961.

137 CONDIT, Carl W. *Chicago, 1930–70: Building, Planning, and Urban Technology*. Chicago, 1974.

138 ELLIOTT, Russell R. *History of Nevada*. Lincoln, Neb., 1973.

139 GOTTMANN, Jean. *Virginia in Our Century*. Charlottesville, Va., 1969.

140 HIGHSAW, Robert B., ed. *The Deep South in Transformation: A Symposium.* University, Ala., 1964.

141 HUBER, Richard M., and Wheaton J. LANE, eds. *The New Jersey Historical Series.* 31 Vols. Princeton, N.J., 1964–1965.

142 HULLEY, Clarence C. *Alaska: Past and Present.* Portland, Ore., 1970.

143 KLEIN, Philip S., and Ari HOOGENBOOM. *A History of Pennsylvania.* New York, 1973.

144 LANDER, Ernest McPherson. *A History of South Carolina, 1865–1960.* Chapel Hill, N.C., 1970.†

145 LARSON, T. A. *Wyoming's War Years, 1941–1945.* Laramie, Wyo., 1954.

146 LUBOVE, Roy. *Twentieth Century Pittsburgh: Government, Business and Environmental Change.* New York, 1969.†

147 MCKELVEY, Blake. *Rochester: An Emerging Metropolis, 1925–1961.* Rochester, N.Y., 1961.

148 MCREYNOLDS, Edwin C. *Missouri: A History of the Crossroads State.* Norman, Okla., 1962.

149 MILLER, William Lee. *The Fifteenth Ward and the Great Society: An Encounter with a Modern City.* Boston, 1966.

150 NASH, Gerald D. *The American West in the Twentieth Century: A Short History of an Urban Oasis.* Englewood Cliffs, N.J., 1973.†

151 NESBIT, Robert C. *Wisconsin: A History.* Madison, Wis., 1973.

152 NICHOLLS, William H. *Southern Tradition and Regional Progress.* Chapel Hill, N.C., 1960.

153 PERRIGO, Lynn I. *The American Southwest: Its Peoples and Cultures.* New York, 1971.

154 RESCHENTHALER, Patricia. "Postwar Readjustment in El Paso, 1945–1950." *S W Stud,* VI (1968), Monograph No. 21.

155 ROGERS, Ben F. "Florida in World War II: Tourists and Citrus." *Fla Hist Q,* XXXIX (1960), 34–41.

156 ROLLE, Andrew F. *California: A History.* New York, 1969.

157 SCHLEGEL, Marvin W. *Conscripted City: Norfolk in World War II.* Norfolk, Va., 1951.

158 SINDLER, Allan P. *Change in the Contemporary South.* Durham, N.C., 1963.

159 TINDALL, George B. *The Emergence of the New South, 1913–1945.* Baton Rouge, La., 1967.†

160 WATTERS, Mary. *Illinois in the Second World War.* 2 Vols. Springfield, Ill., 1951–1952.

161 WATTERS, Pat. *The South and the Nation.* New York, 1969.†

162 WIDICK, B. J. *Detroit: City of Race and Class Violence.* Chicago, 1972.

163 WOLFE, Jonathan James. "Virginia in World War II." Doctoral dissertation, University of Virginia, 1971.

164 WRIGHT, Theon. *The Disenchanted Isles: The Story of the Second Revolution in Hawaii.* New York, 1972.

III. America and the World

A. General Accounts and Foreign Policy Concepts

165 ACHESON, Dean. *Present at the Creation: My Years in the State Department.* New York, 1969.†

166 ACHESON, Dean. *Sketches from Life of Men I Have Known.* New York, 1961.

167 ADAMS, Glen W. "The UNESCO Controversy in Los Angeles, 1951–1953: A Case Study of the Influence of Right-Wing Groups on Urban Affairs." Doctoral dissertation, University of Southern California, 1970.

168 ADLER, Selig. *The Isolationist Impulse: Its Twentieth Century Reaction.* New York, 1957.†

169 AMBROSE, Stephen E. *Rise to Globalism: American Foreign Policy since 1938.* Baltimore, 1971.†

170 AMBROSIUS, Lloyd E. "The Goldwater-Fulbright Controversy." *Ark Hist Q,* XXIX (1970), 252–270.

171 AMUZEGAR, Jahangir. "Point Four: Performance and Prospects." *Pol Sci Q,* LXXIII (1958), 530–546.

172 ARMSTRONG, John P. "The Enigma of Senator Taft and American Foreign Policy." *Rev. Pol,* XVII (1955), 206–231.

173 ARON, Raymond. *The Imperial Republic: The United States and the World, 1945–1973.* Englewood Cliffs, N.J., 1974.

174 BALDWIN, David A. *Economic Development and American Foreign Policy: 1943–1962.* Chicago, 1966.

175 BARBER, Hollis W. *Foreign Policies of the United States.* New York, 1953.

176 BARKER, Charles A., ed. *Power and Law: American Dilemma in World Affairs.* Baltimore, 1971.

177 BARNET, Richard J. *Intervention and Revolution.* New York, 1968.†

178 BARNET, Richard J. *Roots of War.* New York, 1972.†

179 BASKIN, Myron A. "American Planning for World Organization, 1941–1945." Doctoral dissertation, Clark University, 1950.

180 BATEMAN, Herman E. "The Election of 1944 and Foreign Policy." Doctoral dissertation, Stanford University, 1953.

181 BEHRMAN, Jack N. "Political Factors in U.S. International Financial Cooperation, 1945–1950." *Am Pol Sci Rev,* XLVII (1953), 431–460.

182 BEMIS, Samuel Flagg. *The United States as a World Power: A Diplomatic History, 1900–1955.* New York, 1955.

183 BINGHAM, Jonathan B. *Shirt-Sleeve Diplomacy: Point 4 in Action.* New York, 1954.

184 BOHLEN, Charles E. *The Transformation of American Foreign Policy.* New York, 1969.

185 BOHLEN, Charles E. *Witness to History 1929–1969.* New York, 1969.

186 BRAEMAN, John, *et al.,* eds. *Twentieth-Century American Foreign Policy.* Columbus, Ohio, 1971.

187 BROWN, Seyom. *The Faces of Power: Constancy and Change in United States Foreign Policy from Truman to Johnson.* New York, 1968.[†]

188 BRYNIARSKI, Joan Lee. "Against the Tide: Senate Opposition to the Internationalist Foreign Policy of Presidents Franklin D. Roosevelt and Harry S. Truman, 1943–1949." Doctoral dissertation, University of Maryland, 1972.

189 BUHITE, Russell D. *Patrick J. Hurley and American Foreign Policy.* Ithaca, N.Y., 1973.

190 CALLEO, David P., and Benjamin M. ROWLAND. *America and the World Political Economy.* Bloomington, Ind., 1973.[†]

191 CAPITANCHIK, David B. *The Eisenhower Presidency and American Foreign Policy.* New York, 1969.

192 CARLETON, William G. *The Revolution in American Foreign Policy: Its Global Range.* New York, 1967.[†]

193 CAZIER, Stanford O. "CARE: A Study in Cooperative Voluntary Relief." Doctoral dissertation, University of Wisconsin, 1964.

194 CHALLENER, R. D., and John FENTON. "Which Way America? Dulles Always Knew." *Am Her,* XXII (June 1971), 12–13, 84–93.

195 COFFIN, Tristram. *Senator Fulbright: Portrait of a Public Philosopher.* New York, 1966.

196 COLE, Wayne S. *Senator Gerald P. Nye and American Foreign Relations.* Minneapolis, Minn., 1962.

197 CONNALLY, Tom, as told to Alfred STEINBERG. *My Name Is Tom Connally.* New York, 1954.

198 COTTAM, Richard W. *Competitive Interference and Twentieth Century Diplomacy.* Pittsburgh, Pa., 1967.

199 COTTRELL, Leonard Slater, and Sylvia EBERHART. *American Opinion on World Affairs in the Atomic Age.* Princeton, N.J., 1948.

200 CRABB, Cecil V., Jr. "The President, Congress, and American Foreign Relations, 1942–1952: The Quest for a Bi-Partisan Foreign Policy." Doctoral dissertation, Johns Hopkins University, 1953.

201 CURRY, George. *James F. Byrnes.* New York, 1965.

202 DARILEK, Richard E. "A Loyal Opposition in Time of War: The Republican Party and the Politics of Foreign Policy from Pearl Harbor to Yalta." Doctoral dissertation, Princeton University, 1973.

203 DAVIDS, Jules. *America and the World of Our Time: United States Diplomacy in the Twentieth Century.* New York, 1970.

204 DECONDE, Alexander, ed. *Isolation and Security.* Durham, N.C., 1957.

205 DESTLER, I. M. *Presidents, Bureaucrats, and Foreign Policy: The Politics of Organizational Reform.* Princeton, N.J., 1972.[†]

206 DIBACCO, Thomas V. "American Business and Foreign Aid: The Eisenhower Years." *Bus Hist Rev,* XLI (1967), 21–35.

207 DIBACCO, Thomas V. "Return to Dollar Diplomacy? American Business Reaction to the Eisenhower Foreign Aid Program, 1953–1961." Doctoral dissertation, American University, 1965.

208 DIVINE, Robert A., ed. *American Foreign Policy since 1945.* Chicago, 1969.†

209 DIVINE, Robert A., ed. *Causes and Consequences of World War II.* Chicago, 1969.†

210 DIVINE, Robert A. "The Cold War and the Election of 1948." *J Am Hist,* LIX (1972), 90–110.

211 DIVINE, Robert A. *Foreign Policy and U.S. Presidential Elections 1940–1960.* New York, 1974.†

212 DIVINE, Robert A. *Second Chance: The Triumph of Internationalism in America during World War II.* New York, 1967.†

213 DOBNEY, Frederick J., ed. *Selected Papers of Will Clayton.* Baltimore, 1971.

214 DONELAN, Michael. *The Ideas of American Foreign Policy.* Philadelphia, 1965.

215 DRUMMOND, Roscoe, and Gastro COBLENZ. *Duel at the Brink: John Foster Dulles' Command of American Power.* Garden City, N.Y., 1960.

216 DULLES, Eleanor Lansing. *John Foster Dulles: The Last Year.* New York, 1963.

217 DULLES, Foster Rhea. *America's Rise to World Power, 1898–1954.* New York, 1955.†

218 ELDER, Robert E. *The Information Machine: The United States Information Agency and American Foreign Policy.* Syracuse, N.Y., 1968.

219 ETZIONI, Amitai. "The Kennedy Experiment." *W Pol Q,* XX (1967), 361–380.

220 EUBANK, Keith. *The Summit Conferences, 1919–1960.* Norman, Okla., 1966.

221 FARNSWORTH, David N. *The Senate Committee on Foreign Relations (1947–1957).* Urbana, Ill., 1961.

222 FEINGOLD, Henry L. *The Politics of Rescue: The Roosevelt Administration and the Holocaust, 1938–1945.* New Brunswick, N.J., 1970.

223 FERRELL, Robert H. *George C. Marshall.* New York, 1966.

224 FITZSIMONS, Louise. *The Kennedy Doctrine.* New York, 1972.

225 *Foreign Relations of the United States.* Washington, 1957—.

226 FRIEDMAN, Saul S. *No Haven for the Oppressed: United States Policy toward Jewish Refugees, 1938–1945.* Detroit, Mich., 1973.

227 FRIEDMAN, Wolfgang. "Interventionism, Liberalism, and Power-Politics: The Unfinished Revolution in International Thinking." *Pol Sci Q,* LXXXIII (1968), 169–189.

228 GARDNER, Lloyd C. *Architects of Illusion: Men and Ideas in American Foreign Policy, 1941–1949.* Chicago, 1970.†

229 GARDNER, Lloyd C. *Economic Aspects of New Deal Diplomacy.* Madison, Wis., 1964.†

230 GARDNER, Richard N. *Sterling-Dollar Diplomacy: The Origins and the Prospects of Our International Economic Order.* New York, 1969.

231 GAZELL, James A. "Arthur Vandenberg, Internationalism, and the United Nations." *Pol Sci Q,* LXXXVIII (1973), 375–394.

232 GEORGE, Alexander L., *et al. The Limits of Coercive Diplomacy: Laos, Cuba, Vietnam.* Boston, 1971.†

233 GEORGE, James H., Jr. "United States Postwar Relief Planning: The First Phase, 1940–1943." Doctoral dissertation, University of Wisconsin, 1970.

234 GERSON, Louis L. *The Hyphenate in Recent American Politics and Diplomacy.* Lawrence, Kans., 1964.

235 GERSON, Louis L. *John Foster Dulles.* New York, 1967.

236 GEYELIN, Philip. *Lyndon B. Johnson and the World.* New York, 1966.

237 GOOLD-ADAMS, Richard. *John Foster Dulles: A Reappraisal.* New York, 1962.

238 GRABER, D. A. *Crisis Diplomacy: A History of U.S. Intervention Policies and Practices.* Washington, 1959.

239 GRABER, Doris A. "The Truman and Eisenhower Doctrines in the Light of the Doctrine of Non-Intervention." *Pol Sci Q,* LXXIII (1958), 321–334.

240 GRAEBNER, Norman A. *The New Isolationism: A Study in Politics and Foreign Policy since 1950.* New York, 1956.

241 GRAEBNER, Norman A., ed. *An Uncertain Tradition: American Secretaries of State in the Twentieth Century.* New York, 1961.†

242 GRAHAM, Charles J. "Republican Foreign Policy, 1939–1952." Doctoral dissertation, University of Illinois, 1955.

243 GRAUBARD, Stephen R. *Kissinger: Portrait of a Mind.* New York, 1973.

244 GRIMMETT, Richard F. "Who Were the Senate Isolationists?" *Pac Hist Rev,* XLII (1973), 479–498.

245 GRUNDY, Kenneth W. "The Apprenticeship of J. William Fulbright." *Va Q Rev,* XLIII (1967), 382–399.

246 GUHIN, Michael A. "Dulles' Thoughts on International Politics: Myth and Reality." *Orbis,* XIII (1969), 865–889.

247 GUHIN, Michael A. *John Foster Dulles: A Statesman and His Times.* New York, 1972.

248 GUSTAFSON, Milton O. "Congress and Foreign Aid: The First Phase, UNRRA, 1943–1947." Doctoral dissertation, University of Nebraska, 1966.

249 HALPERIN, Morton H., *et al. Bureaucratic Politics and Foreign Policy.* Washington, 1974.

250 HAMMOND, Paul Y. *The Cold War Years: American Foreign Policy since 1945.* New York, 1969.†

251 HERO, Alfred O., Jr. "American Negroes and U.S. Foreign Policy: 1937–1967." *J Con Res,* XIII (1969), 220–251.

252 HERO, Alfred O., Jr. *The Southerner and World Affairs.* Baton Rouge, La., 1965.

253 HILSMAN, Roger. *To Move a Nation: The Politics of Foreign Policy in the Administration of John F. Kennedy.* Garden City, N.Y., 1967.†

254 HOOPES, Townsend. *The Devil and John Foster Dulles: The Diplomacy of the Eisenhower Era.* Boston, 1973.

255 HOWARDS, Irving. "The Influence of Southern Senators on American Foreign Policy from 1939 to 1950." Doctoral dissertation, University of Wisconsin, 1955.

256 HULL, Cordell. *The Memoirs of Cordell Hull.* 2 Vols. New York, 1948.

257 ISRAEL, Fred L., ed. *The War Diary of Breckinridge Long: Selections from the Years 1939-1944.* Lincoln, Neb., 1966.

258 JANIS, Irving L. *Victims of Groupthink: A Psychological Study of Foreign-Policy Decisions and Fiascoes.* Boston, 1972.†

259 JEWELL, Malcolm E. *Senatorial Politics and Foreign Policy.* Lexington, Ky., 1962.

260 JOHNSON, Haynes, and Bernard M. GWERTZMAN. *Fulbright: The Dissenter.* Garden City, N.Y., 1968.

261 JOHNSON, Richard A. *The Administration of United States Foreign Policy.* Austin, Tex., 1971.

262 JOHNSON, Walter, and Francis J. COLLIGAN. *The Fulbright Program: A History.* Chicago, 1965.

263 JOHNSON, Walter, ed. *The Papers of Adlai E. Stevenson: Washington to Springfield, 1941-1948.* Boston, 1973.

264 KALB, Bernard, and Marvin KALB. *Kissinger.* Boston, 1974.

265 KANER, Norman J. "Towards a Minority of One: Vito Marcantonio and American Foreign Policy." Doctoral dissertation, Rutgers University, 1969.

266 KEIM, Albert N. "John Foster Dulles and the Federal Council of Churches, 1937-1949." Doctoral dissertation, Ohio State University, 1971.

267 KENNAN, George F. *American Diplomacy 1900-1950.* Chicago, 1951.†

268 KENNAN, George F. *Memoirs, 1925-1950.* Boston, 1967.

269 KENNAN, George F. *Memoirs, 1950-1963.* Boston, 1972.

270 KOLKO, Gabriel. *The Roots of American Foreign Policy: An Analysis of Power and Purpose.* Boston, 1969.†

271 KOLKO, Gabriel, and Joyce KOLKO. *The Limits of Power: The World and United States Foreign Policy, 1945-1954.* New York, 1972.†

272 KRAMISH, Arnold. *The Peaceful Atom in Foreign Policy.* New York, 1963.

273 KUKLICK, Bruce. "History as a Way of Learning." *Am Q,* XXII (1970), 609-628.

274 LANDAU, David. *Kissinger: The Uses of Power.* Boston, 1972.

275 LEAB, Daniel J. "Dulles at the Brink: Some Diverse Reactions from 10 Years Ago." *Jour Q,* XLIII (1966), 547-550.

276 LERCHE, Charles O., Jr. "Southern Congressmen and the 'New Isolationism'." *Pol Sci Q,* LXXV (1960), 321-337.

277 LERCHE, Charles O., Jr. *The Uncertain South: Its Changing Patterns of Politics in Foreign Policy.* Chicago, 1964.

278 LILLY, Edward P. "The Psychological Strategy Board and Its Predecessors: Foreign Policy Coordination, 1938-1953." *Studies in Modern History.* Ed. Gaetano L. Vincitorio. New York, 1968.

279 LINDBERGH, Charles A. *The Wartime Journals of Charles A. Lindbergh.* New York, 1970.

280 LODGE, Henry Cabot. *The Storm Has Many Faces: A Personal Narrative.* New York, 1973.

281 LORIMER, M. Madeline. "America's Response to Europe's Displaced Persons, 1945–1952: A Preliminary Report." Doctoral dissertation, St. Louis University, 1964.

282 LOWE, Henry Jackson. "The Planning and Negotiation of U.S. Post-War Security, 1942–1943." Doctorial dissertation, University of Virginia, 1972.

283 MCLELLAN, David S., and Charles E. WOODHOUSE. "The Business Elite and Foreign Policy." *W Pol Q*, XIII (1960), 172–190.

284 MAHAJANI, Usha. "Kennedy and the Strategy of Aid: The Clay Report and After." *W Pol Q*, XVIII (1965), 656–668.

285 MAY, Ernest R. *"Lessons" of the Past: The Use and Misuse of History in American Foreign Policy.* New York, 1973.

286 MAZUZAN, George T. "Warren R. Austin: A Republican Internationalist and United States Foreign Policy." Doctoral dissertation, Kent State University, 1969.

287 MILLER, William J. *Henry Cabot Lodge: A Biography.* New York, 1967.

288 MORSE, Arthur D. *While Six Million Died: A Chronicle of American Apathy.* New York, 1968.

289 MULDER, John M. "The Moral World of John Foster Dulles: A Presbyterian Layman and International Affairs." *J Presby Hist,* XLIX (1971), 157–182.

290 MURPHY, Robert. *Diplomat among Warriors.* Garden City, N.Y., 1964.

291 NEUSTADT, Richard E. *Alliance Politics.* New York, 1970.[†]

292 NEVINS, Allan. *The New Deal and World Affairs: A Chronicle of International Affairs, 1933–1945.* New Haven, Conn., 1950.

293 NIEBURG, Harold L. *Nuclear Secrecy and Foreign Policy.* Washington, 1964.

294 NOBLE, G. Bernard. *Christian A. Herter.* New York, 1970.

295 NURSE, Ronald Joseph. "America Must Not Sleep: The Development of John F. Kennedy's Foreign Policy Attitudes, 1947–1960." Doctoral dissertation, Michigan State University, 1971.

296 O'CONNOR, Raymond G. *Force and Diplomacy.* Coral Gables, Fla., 1972.

297 OSGOOD, Robert E. *Alliances and American Foreign Policy.* Baltimore, 1968.[†]

298 OSGOOD, Robert E., *et al. America and the World: From the Truman Doctrine to Vietnam.* Baltimore, 1970.[†]

299 OSGOOD, Robert E. *Limited War: The Challenge to American Strategy.* Chicago, 1957.

300 OSGOOD, Robert E., *et al. Retreat from Empire? The First Nixon Administration.* Baltimore, 1973.[†]

301 PACKENHAM, Robert A. *Liberal America and the Third World: Political Development Ideas in Foreign Aid and Social Science.* Princeton, N.J., 1973.

302 PATERSON, Thomas G. "Foreign Aid under Wraps: The Point Four Program." *Wis Mag Hist,* LVI (1972–1973), 119–126.

303 PENROSE, E. F. *Economic Planning for the Peace.* Princeton, N.J., 1953.

304 PERKINS, Dexter. *The American Approach to Foreign Policy.* Cambridge, Mass., 1962.[†]

305 PERKINS, Dexter. *The Diplomacy of a New Age: Major Issues in U.S. Policy since 1945.* Bloomington, Ind., 1967.[†]

306 PERLMUTTER, Oscar William. "Acheson *vs.* Congress." *Rev Pol,* XXII (1960), 5–44.

307 PERLMUTTER, O. William. "The 'Neo-Realism' of Dean Acheson." *Rev Pol,* XXVI (1964), 100–123.

308 PHILIPOSE, Thomas. "The 'Loyal Opposition': Republican Leaders and Foreign Policy, 1943–1946." Doctoral dissertation, University of Denver, 1972.

309 POOLE, Walter S. "The Quest for a Republican Foreign Policy, 1941–1951." Doctoral dissertation, University of Pennsylvania, 1968.

310 POWERS, Richard J. "Containment: From Greece to Vietnam—and Back?" *W Pol Q,* XXII (1969), 846–861.

311 PRATT, Julius W. *Cordell Hull, 1933–44.* 2 Vols. New York, 1964.

312 PRATT, Virginia Anne. "The Influence of Domestic Controversy on American Participation in the United Nations Commission on Human Rights, 1946–1953." Doctoral dissertation, University of Minnesota, 1971.

313 RADOSH, Ronald. *American Labor and United States Foreign Policy: The Cold War in the Unions from Gompers to Lovestone.* New York, 1969.[†]

314 RANGE, Willard, *Franklin D. Roosevelt's World Order.* Athens, Ga., 1959.

315 REES, David. *Harry Dexter White: A Study in Paradox.* New York, 1973.

316 REESE, Trevor R. *Australia, New Zealand, and the United States: A Survey of International Relations, 1941–1968.* New York, 1969.

317 REIFF, Henry. *The United States and the Treaty Law of the Sea.* Minneapolis, Minn., 1959.

318 ROBINS, Dorothy B. *Experiment in Democracy: The Story of U.S. Citizen Organizations in Forging the Charter of the United Nations.* New York, 1971.

319 ROOSEVELT, Eleanor. *On My Own.* New York, 1958.

320 ROSTOW, Walt W. *The United States in the World Arena.* New York, 1960.[†]

321 RUETTEN, Richard. "Harry Elmer Barnes and the 'Historical Blackout.' " *Hist,* XXXIII (1971), 202–214.

322 RUSSELL, Ruth B. *The United Nations and United States Security Policy.* Washington, 1968.

323 SCHLESINGER, Arthur M., Jr., gen. ed. *The Dynamics of World Power: A Documentary History of United States Foreign Policy 1945–1973.* 5 Vols. New York, 1973.

324 SCHLESINGER, Arthur M., Jr. *The Imperial Presidency.* Boston, 1973.

325 SELLEN, Robert W. "Old Assumptions versus New Realities: Lyndon Johnson and Foreign Policy." *Int J,* XXVIII (1973), 205–229.

326 SERAFTY, Simon. *The Elusive Enemy: American Foreign Policy since World War II.* Boston, 1972.[†]

327 SILVERMAN, Sheldon A. "At the Water's Edge: Arthur Vandenberg and the Foundation of American Bipartisan Foreign Policy." Doctoral dissertation, University of California at Los Angeles, 1967.

328 SIRACUSA, Joseph M. *New Left Diplomatic Histories and Historians: The American Revisionists.* Port Washington, N.Y., 1973.

329 SKOLNIKOFF, Eugene B. *Science, Technology, and American Foreign Policy.* Cambridge, Mass., 1967.†

330 SMITH, A. Merriman. *A President's Odyssey.* New York, 1961. Dwight D. Eisenhower.

331 SMITH, Gaddis. *Dean Acheson.* New York, 1972.

332 SMITH, Glenn H. "Senator William Langer: A Study of Isolationism." Doctoral dissertation, State University of Iowa, 1968.

333 SPAIN, August O. "International Federalism in Recent American Thought." *S W Soc Sci Q,* XXXIII (1952), 187–205.

334 SPANIER, John. *American Foreign Policy since World War II.* New York, 1968.†

335 STILLMAN, Edmund, and William PFAFF. *The New Politics: America and the End of the Postwar Era.* New York, 1961.

336 STROMBERG, Roland N. *Collective Security and American Foreign Policy: From the League of Nations to NATO.* New York, 1963.

337 SULLIVAN, Robert R. "The Politics of Altruism: An Introduction to the Food-For-Peace Partnership between the United States Government and Voluntary Relief Agencies." *W Pol Q,* XXIII (1970), 762–768.

338 SULZBERGER, C. L. *An Age of Mediocrity: Memoirs and Diaries, 1963–1972.* New York, 1973.

339 SULZBERGER, C. L. *The Last of the Giants.* New York, 1970. Foreign policy of the 1950's and 1960's.

340 SULZBERGER, C. L. *A Long Row of Candles: Memoirs and Diaries.* New York, 1969.

341 THEOHARIS, Athan. "The Republican Party and Yalta: Partisan Exploitation of the Polish American Concern over the Conference, 1945–1960." *Pol Am Stud,* XXVIII (1971), 5–19.

342 THEOHARIS, Athan G. *The Yalta Myths: An Issue in U.S. Politics, 1945–1955.* Columbia, Mo., 1970.

343 TOMPKINS, C. David. *Senator Arthur H. Vandenberg: The Evolution of a Modern Republican, 1884–1945.* East Lansing, Mich., 1970.

344 TRASK, David F. *Victory without Peace: American Foreign Relations in the Twentieth Century.* New York, 1968.

345 TRIVERS, Howard. *Three Crises in American Foreign Affairs and a Continuing Revolution.* Carbondale, Ill., 1972. The Berlin Wall, Cuban Missile, and Vietnam crises.

346 TUCKER, Robert W. *Nation or Empire? The Debate over American Foreign Policy.* Baltimore, 1968.†

347 TUCKER, Robert W. *The Radical Left and American Foreign Policy.* Baltimore, 1971.†

348 TUTTLE, William M., Jr. "James B. Conant, Pressure Groups, and the National Defense, 1933–1945." Doctoral dissertation, University of Wisconsin, 1967.

349 VAN ALSTYNE, Richard W. *American Crisis Diplomacy: The Quest for Collective Security, 1918–1952.* Stanford, Cal., 1952.

350 VAN DYKE, Vernon, and Edward LANE. "Senator Taft and American Security." *J Pol,* XIV (1952), 177–202.

351 VANDENBERG, Arthur H., Jr., ed. *The Private Papers of Senator Vandenberg.* Boston, 1952.

352 WALKER, Richard L. *E. R. Stettinius, Jr.* New York, 1965.

353 WALTON, Richard J. *Cold War and Counterrevolution: The Foreign Policy of John F. Kennedy.* New York, 1972.†

354 WALTON, Richard J. *The Remnants of Power: The Tragic Last Years of Adlai E. Stevenson,* New York, 1968.

355 WARREN, Sidney. *The President as World Leader.* Philadelphia, 1964.

356 WESTERFIELD, H. Bradford. *Foreign Policy and Party Politics: Pearl Harbor to Korea.* New Haven, Conn., 1955.

357 WHELAN, Joseph G. "George Kennan and His Influence on American Foreign Policy." *Va Q Rev,* XXXV (1959), 196–220.

358 WHITEFORD, Daniel F. "The American Legion and American Foreign Policy, 1950–1963." Doctoral dissertation, University of Maryland, 1967.

359 WILLIAMS, William Appleman. *The Tragedy of American Diplomacy.* New York, 1962.†

360 WILLOUGHBY, William R. *The St. Lawrence Waterway: A Study in Politics and Diplomacy.* Madison, Wis., 1961.

361 WINDMULLER, John P. "The Foreign Policy Conflict in American Labor." *Pol Sci Q,* LXXXII (1967), 205–234.

362 WOOLEY, Wesley T., Jr. "The Quest for Permanent Peace—American Supranationalism, 1945–1947." *Hist,* XXXV (1972), 18–31.

363 WRIGHT, C. Ben. "George F. Kennan, Scholar-Diplomat: 1926–1946." Doctoral dissertation, University of Wisconsin, 1972.

364 WRIGHT, Theodore Paul. *American Support of Free Elections Abroad.* Washington 1964.

365 WYMAN, David S. *Paper Walls: America and the Refugee Crisis, 1938–1941.* Amherst, Mass., 1968.

366 YODER, Jon A. "The United World Federalists: Liberals for Law and Order." *Am Stud,* XIII (Spring 1972), 109–129.

367 YOST, Charles W. *The Conduct and Misconduct of Foreign Affairs.* New York, 1972.

B. Entry into the Second World War

368 BAKER, Leonard. *Roosevelt and Pearl Harbor.* New York, 1970.

369 BARRON, Gloria. *Leadership in Crisis: FDR and the Path to Intervention.* Port Washington, N.Y., 1973.

370 BEARD, Charles A. *President Roosevelt and the Coming of the War 1941: A Study in Appearances and Realities.* New Haven, Conn., 1948.

371 BLUM, John Morton. *From the Morgenthau Diaries: Years of Urgency, 1938–1941.* Boston, 1965.

372 BOYLE, John H. "The Drought-Walsh Mission to Japan." *Pac Hist Rev,* XXXIV (1965), 141–161.

373 BUTOW, R. J. C. "Backdoor Diplomacy in the Pacific: The Proposal for a Konoye-Roosevelt Meeting, 1941." *J Am Hist,* LIX (1972), 48–72.

374 BUTOW, Robert J. C. "The Hull-Nomura Conversations: A Fundamental Misconception." *Am Hist Rev,* LXV (1960), 822–836.

375 CHADWIN, Mark Lincoln. *The Hawks of World War II.* Chapel Hill, N.C., 1968.†

376 CHERNY, Robert W. "Isolationist Voting in 1940: A Statistical Analysis." *Neb Hist,* LII (1971), 293–310.

377 CLEARY, Robert E. "Executive Agreements in the Conduct of United States Foreign Policy: A Case Study: The Destroyer-Base Deal." Doctoral dissertation, Rutgers University, 1969.

378 COLE, Wayne S. "America First and the South, 1940–1941." *J S Hist,* XXII (1956), 36–47.

379 COLE, Wayne S. "The America First Committee." *J Ill State Hist Soc,* XLIV (1951), 305–322.

380 COLE, Wayne S. *America First: The Battle against Intervention, 1940–1941.* Madison, Wis., 1953.

381 COLE, Wayne S. "American Entry into World War II: A Historiographical Appraisal." *Miss Val Hist Rev,* XLIII (1957), 595–617.

382 COMPTON, James V. *The Swastika and the Eagle: Hitler, the United States, and the Origins of World War II.* Boston, 1967.

383 CONROY, Hilary. "The Strange Diplomacy of Admiral Nomura." *Proc Am Philos Soc,* CXIV (1970), 205–216.

384 CURRENT, Richard N. "How Stimson Meant to 'Maneuver' the Japanese." *Miss Val Hist Rev,* XL (1953), 67–74.

385 DIVINE, Robert A. *The Reluctant Belligerent: American Entry into World War II.* New York, 1965.†

386 ESTHUS, Raymond A. "President Roosevelt's Commitment to Britain to Intervene in a Pacific War." *Miss Val Hist Rev,* L (1963), 28–38.

387 FEIS, Herbert. *The Road to Pearl Harbor: The Coming of the War between the United States and Japan.* Princeton, N.J., 1950.†

388 FEIS, Herbert. *Three International Episodes: Seen from E. A.* New York, 1966. Economic Advisor to the Department of State.†

389 FRIEDLÄNDER, Saul. *Prelude to Downfall: Hitler and the United States, 1939–1941.* New York, 1967.

390 FRIEDMAN, Donald J. *The Road from Isolation: The Campaign of the American Committee for Non-Participation in Japanese Aggression, 1938–1941.* Cambridge, Mass., 1968.†

391 GARLID, George W. "Minneapolis Unit of the Committee to Defend America by Aiding the Allies." *Minn Hist,* XLI (1969), 267–283.

392 GOODHART, Philip. *Fifty Ships That Saved the World: The Foundation of the Anglo-American Alliance.* Garden City, N.Y., 1965.

393 GOTTLIEB, Moshe. "In the Shadow of War: The American Anti-Nazi Boycott Movement in 1939–1941." *Am Jew Hist Q*, LXII (1972), 146–161.

394 GUINSBURG, Thomas N. "The George W. Norris 'Conversion' to Internationalism, 1939–1941." *Neb Hist*, LIII (1972), 477–490.

395 HAIGHT, John McVickar, Jr. *American Aid to France, 1938–1940*. New York, 1970.

396 HALSTEAD, Charles R. "Diligent Diplomat: Alexander W. Weddell as American Ambassador to Spain, 1939–1942." *Va Mag Hist Biog*, LXXXII (1974), 3–38.

397 HEINRICHS, Waldo H., Jr. *American Ambassador: Joseph C. Grew and the Development of the United States Diplomatic Tradition*. Boston, 1966.

398 HERZOG, James H. "Influence of the United States Navy in the Embargo of Oil to Japan, 1940–1941." *Pac Hist Rev*, XXXV (1966), 317–328.

399 HILTON, Stanley E. "The Welles Mission to Europe, February–March 1940: Illusion or Realism?" *J Am Hist*, LVIII (1971), 93–120.

400 JOHNSON, Walter. *The Battle against Isolation*. Chicago, 1944.

401 JONAS, Manfred. *Isolationism in America, 1935–1941*. Ithaca, N.Y., 1966.†

402 JONES, Alfred Haworth. "The Making of an Interventionist on the Air: Elmer Davis and CBS News, 1939–1941." *Pac Hist Rev*, XLII (1973), 74–93.

403 KIMBALL, Warren F. " 'Beggar My Neighbor': America and the British Interim Finance Crisis 1940–1941." *J Econ Hist*, XXIX (1969), 758–772.

404 KIMBALL, Warren F. "Lend-Lease and the Open Door: The Temptation of British Opulence, 1937–1942." *Pol Sci Q*, LXXXVI (1971), 232–259.

405 KIMBALL, Warren F. *The Most Unsordid Act: Lend-Lease, 1939–1941*. Baltimore, 1969.

406 LANE, Peter Barry. "The United States and the Balkan Crisis of 1940–1941." Doctoral dissertation, University of Washington, 1972.

407 LANGER, William L., and S. E. GLEASON. *The Undeclared War, 1940–1941: The World Crisis and American Foreign Policy*. New York, 1953.

408 LINDLEY, William R. "The Atlantic Charter: Press Release or Historic Document?" *Jour Q*, XLI (1964), 375–379, 394.

409 MCBANE, Richard L. "The Crisis in the White Committee." *Midcon Am Stud J*, IV (Fall 1963), 28–38.

410 MCCANN, Frank D., Jr. "Aviation Diplomacy: The United States and Brazil, 1939–1941." *Inter-Am Eco Aff*, XXI (Spring 1968), 35–50.

411 MILLIS, Walter. *This Is Pearl! The United States and Japan—1941*. New York, 1947.

412 RAUCH, Basil. *Roosevelt from Munich to Pearl Harbor: A Study in the Creation of a Foreign Policy*. New York, 1950.

413 RUSSETT, Bruce M. *No Clear and Present Danger: A Skeptical View of the United States Entry into World War II*. New York, 1972.†

414 RYANT, Carl G. "From Isolation to Intervention: *The Saturday Evening Post*, 1939–42." *Jour Q*, XLVIII (1971), 679–687.

415 SCHROEDER, Paul W. *The Axis Alliance and Japanese-American Relations, 1941*. Ithaca, N.Y., 1958.

416 SHERWOOD, Robert E. *Roosevelt and Hopkins.* See 122.

417 STEELE, Richard W. "Preparing the Public for War: Efforts to Establish a National Propaganda Agency, 1940–41." *Am Hist Rev,* LXXV (1970), 1640–1653.

418 TREFOUSSE, H. L. *Germany and American Neutrality, 1939–1941.* New York, 1951.

419 TUTTLE, William M., Jr. "Aid-to-the-Allies Short-of-War versus American Intervention: A Reappraisal of William Allen White's Leadership." *J Am Hist,* LVI (1970), 840–858.

420 WALKER, Samuel. "Communists and Isolationism: The American Peace Mobilization, 1940–1941." *Md Hist,* IV (1973), 1–12.

421 WILSON, Theodore A. *The First Summit: Roosevelt and Churchill at Placentia Bay 1941.* Boston, 1969.

C. Diplomacy of the Second World War

422 ARMSTRONG, Anne. *Unconditional Surrender.* New Brunswick, N.J., 1961.

423 BEITZELL, Robert. *The Uneasy Alliance: America, Britain, and Russia, 1941–1943.* New York, 1973.

424 BELLUSH, Bernard, *He Walked Alone: A Biography of John Gilbert Winant.* The Hague, 1968.

425 BLAIR, Leon Borden. "Amateurs in Diplomacy: The American Vice Consuls in North Africa, 1941–1943." *Hist,* XXXV (1973), 607–620.

426 BLASIER, Cole. "The United States, Germany, and the Bolivian Revolutionaries (1941–1946)." *His-Am Hist Rev,* LII (1972), 26–54.

427 BLUM, John Morton. *From the Morgenthau Diaries: Years of War, 1941–1945.* Boston, 1967.

428 BUHITE, Russell D. "Patrick J. Hurley and the Yalta Far Eastern Agreement." *Pac Hist Rev,* XXXVII (1968), 343–353.

429 CALDWELL, Oliver J. *A Secret War: Americans in China, 1944–1945.* Carbondale, Ill. 1972.†

430 CALLCOTT, Wilfrid Hardy. *The Western Hemisphere: Its Influence on United States Policies to the End of World War II.* Austin, Tex., 1968.

431 CAMPBELL, Thomas M. *Masquerade Peace: America's UN Policy, 1944–1945.* Tallahassee, Fla., 1973.

432 CHASE, John L. "The Development of the Morgenthau Plan through the Quebec Conference." *J Pol,* XVI (1954), 324–359.

433 CHASE, John L. "Unconditional Surrender Reconsidered." *Pol Sci Q,* LXX (1955), 258–279.

434 CLASH, Thomas Wood. "United States-Mexican Relations, 1940–1946: A Study of U.S. Interests and Policies." Doctoral dissertation, State University of New York at Buffalo, 1972.

435 CORTADA, James W. *United States-Spanish Relations, Wolfram and World War II.* Barcelona, 1971.

436 DAWSON, Raymond H. *The Decision to Aid Russia, 1941: Foreign Policy and Domestic Politics.* Chapel Hill, N.C., 1959.

437 DEANE, John R. *The Strange Alliance: The Story of Our Efforts at Wartime Cooperation with Russia.* New York, 1947.[†]

438 DIVINE, Robert A. *Roosevelt and World War II.* Baltimore, 1969.[†]

439 DRACHMAN, Edward R. *United States Policy toward Vietnam, 1940–1945.* Rutherford, N.J., 1970.

440 DULLES, Foster R., and Gerald RIDINGER. "The Anti-Colonial Policies of Franklin D. Roosevelt." *Pol Sci Q,* LXX (1955), 1–18.

441 DURRENCE, James Larry. "Ambassador Clarence E. Gauss and United States Relations with China, 1941–1944." Doctoral dissertation, University of Georgia, 1971.

442 ECKES, Alfred E., Jr. "Bretton Woods: America's New Deal for an Open World." Doctoral dissertation, University of Texas, 1969.

443 ECKES, Alfred E., Jr. "Open Door Expansionism Reconsidered: The World War II Experience." *J Am Hist,* LIX (1973), 909–924.

444 ESHERICK, Joseph W., ed. *Lost Chance in China: The World War II Despatches of John S. Service.* New York, 1974.

445 EUBANKS, Richard Kay. "The Diplomacy of Postponement: The United States and Russia's Western Frontier Claims during World War II." Doctoral dissertation, University of Texas, 1971.

446 FEIS, Herbert. *The Atomic Bomb and the End of World War II.* Princeton, N.J., 1966.

447 FEIS, Herbert. *The China Tangle: The American Effort in China from Pearl Harbor to the Marshall Mission.* Princeton, N.J., 1953.[†]

448 FEIS, Herbert. *Churchill, Roosevelt, Stalin: The War They Waged and the Peace They Sought.* Princeton, N.J., 1967.[†]

449 FEIS, Herbert. *Three International Episodes.*[†] See 388.

450 GARLOCK, Peter David. "The United States and the Indian Crisis, 1941–1943: The Limits of Anti-Colonialism." Doctoral dissertation, Yale University, 1972.

451 GLENNON, John P. " 'This Time Germany Is a Defeated Nation': The Doctrine of Unconditional Surrender and Some Unsuccessful Attempts to Alter It, 1943–1944." *Statesmen and Statecraft of the Modern West.* Ed. Gerald N. Grob. Barre, Mass., 1967.

452 GORDON, Leonard. "American Planning for Taiwan, 1942–1945." *Pac Hist Rev,* XXXVII (1968), 201–228.

453 GUERRANT, Edward O. *Roosevelt's Good Neighbor Policy.* Albuquerque, N. Mex., 1950.

454 HALPERIN, Samuel, and Irvin ODER. "The United States in Search of a Policy: Franklin D. Roosevelt and Palestine." *Rev Pol,* XXIV (1962), 320–341.

455 HARRIS, Dennis E. "The Diplomacy of the Second Front: America, Britain, Russia and the Normandy Invasion." Doctoral dissertation, University of California at Santa Barbara, 1969.

456 HAYES, Carlton J. H. *Wartime Mission to Spain, 1942–1945.* New York, 1946.

457 HEINRICHS, Waldo H., Jr. *American Ambassador.* See 397.

458 HERRING, George C., Jr. "The United States and British Bankruptcy, 1944–1945: Responsibilities Deferred." *Pol Sci Q,* LXXXVI (1971), 260–280.

459 HESS, Gary R. *America Encounters India,* 1941–1947. Baltimore, 1971.

460 HESS, Gary R. "Franklin Roosevelt and Indochina." *J Am Hist,* LIX (1972), 353–368.

461 HINES, Calvin W. "United States Diplomacy in the Caribbean during World War II." Doctoral dissertation, University of Texas, 1968.

462 JONES, Robert Huhn. *The Roads to Russia: United States Lend-Lease to the Soviet Union.* Norman, Okla., 1969.

463 KOLKO, Gabriel. *The Politics of War: The World and United States Foreign Policy, 1943–1945.* New York, 1968.†

464 LANGER, William L. *Our Vichy Gamble.* New York, 1947.†

465 LIANG, Chin-tung. *General Stilwell in China, 1942–1944: The Full Story.* New York, 1972.

466 LUKAS, Richard C. "Soviet Stalling Tactics in the Forties." *Aero Hist,* XIV (1967), 51–56.

467 MCCANN, Frank D., Jr. *The Brazilian-American Alliance, 1937–1945.* Princeton, N.J., 1973.

468 MCNEILL, William H. *America, Britain, and Russia: Their Cooperation and Conflict, 1941–1946.* New York, 1953.

469 MARTIN, James V. "Thai-American Relations in World War II." *J Asian Stud,* XXII (1963), 451–467.

470 MATHES, Michael. "The Two Californias during World War II." *Calif Hist Soc Q,* XLIV (1965), 323–331.

471 MAY, Ernest R. "The United States, the Soviet Union, and the Far Eastern War, 1941–1945." *Pac Hist Rev,* XXIV (1955), 153–174.

472 MEIER, Heinz K. *Friendship under Stress: U.S.-Swiss Relations 1900–1950.* Bern, 1970.

473 NEUMANN, William L. *After Victory: Churchill, Roosevelt, Stalin and the Making of the Peace: U.S. and Allied Diplomacy in World War II.* New York, 1967.

474 O'CONNOR, Raymond G. *Diplomacy for Victory: FDR and Unconditional Surrender.* New York, 1971.†

475 PARZEN, Herbert. "The Roosevelt Palestine Policy, 1943–1945." *Am Jew Arch,* XXVI (1974), 31–65.

476 PERLMUTTER, Oscar. "Acheson and the Diplomacy of World War II." *W Pol Q,* XIV (1961), 896–911.

477 REED, John J. "American Diplomatic Relations with Australia during the Second World War." Doctoral dissertation, University of Southern California, 1970.

478 SADLER, Charles Gill. "The Expendable Frontier: United States Policy on the Polish-German Frontier during the Second World War." Doctoral dissertation, Northwestern University, 1971.

479 SANTORO, Carmela E. "United States and Mexican Relations during World War II." Doctoral dissertation, Syracuse University, 1967.

480 SHERWOOD, Robert E. *Roosevelt and Hopkins.* See 122.

481 SHEWMAKER, Kenneth E. "The Mandate of Heaven vs. U.S. Newsmen in China, 1941–45." *Jour Q,* XLVI (1969), 274–280.

482 SMITH, Charles. "Lend-Lease to Great Britain 1941–1945." *South Q,* X (1972), 195–208.

483 SMITH, Gaddis. *American Diplomacy during the Second World War, 1941–1945.* New York, 1965.[†]

484 SMITH, Robert T. "Alone in China: Patrick J. Hurley's Attempt to Unify China, 1944–1945." Doctoral dissertation, University of Oklahoma, 1966.

485 SNELL, John L. *Illusion and Necessity: The Diplomacy of Global War, 1939–1945.* Boston, 1963.[†]

486 STANDLEY, William H., and Arthur A. AGETON. *Admiral Ambassador to Russia.* Chicago, 1955.

487 STOLER, Mark Alan. "The Politics of the Second Front: American Military Planning and Diplomacy 1941–44." Doctoral dissertation, University of Wisconsin, 1971.

488 SWEENEY, J. K. "The Framework of Luso-American Diplomatic Relations during the Second World War." *Rocky Mt Soc Sci J,* X (October 1973), 93–100.

489 SWEENEY, J. K. "Portugal, the United States and Aviation, 1945." *Rocky Mt Soc Sci J,* IX (April 1972), 77–84.

490 SWEENEY, Jerry K. "United States' Policy toward Portugal during the Second World War." Doctoral dissertation, Kent State University, 1970.

491 TUCHMAN, Barbara W. *Stilwell and the American Experience in China, 1911–1945.* New York, 1971.[†]

492 VENKATARAMANI, M. S., and B. K. SHRIVASTAVA. "The President and the Mahatma: America's Response to Gandhi's Fast, February-March 1943." *Int Rev Soc Hist,* XIII (1968), 141–173.

493 WEATHERS, Bynum Edgar, Jr. "A Study of the Methods Employed in the Acquisition of Air Bases in Latin America for the Army Air Forces in World War II." Doctoral dissertation, University of Denver, 1971.

494 WILLSON, John P. "Carlton J. H. Hayes, Spain, and the Refugee Crisis, 1942–1945." *Am Jew Hist Q,* LXII (1972), 99–110.

495 WOODS, Randall Bennett. "United States' Policy toward Argentina from Pearl Harbor to San Francisco." Doctoral dissertation, University of Texas, 1972.

496 YOUNG, Arthur. *China and the Helping Hand, 1937–1945.* Cambridge, Mass., 1963.

D. Europe, Russia, and the Cold War

497 ABEL, Elie. *The Missile Crisis.* Philadelphia, 1966.

498 ALLISON, Graham T. "Conceptual Models and the Cuban Missile Crisis." *Am Pol Sci Rev,* LXIII (1969), 689–718.

499 ALLISON, Graham T. *Essence of Decision: Explaining the Cuban Missile Crisis.* Boston, 1971.[†]

500 ALPEROVITZ, Gar. *Atomic Diplomacy: Hiroshima and Potsdam. The Use of the Atomic Bomb and the American Confrontation with Soviet Power.* New York, 1965.

501 ARKES, Hadley. *Bureaucracy, The Marshall Plan, and the National Interest.* Princeton, N.J., 1973.

502 BADER, William B. *The United States and the Spread of Nuclear Weapons.* New York, 1968.†

503 BAILEY, Thomas A. *America Faces Russia: Russian-American Relations from Early Times to Our Day.* Ithaca, N.Y., 1950.

504 BERNSTEIN, Barton J. "American Foreign Policy and the Origins of the Cold War." *Politics and Policies of the Truman Administration.* Ed. Barton J. Bernstein. Chicago, 1970.†

505 BERNSTEIN, Barton J. "The Quest for Security: American Foreign Policy and International Control of Atomic Energy, 1942-1946." *J Am Hist,* LX (1974), 1003-1044.

506 BLAND, Larry Irvin. "W. Averell Harriman: Businessman and Diplomat, 1891–1945." Doctoral dissertation, University of Wisconsin, 1972.

507 BUHITE, Russell D. "Soviet-American Relations and the Repatriation of Prisoners of War, 1945." *Hist,* XXXV (1973), 384–397.

508 BYRNES, James F. *All in One Lifetime.* New York, 1958.

509 BYRNES, James F. *Speaking Frankly.* New York, 1947. Origins of the Cold War.

510 CABLE, John N. "Arthur Bliss Lane: Cold Warrior in Warsaw, 1945." *Pol Am Stud,* XXX (1973), 66–82.

511 CABLE, John Nathaniel. "The United States and the Polish Question, 1939–1948." Doctoral dissertation, Vanderbilt University, 1972.

512 CLAY, Lucius D. *Decision in Germany.* Garden City, N.Y., 1950.

513 CLEMENS, Diane Shaver. *Yalta.* New York, 1970.†

514 CRADDOCK, Walter R. "United States Diplomacy and the Saar Dispute, 1949–1955." *Orbis,* XII (1968), 247–267.

515 DAVIS, Lynn Etheridge. *The Cold War Begins: Soviet American Conflict over Eastern Europe.* Princeton, N.J., 1974.

516 DAVISON, Walter Phillips. *The Berlin Blockade: A Study in Cold War Politics.* Princeton, N.J., 1958.

517 DECONDE, Alexander. *Half Bitter, Half Sweet: An Excursion into Italian-American History.* New York, 1971.

518 DOENECKE, Justus D. "Lawrence Dennis: Revisionist of the Cold War." *Wis Mag Hist,* LV (1972), 275–286.

519 DORN, Walter L. "The Debate over American Occupation Policy in Germany in 1944–1945." *Pol Sci Q,* LXXII (1957), 481–501.

520 DRUKS, Herbert. *Harry S. Truman and the Russians, 1945-1953.* New York, 1966.

521 DUNCAN, Francis. "Atomic Energy and Anglo-American Relations, 1946–1954." *Orbis,* XII (1969), 1188–1203.

522 ELLIOTT, Mark. "The United States and Forced Repatriation of Soviet Citizens, 1944–47." *Pol Sci Q,* LXXXVIII (1973), 253–275.

523 FEIS, Herbert. *Between War and Peace: The Potsdam Conference.* Princeton, N.J., 1960.†

524 FEIS, Herbert. *Contest over Japan.* New York, 1967.†

525 FEIS, Herbert. *From Trust to Terror: The Onset of the Cold War, 1945–1950.* New York, 1970.†

526 FLEMING, D. F. *The Cold War and Its Origins, 1917–1960.* 2 Vols. Garden City, N.Y., 1961.

527 GADDIS, John Lewis. *The United States and the Origins of the Cold War, 1941–1947.* New York, 1972.†

528 GAMSON, William A., and Andre MODIGLIANI. *Untangling the Cold War: A Strategy for Testing Rival Theories.* Boston, 1971.

529 GARDNER, Lloyd C., et al. *The Origins of the Cold War.* Waltham, Mass., 1970.†

530 GELBER, Lionel. *America in Britain's Place: The Leadership of the West and Anglo-American Unity.* New York, 1961.

531 GIMBEL, John. "American Military Government and the Education of a New German Leadership." *Pol Sci Q,* LXXXIII (1968), 248–267.

532 GIMBEL, John. *The American Occupation of Germany: Politics and the Military, 1945–1949.* Stanford, Cal., 1968.

533 GIMBEL, John. "On the Implementation of the Potsdam Agreement: An Essay on U.S. Postwar German Policy." *Pol Sci Q,* LXXXVII (1972), 242–269.

534 GOLDEN, Anne T. "Attitudes to the Soviet Union as Reflected in the American Press, 1944–1948." Doctoral dissertation, University of Toronto, 1970.

535 GORDON, Gerald R. "The Coming of the Cold War: The American Labor Movement and the Problem of Peace, 1945–1946." *Sus Univ Stud,* VIII (1968), 14–29.

536 GRAEBNER, Norman. *Cold War Diplomacy: American Foreign Policy, 1945–1960.* Princeton, N.J., 1962.†

537 HALLE, Louis J. *The Cold War as History.* New York, 1967.†

538 HAMBY, Alonzo L. "Henry A. Wallace, the Liberals, and Soviet-American Relations." *Rev Pol,* XXX (1968), 153–169.

539 HARRIMAN, W. Averell. *America and Russia in a Changing World: A Half Century of Personal Observations.* Garden City, N.Y., 1971.

540 HERRING, George C., Jr. *Aid to Russia 1941–1946: Strategy, Diplomacy, the Origins of the Cold War.* New York, 1973.

541 HERRING, George C., Jr. "Lend-Lease to Russia and the Origins of the Cold War, 1944–1945." *J Am Hist,* LVI (1969), 93–114.

542 HERZ, Martin F. *Beginnings of the Cold War.* Bloomington, Ind., 1966.†

543 HITCHENS, Harold L. "Influences on the Congressional Decision to Pass the Marshall Plan." *W Pol Q,* XXI (1968), 51–68.

544 HOGEBOOM, Willard L. "The Cold War and Revisionist Historiography." *Soc Stud,* LXI (1970), 314–318.

545 HOROWITZ, David. *Free World Colossus: A Critique of American Foreign Policy in the Cold War.* New York, 1971.†

546 IRONS, Peter Hanlon. "America's Cold War Crusade: Domestic Politics and Foreign Policy, 1942–1948." Doctoral dissertation, Boston University, 1973.

547 IRONS, Peter H. " 'The Test Is Poland': Polish Americans and the Origins of the Cold War." *Pol Am Stud,* XXX (1973), 5–63.

548 JACOBSON, Harold Karan, and Eric STEIN. *Diplomats, Scientists, and Politicians: The United States and the Nuclear Test Ban Negotiations.* Ann Arbor, Mich., 1966.

549 JESSUP, Philip C. "Park Avenue Diplomacy—Ending the Berlin Blockade." *Pol Sci Q,* LXXXVII (1972), 377–400.

550 JONES, Joseph Marion. *The Fifteen Weeks.* New York, 1955.† Development of the Truman Doctrine and Marshall Plan.

551 KAHAN, Jerome H., and Anne K. LONG. "The Cuban Missile Crisis: A Study of Its Strategic Context." *Pol Sci Q,* LXXXVII (1972), 564–590.

552 KAPLAN, Lawrence S. "The United States and the Origins of NATO," *Rev Pol,* XXXI (1969), 210–222.

553 KENNEDY, Robert F. *Thirteen Days: A Memoir of the Cuban Missile Crisis.* New York, 1969.

554 KOVACS, Arpad F. "The Roots of the Cold War: The End of the Balance of Power and the New American Policy of Collective Security, 1943–1945." *Studies in Modern History.* Ed. Gaetano L. Vincitorio. New York, 1968.

555 KUKLICK, Bruce. *American Policy and the Division of Germany: The Clash with Russia over Reparations.* Ithaca, N.Y., 1972.

556 KUKLICK, Bruce. "The Division of Germany and American Policy on Reparations." *W Pol Q,* XXIII (1970), 276–293.

557 LAFEBER, Walter. *America, Russia, and the Cold War, 1945–1971.* New York, 1972.†

558 LANDA, Ronald Dean. "The Triumph and Tragedy of American Containment: When the Lines of the Cold War Were Drawn in Europe, 1947–48." Doctoral dissertation, Georgetown University, 1971.

559 LEIGH, Michael. "Is There a Revisionist Thesis on the Origins of the Cold War?" *Pol Sci Q,* LXXXIX (1974), 101–116.

560 LEVERING, Ralph Brooks. "Prelude to Cold War: American Attitudes toward Russia during World War II." Doctoral dissertation, Princeton University, 1971.

561 LIEBERMAN, Joseph I. *The Scorpion and the Tarantula: The Struggle to Control Atomic Weapons, 1945–1949.* Boston, 1970.

562 LUKACS, John. *A New History of the Cold War.* Garden City, N.Y., 1966.†

563 MACDONALD, William W. "The Revisionist Cold War Historians." *Mid W Q,* XI (1969), 37–49.

564 MCNEILL, William H. *America, Britain, and Russia.* See 468.

565 MCNEILL, William Hardy. *Greece: American Aid in Action, 1947–1956.* New York, 1957.

566 MADDOX, Robert James. "*Atomic Diolomacy:* A Study in Creative Writing." *J Am Hist,* LIX (1973), 925–934.

567 MADDOX, Robert James. *The New Left and the Origins of the Cold War.* Princeton, N.J., 1973.†

568 MAIER, Charles S. "Revisionism and Beyond: Considerations on the Origins of the Cold War." *Pers Am Hist,* IV (1970), 313–347.

569 MALLALIEU, William C. "The Origin of the Marshall Plan: A Study in Policy Formation and National Leadership." *Pol Sci Q,* LXXIII (1958), 481–504.

570 MAY, Joseph T. "John Foster Dulles and the European Defense Community." Doctoral dissertation, Kent State University, 1969.

571 MOSELY, Philip E. "Hopes and Failures: American Policy toward East Central Europe, 1941–1947." *Rev Pol,* XVII (1955), 461–485.

572 NICHOLAS, Herbert. *Britain and the U.S.A.* Baltimore, 1963.

573 OSGOOD, Robert E. *NATO: The Entangling Alliance.* Chicago, 1962.

547 PATERSON, Thomas G. "The Abortive American Loan to Russia and the Origins of the Cold War, 1943–1946." *J Am Hist,* LVI (1969), 70–92.

575 PATERSON, Thomas G., ed. *Cold War Critics: Alternatives to American Foreign Policy in the Truman Years.* Chicago, 1971.[†]

576 PATERSON, Thomas G. "Potsdam, the Atomic Bomb, and the Cold War: A Discussion with James F. Byrnes." *Pac Hist Rev,* XLI (1972), 225–230.

577 PATERSON, Thomas G. "The Quest for Peace and Prosperity: International Trade, Communism, and the Marshall Plan." *Politics and Policies of the Truman Administration.* Ed. Barton J. Bernstein. Chicago, 1970.[†]

578 PATERSON, Thomas G. *Soviet-American Confrontation: Postwar Reconstruction and the Origins of the Cold War.* Baltimore, 1974.

579 PETERSON, Frank Ross. "Harry S. Truman and His Critics: The 1948 Progressives and the Origins of the Cold War." *Essays on Radicalism in Contemporary America.* Ed. Leon Borden Blair. Austin, Tex., 1972.

580 PLISCHKE, Elmer. "Eisenhower's 'Correspondence Diplomacy' with the Kremlin: Case Study in Summit Diplomatics." *J Pol,* XXX (1968), 137–159.

581 POWERS, Francis Gary, and Curt GENTRY. *Operation Overflight: The U-2 Spy Pilot Tells His Story for the First Time.* New York, 1970.[†]

582 PRICE, Harry Bayard. *The Marshall Plan and Its Meaning.* Ithaca, N.Y. 1955.

583 QUADE, Quentin L. "The Truman Administration and the Separation of Powers: The Case of the Marshall Plan." *Rev Pol,* XXVII (1965), 58–77.

584 ROBERTS, Chalmers M. *The Nuclear Years: The Arms Race and Arms Control, 1945–70.* New York, 1970.

585 ROSE, Lisle A. *After Yalta: America and the Origins of the Cold War.* New York, 1973.

586 ROSE, Lisle A. *The Coming of the American Age, 1945–1946: The United States and the End of World War II.* Kent, Ohio, 1973.

587 ROSI, Eugene J. "How 50 Periodicals and the *Times* Interpreted the Test Ban Controversy." *Jour Q,* XLI (1964), 545–556.

588 RUBINSTEIN, Alvin Z., and George GINSBURGS, eds. *Soviet and American Policies in the United Nations.* New York, 1971.

589 SCHLAUCH, Wolfgang. "American Policy towards Germany, 1945." *J Contemp Hist,* V (1970), 113–128.

590 SCHLAUCH, Wolfgang. "Representative William M. Colmer and Senator James O. Eastland and the Reconstruction of Germany, 1945." *J Miss Hist,* XXXIV (1972), 193–213.

591 SCHICK, Jack M. "American Diplomacy and the Berlin Negotiations." *W Pol Q,* XVIII (1965), 803–820.

592 SCHICK, Jack M. *The Berlin Crisis, 1958–1962.* Philadelphia, 1971.

593 SCHICK, Jack M. "The Berlin Crisis of 1961 and U.S. Military Strategy." *Orbis,* VIII (1965), 816–831.

594 SCHLESINGER, Arthur M., Jr. "Origins of the Cold War." *For Aff,* XLVI (1967), 22–52.

595 SHERWIN, Martin J. "The Atomic Bomb and the Origins of the Cold War: U.S. Atomic-Energy Policy and Diplomacy, 1941–45." *Am Hist Rev,* LXXVIII (1973), 945–968.

596 SMALL, Melvin. "How We Learned to Love the Russians: American Media and the Soviet Union during World War II." *Hist,* XXXVI (1974), 455–478.

597 SMITH, Frederic N. "The American Role in the Repatriation of Certain Soviet Citizens, Forcible and Otherwise, to the USSR Following World War II." Doctoral dissertation, Georgetown University, 1970.

598 SMITH, Jean Edward, ed. *The Papers of General Lucius D. Clay: Germany 1945–1949.* 2 Vols. Bloomington, Ind., 1974.

599 SMITH, Walter Bedell. *My Three Years in Moscow.* Philadelphia, 1950.

600 SNELL, John L., ed. *The Meaning of Yalta: Big Three Diplomacy and the New Balance of Power.* Baton Rouge, La., 1956.†

601 SNELL, John L. *Wartime Origins of the East-West Dilemma over Germany.* New Orleans, La., 1959.

602 SPENCER, Frank. "The United States and Germany in the Aftermath of War: II. The Second World War." *Int Aff,* XLIV (1968), 48–62.

603 STETTINIUS, Edward R., Jr. *Roosevelt and the Russians: The Yalta Conference.* Ed. Walter Johnson. Garden City, N.Y., 1949.

604 SYLVESTER, Harold J. "American Public Reaction to Communist Expansion: From Yalta to NATO." Doctoral dissertation, University of Kansas, 1970.

605 THEOHARIS, Athan. "James F. Byrnes: Unwitting Yalta Myth-Maker." *Pol Sci Q,* LXXXI (1966), 581–592.

606 THEOHARIS, Athan. "Roosevelt and Truman on Yalta: The Origins of the Cold War." *Pol Sci Q,* LXXXVII (1972), 210–241.

607 TURNER, Arthur Campbell. *The Unique Partnership: Britain and the United States.* New York, 1971.†

608 WHEELER-BENNETT, John, and Anthony NICHOLLS. *The Semblance of Peace: The Political Settlement after the Second World War.* New York, 1972.†

609 WHITESIDE, Henry O. "Kennedy and the Kremlin: Soviet-American Relations, 1961–1963." Doctoral dissertation, Stanford University, 1969.

610 WIEGELE, Thomas C. "The Origins of the MLF Concept, 1957–1960." *Orbis,* XII (1968), 465–489.

611 WILLEN, Paul. "Who 'Collaborated' with Russia?" *Ant Rev,* XIV (1954), 259–283.

AMERICA AND THE WORLD

612 WILLIAMS, William Appleman. *American-Russian Relations 1781–1947.* New York, 1952.

613 WISE, David, and Thomas B. ROSS. *The U-2 Affair.* New York, 1962.

614 WRIGHT, Theodore P. "The Origins of the Free Elections Dispute in the Cold War." *W Pol Q,* XIV (1961), 850–864.

615 XYDIS, Stephen G. "America, Britain, and the USSR in the Greek Arena, 1944–1947." *Pol Sci Q,* LXXVIII (1963), 581–596.

616 ZINK, Harold. *The United States in Germany, 1944–55.* Princeton, N.J., 1957.

E. Africa and Asia

617 ARSENAULT, Raymond. "White on Chrome: Southern Congressmen and Rhodesia 1962–1971." *Issue,* II (Winter 1972), 46–57.

618 AUSTIN, Anthony. *The President's War: The Story of the Tonkin Gulf Resolution and How the Nation Was Trapped in Vietnam.* Philadelphia, 1971.

619 BATOR, Victor. *Vietnam: A Diplomatic Tragedy. The Origins of the United States Involvement.* Dobbs Ferry, N.Y., 1965.

620 BEAL, John Robinson. *Marshall in China.* Garden City, N.Y., 1970.

621 BERGER, Carl. *The Korea Knot: A Military-Political History.* Philadelphia, 1964.

622 BICKERTON, Ian J. "President Truman's Recognition of Israel." *Am Jew Hist Q,* LVIII (1969), 173–240.

623 BIERBRIER, Doreen. "The American Zionist Emergency Council: An Analysis of a Pressure Group." *Am Jew Hist Q,* LX (1970), 82–105.

624 BLAIR, Leon Borden. *Western Window in the Arab World.* Austin, Tex., 1970.

625 BOWLES, Chester. *Promises to Keep: My Years in Public Life, 1941–1969.* New York, 1971.†

626 BRANDON, Henry. *Anatomy of Error: The Inside Story of the Asian War on the Potomac, 1954–1969.* Boston, 1969.

627 BRODKIN, E. I. "United States Aid to India and Pakistan: The Attitudes of the Fifties." *Int Aff,* XLIII (1967), 664–677.

628 BURTON, William L. "Protestant America and the Rebirth of Israel." *Jew Soc Stud,* XXVI (1964), 203–214.

629 CARIDI, Ronald J. *The Korean War and American Politics.* Philadelphia, 1969.

630 CARIDI, Ronald James. "The GOP and the Korean War." *Pac Hist Rev,* XXXVII (1968), 423–443.

631 CLIFFORD, Clark. "A Viet Nam Reappraisal: The Personal History of One Man's View and How It Evolved." *For Aff,* XLVII (1969), 601–622.

632 COHEN, Bernard C. *The Political Process and Foreign Policy: The Making of the Japanese Peace Settlement.* Princeton, N.J., 1957.

633 COHEN, Warren I. *America's Response to China: An Interpretive History of Sino-American Relations.* New York, 1971.†

634 COOPER, Chester L. *The Lost Crusade: America in Vietnam.* New York, 1970.†

28

635 DIBACCO, Thomas V. "The Business Press and Vietnam: Ectasy or Agony?" *Jour Q*, XLV (1968), 426–435.

636 DOUGLASS, Bruce, and Ross TERRILL, eds. *China and Ourselves: Explorations and Revisions by a New Generation.* Boston, 1970.[†]

637 DRAPER, Theodore. *Abuse of Power.* New York, 1967.[†] The Vietnam War.

638 DULLES, Foster Rhea. *American Policy toward Communist China 1949–1969.* New York, 1972.[†]

639 DUNN, Frederick S. *Peace-Making and the Settlement with Japan.* Princeton, N.J., 1963.

640 FAIRBANK, John K. *China: The People's Middle Kingdom and the U.S.A.* Cambridge, Mass., 1967.

641 FAIRBANK, John King. *The United States and China.* Cambridge, Mass., 1971. [†]

642 FALK, Richard A., ed. *The Vietnam War and International Law.* 3 Vols. Princeton, N.J., 1967–1972.[†]

643 FALL, Bernard B., and Roger SMITH, eds. *Anatomy of a Crisis: The Laotian Crisis of 1960–1961.* Garden City, N.Y., 1969.

644 FEIS, Herbert. *The Birth of Israel: The Tousled Diplomatic Bed.* New York, 1969.

645 FETZER, James A. "Congress and China, 1941–1950." Doctoral dissertation, Michigan State University, 1969.

646 FETZER, James. "Senator Vandenberg and the American Commitment to China, 1945–1950." *Hist,* XXXVI (1974), 283–303.

647 FINER, Herman. *Dulles over Suez: The Theory and Practice of His Diplomacy.* Chicago, 1964.

648 FITZGERALD, Frances. *Fire in the Lake: The Vietnamese and the Americans in Vietnam.* Boston, 1972.[†]

649 GALBRAITH, John Kenneth. *Ambassador's Journal: A Personal Account of the Kennedy Years.* Boston, 1969.

650 GALLOWAY, John. *The Gulf of Tonkin Resolution.* Rutherford, N.J., 1970.

651 GOLDBERG, Ronald Allen. "The Senate and Vietnam: A Study in Acquiescence." Doctoral dissertation, University of Georgia, 1972.

652 GOODMAN, Grant K., comp. *The American Occupation of Japan: A Retrospective View.* Lawrence, Kans., 1968.[†]

653 GOODRICH, Leland M. *Korea: A Study of U.S. Policy in the United Nations.* New York, 1956.

654 GRAEBNER, Norman A. "Consequences of the China Debate." *W Aff Q,* XXVI (1955), 255–274.

655 GRAFF, Henry F. *The Tuesday Cabinet: Deliberation and Decision on Peace and War under Lyndon Johnson.* Englewood Cliffs, N.J., 1970.

656 GUHIN, Michael A. "The United States and the Chinese People's Republic: The Non-Recognition Policy Reviewed." *Int Aff,* XLV (1969), 44–63.

657 GURTOV, Melvin. *The First Vietnam Crisis: Chinese Communist Strategy and United States Involvement, 1953–54.* New York, 1967.[†]

658 HALBERSTAM, David. *The Best and the Brightest.* New York, 1972.† Origins of the Vietnam War.

659 HALL, Luella. *The United States and Morocco, 1776–1956.* Metuchen, N.J., 1971.

660 HALPERIN, Samuel. *The Political World of American Zionism.* Detroit, Mich., 1961.

661 HART, Parker T., ed. "America and the Middle East." *Ann Am Acad Pol Soc Sci,* CCCCI (1972), 1–142.

662 HESS, Gary R. *America Encounters India.* See 459.

663 HESS, Gary R. "The Iranian Crisis of 1945–46 and the Cold War." *Pol Sci Q,* LXXXIX (1974), 117–146.

664 HILL, Kenneth L. "President Kennedy and the Neutralization of Laos." *Rev Pol,* XXXI (1969), 353–369.

665 HOOPES, Townsend. *The Limits of Intervention (An Inside Account of How the Johnson Policy of Escalation in Vietnam Was Reversed).* New York, 1970.†

666 HOPE, A. Guy. *America and Swaraj: The U.S. Role in Indian Independence.* Washington, 1968.

667 HOSTETTER, John Harold. "John Foster Dulles and the French Defeat in Indochina." Doctoral dissertation, Rutgers University, 1972.

668 HUFF, Earl D. "A Study of a Successful Interest Group: The American Zionist Movement." *W Pol Q,* XXV (1972), 109–124.

669 HURLEY, Robert Michael. "President John F. Kennedy and Vietnam, 1961–1963." Doctoral dissertation, University of Hawaii, 1970.

670 IRIYE, Akira. *Across the Pacific: An Inner History of American-East Asian Relations.* New York, 1967.†

671 JAUHRI, R. C. *American Diplomacy and Independence for India.* Bombay, 1970.

672 JOYNT, Carey B. "John Foster Dulles and the Suez Crisis." *Statesmen and Statecraft of the Modern West.* Ed. Gerald N. Grob. Barre, Mass., 1967.

673 KAHIN, George M., and John W. LEWIS *The United States in Vietnam.* New York, 1967.†

674 KAHLER, John K. "The Genesis of the American Involvement in Indo-China, 1940–1954." Doctoral dissertation, University of Chicago, 1964.

675 KAIL, F. M. *What Washington Said: Administration Rhetoric and the Vietnam War, 1949–1969.* New York, 1973.

676 KALB, Marvin, and Elie ABEL. *Roots of Involvement: The U.S. in Asia 1784–1971.* New York, 1971.

677 KAPLAN, Lawrence S. "The United States, Belgium, and the Congo Crisis of 1960." *Rev Pol,* XXIX (1967), 239–256.

678 KHAIR, Mohammed Abul. "United States Foreign Policy in the Indo-Pakistan Subcontinent, 1940–1955." Doctoral dissertation, University of California at Berkeley, 1962.

679 KIM, Sung Yong. *United States-Philippine Relations, 1946–1956.* Washington, 1968.

680 KINSEY, Winston L. "The United States and Ghana, 1951–1966." Doctoral dissertation, Texas Tech University, 1969.

681 KOEN, Ross Y. *The China Lobby in American Politics.* New York, 1960.

682 KRASLOW, David, and Stuart H. LOORY. *The Secret Search for Peace in Vietnam.* New York, 1968.

683 KSHIRSAGAR, Shiwaran K. "Development of Relations between India and the United States, 1941-52." Doctoral dissertation, American University, 1957.

684 LANSDALE, Edward Geary. *In the Midst of Wars: An American's Mission to Southeast Asia.* New York, 1972.

685 LATOURETTE, Kenneth Scott. *The American Record in the Far East, 1945-1951.* New York, 1952.

686 LEFEVER, Ernest W. "U.S. Policy, the UN and the Congo." *Orbis,* XI (1967), 394-413.

687 LOFGREN, Charles A. "Congress and the Korean Conflict." Doctoral dissertation, Stanford University, 1966.

688 LOFGREN, Charles A. "Mr. Truman's War: A Debate and Its Aftermath." *Rev Pol,* XXXI (1969), 223-241.

689 LONG, Ronald B. "The Role of American Diplomats in the Fall of China, 1941-1949." Doctoral dissertation, St. John's University, 1961.

690 LYONS, Gene M. *Military Policy and Economic Aid: The Korean Case, 1950-1953.* Columbus, Ohio, 1961.

691 MCLELLAN, David S. "Dean Acheson and the Korean War." *Pol Sci Q,* LXXXIII (1968), 16-39.

692 MANTELL, Matthew Edwin. "Opposition to the Korean War: A Study in American Dissent." Doctoral dissertation, New York University, 1973.

693 MAY, Ernest R., and James C. THOMSON, Jr., eds. *American-East Asian Relations: A Survey.* Cambridge, Mass., 1972.

694 MEADE, E. Grant. *American Military Government in Korea.* New York, 1951.

695 MELBOURNE, Roy M. "The American Response to the Nigerian Conflict, 1968." *Issue,* III (Summer 1973), 33-42.

696 MINEAR, Richard H. *Victors' Justice: The Tokyo War Crimes Trial.* Princeton, N.J., 1971.†

697 MOORE, John Norton. *Law and the Indo-China War.* Princeton, N.J., 1972.†

698 MUELLER, John E. "Trends in Popular Support for the Wars in Korea and Vietnam." *Am Pol Sci Rev,* LXV (1971), 358-375.

699 MULCH, Barbara E. Gooden. "A Chinese Puzzle: Patrick J. Hurley and the Foreign Service Officer Controversy." Doctoral dissertation, University of Kansas, 1972.

700 NEUMANN, William L. *America Encounters Japan: From Perry to MacArthur.* Baltimore, 1963.†

701 NICHOLS, Jeanette P. "United States Aid to South and Southeast Asia, 1950-1960." *Pac Hist Rev,* XXXII (1963), 171-184.

702 OH, John Kie-Chiang. "Role of the United States in South Korea's Democratization." *Pac Aff,* XLII (1969), 164-177.

703 *The Pentagon Papers as Published by the "New York Times."* New York, 1971.†

704 The Pentagon Papers: The Defense Department History of United States Decision-making on Vietnam. The Gravel Edn. 4 Vols. Boston, 1971.†

705 POLK, William R. The United States and the Arab World. Cambridge, Mass., 1969.

706 RANKIN, Karl Lott. China Assignment. Seattle, Wash., 1964.

707 REISCHAUER, Edwin O. The United States and Japan. Cambridge, Mass., 1965.†

708 RIGGS, James Richard. "Congress and the Conduct of the Korean War." Doctoral dissertation, Purdue University, 1972.

709 ROCHE, George C., III. "Public Opinion and the China Policy of the United States, 1941–1951." Doctoral dissertation, University of Colorado, 1965.

710 SAWYER, Robert K. Military Advisors in Korea: KMAG in Peace and War. Washington, 1962.

711 SCHLESINGER, Arthur M., Jr. The Bitter Heritage: Vietnam and American Democracy, 1941–1966. Boston, 1967.†

712 SHAPLEN, Robert. The Lost Revolution: The U.S. in Vietnam, 1946–1966. New York, 1966.†

713 SHEWMAKER, Kenneth E. Americans and Chinese Communists, 1927–1945: A Persuading Encounter. Ithaca, N.Y., 1971.

714 SILVERBERG, Robert. If I Forget Thee O Jerusalem: American Jews and the State of Israel. New York, 1970.

715 SMYLIE, James H. "American Religious Bodies, Just War, and Vietnam." J Ch State, XI (1969), 383–408.

716 SNETSINGER, John. Truman, the Jewish Vote, and the Creation of Israel. Stanford, Cal., 1974.

717 THOMAS, John N. The Institute of Pacific Relations: Asian Scholars and American Politics. Seattle, Wash., 1974.

718 TOZER, Warren W. "The Foreign Correspondents' Visit to Yenan in 1944: A Reassessment." Pac Hist Rev, XLI (1972), 207–224.

719 TSOU, Tang. America's Failure in China, 1941–50. Chicago, 1963.†

720 VAN ALSTYNE, Richard W. The United States and East Asia. New York, 1973.†

721 VARG, Paul. The Closing of the Door: Sino-American Relations, 1936–1946. East Lansing, Mich., 1973.

722 VINACKE, Harold M. The United States and the Far East, 1945–1951. Stanford, Cal., 1952.

723 WEISSMAN, Stephen R. American Foreign Policy in the Congo, 1960–1964. Ithaca, N.Y., 1974.

724 WILDES, Harry Emerson. Typhoon in Tokyo: The Occupation and Its Aftermath. New York, 1954.

725 WILLIAMS, Justin. "Completing Japan's Political Reorientation, 1947–1952: Crucial Phase of the Allied Occupation." Am Hist Rev, LXXIII (1968), 1454–1469.

726 WILSON, Wesley C. "1946: General George C. Marshall and the United States Army Mediate China's Civil War." Doctoral dissertation, University of Colorado, 1965.

727 WITTNER, Lawrence S. "MacArthur and the Missionaries: God and Man in Occupied Japan." *Pac Hist Rev,* XL (1971), 77–98.

728 YOUNG, Kenneth T. *Negotiating with the Chinese Communists: The United States Experience, 1953–1967.* New York, 1968.†

F. Latin America

729 ATKINS, G. Pope, and Larman C. WILSON. *The United States and the Trujillo Regime.* New Brunswick, N.J., 1972.

730 BERGER, Henry W. "Union Diplomacy: American Labor's Foreign Policy in Latin America, 1932–1955." Doctoral dissertation, University of Wisconsin, 1966.

731 BLUMENTHAL, Michael D. "The Economic Good Neighbor: Aspects of United States Economic Policy toward Latin America in the Early 1940's as Revealed by the Activities of the Office of Inter-American Affairs." Doctoral dissertation, University of Wisconsin, 1968.

732 BONSAL, Philip W. *Cuba, Castro, and the United States.* Pittsburgh, Pa., 1971.

733 BRADSHAW, James Stanford. "The 'Lost' Conference: The Economic Issue in United States–Latin American Relations, 1945–1957." Doctoral dissertation, Michigan State University, 1972.

734 CAREY, James C. *Peru and the United States, 1900–1962.* Notre Dame, Ind., 1964.

735 CHARDKOFF, Richard B. "Communist Toehold in the Americas: A History of Official United States Involvement in the Guatemalan Crisis, 1954." Doctoral dissertation, Florida State University, 1967.

736 CONNELL-SMITH, Gordon. *The Inter-American System.* New York, 1966.

737 COOLEY, John Andrew. "The United States and the Panama Canal, 1938–1947: Policy Formulation and Implementation from Munich through the Early Years of the Cold War." Doctoral dissertation, Ohio State University, 1972.

738 CRAIG, Richard B. *The Bracero Program: Interest Groups and Foreign Policy.* Austin, Tex., 1971.

739 CRONON, E. David. *Josephus Daniels in Mexico.* Madison, Wis., 1960.†

740 DOZER, Donald Marquand. *Are We Good Neighbors? Three Decades of Inter-American Relations, 1930–1960.* Gainesville, Fla., 1959.

741 DRAPER, Theodore. "The Dominican Intervention Reconsidered." *Pol Sci Q,* LXXXVI (1971), 1–36.

742 DRAPER, Theodore. *The Dominican Revolt: A Case Study in American Policy.* New York, 1968.

743 FRANCIS, Michael J. "The United States and the Act of Chapultepec." *S W Soc Sci Q,* XLV (1964), 249–257.

744 FRANCIS, Michael J. "The U.S. Press and Castro: A Study in Declining Relations." *Jour Q,* XLIV (1967), 257–266.

745 GIVENS, Larry Dale. "Official United States' Attitudes Toward Latin American Military Regimes, 1933–1960." Doctoral dissertation, University of California at Davis, 1970.

746 GREEN, David. "The Cold War Comes to Latin America." *Politics and Policies of the Truman Administration.* Ed. Barton J. Bernstein. Chicago, 1970.†

747 GREEN, David. *The Containment of Latin America: A History of the Myths and Realities of the Good Neighbor Policy.* Chicago, 1971.

748 GUERRANT, Edward O. *Roosevelt's Good Neighbor Policy.* See 453.

749 HUNDLEY, Norris, Jr. *Dividing the Waters: A Century of Controversy Between the United States and Mexico.* Berkeley, Cal., 1966.

750 HUNDLEY, Norris, Jr. "The Politics of Water and Geography: California and the Mexican-American Treaty of 1944." *Pac Hist Rev,* XXXVI (1967), 209–226.

751 JOHNSON, Haynes, et al. *The Bay of Pigs: The Leaders' Story of Brigade 2506.* New York, 1964.

752 LANGLEY, Lester D. *The Cuban Policy of the United States: A Brief History.* New York, 1968.

753 LANGLEY, Lester D. "U.S.-Panamanian Relations since 1941." *J Inter-Am Stud W Aff,* XII (1970), 339–366.

754 LEVENSTEIN, Harvey A. *Labor Organizations in the United States and Mexico: A History of Their Relations.* Westport, Conn., 1971.

755 LEVINSON, Jerome, and Juan DE ONIS, eds. *The Alliance That Lost Its Way: A Critical Report on the Alliance for Progress.* Chicago, 1970.†

756 LOWENTHAL, Abraham F. *The Dominican Intervention.* Cambridge, Mass., 1972.

757 MCCAIN, Johnny M. "Contract Labor as a Factor in United States-Mexican Relations, 1942–1947." Doctoral dissertation, University of Texas, 1970.

758 MCDERMOTT, Louis M. "Guatemala, 1954: Intervention or Aggression?" *Rocky Mt Soc Sci J,* IX (January 1972), 79–88.

759 MARTIN, John Bartlow. *Overtaken by Events: The Dominican Crisis from the Fall of Trujillo to the Civil War.* Garden City, N.Y., 1966.

760 MECHAM, John Lloyd. *A Survey of United States-Latin American Relations.* Boston, 1965.

761 MECHAM, J. Lloyd. *The United States and Inter-American Security, 1889–1960.* Austin, Tex., 1961.

762 PERKINS, Dexter. *The United States and the Caribbean.* Cambridge, Mass., 1966.

763 PETERSON, Harold F. *Argentina and the United States, 1810–1960.* New York, 1964.

764 ROGERS, William D. *The Twilight Struggle: The Alliance for Progress and the Politics of Development in Latin America.* New York, 1967.

765 SCRUGGS, Otey M. "Evolution of the Mexican Farm Labor Agreement of 1942." *Ag Hist,* XXXIV (1960), 140–149.

766 SCRUGGS, Otey. "Texas, Good Neighbor?" *S W Soc Sci Q,* XLIII (1962), 118–125.

767 SCRUGGS, Otey M. "The United States, Mexico, and the Wetbacks, 1942–1947." *Pac Hist Rev,* XXX (1961), 149–164.

768 SLATER, Jerome. *Intervention and Negotiation: The United States and the Dominican Revolution.* New York, 1970.

769 SMETHERMAN, Robert. "U.S. Aid to Latin America: An Appraisal." *Mid W Q,* X (1969), 263–272.

770 SMETHERMAN, Robert M. "U.S. Aid to Latin America, 1945–1960." Doctoral dissertation, Claremont Graduate School, 1967.

771 SMITH, Earl E. T. *The Fourth Floor: An Account of the Castro Communist Revolution.* New York, 1963.

772 SMITH, Robert F. *The United States and Cuba: Business and Diplomacy, 1917–1960.* New York, 1960.[†]

773 SPECTOR, Stephen D. "United States Attempts at Regional Security and the Extension of the Good Neighbor Policy in Latin America, 1945–1952." Doctoral dissertation, New York University, 1970.

774 SZULC, Tad, and Karl E. MEYER. *The Cuban Invasion: The Chronicle of Disaster.* New York, 1962.

775 TAYLOR, Phillip B., Jr. "The Guatemalan Affair: A Critique of United States Foreign Policy." *Am Pol Sci Rev,* L (1956), 787–806.

776 WAGNER, R. Harrison. *United States Policy toward Latin America: A Study in Domestic and International Politics.* Stanford, Cal., 1970.

777 WHITAKER, Arthur P. *The Western Hemisphere Idea: Its Rise and Decline.* Ithaca, N.Y., 1954.[†]

778 WILLIAMS, William Appleman. *The United States, Cuba, and Castro.* New York, 1962.

779 WOOD, Bryce. *The Good Neighbor Policy.* New York, 1961.[†]

IV. National Defense and Military Policy

A. General

780 ALBION, Robert Greenhalgh, and Robert Howe CONNERY. *Forrestal and the Navy.* New York, 1962.

781 ALEXANDER, Thomas G. "Brief Histories of Three Federal Military Installations in Utah: Kearns Army Base, Hurricane Mesa, and Green River Test Complex." *Utah Hist Q,* XXXIV (1966), 121–137.

782 ALEXANDER, Thomas G. "Ogden's 'Arsenal of Democracy,' 1920–1955." *Utah Hist Q,* XXXIII (1965), 237–247.

783 AMBROSE, Stephen E., and James Alden BARBER, Jr., eds. *The Military and American Society.* New York, 1971.[†]

784 ARMACOST, Michael H. *The Politics of Weapons Innovation: The Thor-Jupiter Controversy.* New York, 1969.

785 ARRINGTON, Leonard J., et al. "Utah's Biggest Business: Ogden Air Materiel Area at Hill Air Force Base, 1938–1965." *Utah Hist Q,* XXXIII (1965), 9–33.

786 ARRINGTON, Leonard J., and Thomas G. ALEXANDER. "Sentinels on the Desert: The Dugway Proving Ground (1942–1963) and Deseret Chemical Depot (1942–1955)" *Utah Hist Q,* XXXII (1964), 32–43.

787 ARRINGTON, Leonard J., and Thomas G. ALEXANDER. "They Kept 'Em Rolling: The Tooele Army Depot, 1942–1962." *Utah Hist Q,* XXXI (1963), 3–25.

788 ARRINGTON, Leonard J., and Thomas G. ALEXANDER. "Utah's First Line of Defense: The Utah National Guard and Camp W. G. Williams: 1926–1965." *Utah Hist Q,* XXXIII (1965), 141–156.

789 ARRINGTON, Leonard J., and Archer L. DURHAM. "Anchors Aweigh in Utah: The U.S. Naval Depot at Clearfield, 1942–1962." *Utah Hist Q,* XXXI (1963), 109–126.

790 ART, Robert J. *The TFX Decision: McNamara and the Military.* Boston, 1968.

791 BANTELL, John F. "The Search for Military Preparedness in the Postwar Era." *Soc Stud,* LXIII (1972), 262–270.

792 BENDER, Averam B. "From Tanks to Missiles, Camp Cooke/Cooke Air Force Base, 1941–1958." *Ariz West,* IX (1967), 219–242.

793 BENSON, Charles Dunlap. "The U.S. Armed Services' Examination of Their Role, 1945–1950." Doctoral dissertation, University of Florida, 1970.

794 BORKLUND, C. W. *The Department of Defense.* New York, 1968.

795 BORKLUND, C. W. *Men of the Pentagon: From Forrestal to McNamara.* New York, 1966.

796 BOTTOME, Edgar M. *The Missile Gap: A Study of the Formulation of Military and Political Policy.* Rutherford, N.J., 1971.

797 BRAYTON, Abbott A. "American Reserve Policies since World War II." *Mil Aff,* XXXVI (1972), 139–144.

798 CARALEY, Demetrios. *The Politics of Military Unification: A Study of Conflict and the Policy Process.* New York, 1966.

799 CARRISON, Daniel J. *The United States Navy.* New York, 1968.

800 CHRISTMAN, Albert B. *Sailors, Scientists, and Rockets: Origins of the Navy Rocket Program and of the Naval Ordnance Test Station, Inyokern.* Washington, 1971.

801 CLARK, Keith C., and Laurence J. LEGERE, eds. *The President and the Management of National Security: A Report by the Institute for Defense Analyses.* New York, 1969.

802 CONANT, James B. *My Several Lives.* New York, 1970.

803 COOLING, B. Franklin. "Civil Defense and the Army: The Quest for Responsibility, 1946–1948." *Mil Aff,* XXXVI (1972), 11–14.

804 DAVIS, Vincent. *The Admirals Lobby.* Chapel Hill, N.C., 1967.

805 DAVIS, Vincent. *Postwar Defense Policy and the U.S. Navy, 1943–1946.* Chapel Hill, N.C., 1966.

806 DERTHICK, Martha. *The National Guard in Politics.* Cambridge, Mass., 1965.

807 DICK, James C. "The Strategic Arms Race, 1957–61: Who Opened a Missile Gap?" *J Pol,* XXXIV (1972), 1062–1110.

808 EASTMAN, James N., Jr. "Location and Growth of Tinker Air Force Base and Oklahoma City Air Materiel Area." *Chron Okla,* L (1972), 326–346.

809 EKIRCH, Arthur A., Jr. *The Civilian and the Military.* New York, 1956.†

810 EMME, Eugene M., ed. *The History of Rocket Technology: Essays on Research, Development, and Utility.* Detroit, Mich., 1964.

811 EPSTEIN, Laurence B. "The American Philosophy of War, 1945–1967." Doctoral dissertation, University of Southern California, 1967.

812 FALK, Stanley L. "The National Security Council under Truman, Eisenhower, and Kennedy." *Pol Sci Q,* LXXIX (1964), 403–434.

813 FRENCH, Thomas A. "Unification and the American Military Establishment, 1945–1950." Doctoral dissertation, State University of New York at Buffalo, 1972.

814 FURGURSON, Ernest B. *Westmoreland: The Inevitable General.* Boston, 1968.

815 GENEROUS, William T., Jr. *Swords and Scales: The Development of the Uniform Code of Military Justice.* Port Washington, N.Y., 1973.

816 GILLAM, Richard. "The Peacetime Draft: Voluntarism to Coercion." *Yale Rev,* LVII (1968), 495–517.

817 GILPIN, Robert. *American Scientists and Nuclear Weapons Policy.* Princeton, N.J., 1962.†

818 GLINES, Carroll V., Jr. *The Compact History of the United States Air Force.* New York, 1973.

819 GOLDBERG, Alfred, ed. *A History of the United States Air Force, 1907–1957.* Princeton, N.J., 1957.

820 HALPERIN, Morton H. "The Decision to Deploy the ABM: Bureaucratic and Domestic Politics in the Johnson Administration." *World Pol,* XXV (1972), 62–95.

821 HAMMOND, Paul Y. "A Functional Analysis of Defense Department Decision-Making in the McNamara Administration." *Am Pol Sci Rev,* LXII (1968), 57–69.

822 HAMMOND, Paul Y. *Organizing for Defense: The American Military Establishment in the Twentieth Century.* Princeton, N.J., 1961.

823 HAYNES, Richard F. *The Awesome Power: Harry S. Truman as Commander in Chief.* Baton Rouge, La., 1973.

824 HEWLETT, Richard G., and Oscar E. ANDERSON, Jr. *A History of the United States Atomic Energy Commission: The New World, 1939–1946.* University Park, Pa., 1962.

825 HEWLETT, Richard G., and Francis DUNCAN. *A History of the United States Atomic Energy Commission: Atomic Shield 1947/1952.* University Park, Pa., 1969.

826 HUNTINGTON, Samuel P. *The Common Defense: Strategic Programs in National Politics.* New York, 1961.†

827 HUNTINGTON, Samuel P. *The Soldier and the State: The Theory and Politics of Civil-Military Relations.* Cambridge, Mass., 1957.†

828 KANTER, Arnold. "Congress and the Defense Budget: 1960–1970." *Am Pol Sci Rev,* LXVI (1972), 129–143.

829 KAUFMANN, William W. *The McNamara Strategy.* New York, 1964.

830 KIRKPATRICK, Lyman B., Jr. *The Real CIA.* New York, 1968.

831 KOLODZIEJ, Edward A. *The Uncommon Defense and Congress, 1945–1963.* Columbus, Ohio, 1966.

832 KORB, Lawrence J. "Robert McNamara's Impact on the Budget Strategies of the Joint Chiefs of Staff." *Aero Hist,* XVII (1970), 132–136.

833 LECKIE, Robert. *The Wars of America.* New York, 1968.

834 LEE, R. Alton. "The Army 'Mutiny' of 1946." *J Am Hist,* LIII (1966), 555–571.

835 LEMAY, Curtis E., with MacKinlay KANTOR. *Mission with LeMay: My Story.* New York, 1965.

836 LICKLIDER, Roy E. "The Missile Gap Controversy." *Pol Sci Q,* LXXXV (1970), 600–615.

837 LILIENTHAL, David E. *The Journals of David E. Lilienthal: The Atomic Energy Years, 1945–1950.* New York, 1964.

838 LOWE, George E. *The Age of Deterrence.* Boston, 1964.

839 LYONS, Gene M. *Schools for Strategy: Education and Research in National Security Affairs.* New York, 1965.

840 MACARTHUR, Douglas. *Reminiscences.* New York, 1964.

841 MCCAHILL, William P., et al. *The Marine Corps Reserve: A History.* Washington, 1966.

842 MILLIS, Walter. *Arms and Men.* New York, 1956.†

843 MILLIS, Walter, *et al., Arms and the State: Civil-Military Elements in National Policy.* New York, 1958.

844 MILLIS, Walter, ed. *The Forrestal Diaries.* New York, 1951.

845 MOULTON, Harland B. "American Strategic Power: Two Decades of Nuclear Strategy and Weapon Systems, 1945–1965." Doctoral dissertation, University of Minnesota, 1969.

846 MOULTON, Harland B. *From Superiority to Parity: The United States and the Strategic Arms Race, 1961–1971.* Westport, Conn., 1973.

847 MROZEK, Donald John. "Peace through Strength: Strategic Air Power and the Mobilization of the United States for the Pursuit of Foreign Policy, 1945–1955." Doctoral dissertation, Rutgers University, 1972.

848 MROZEK, Donald J. "The Truman Administration and the Enlistment of the Aviation Industry in Postwar Defense." *Bus Hist Rev,* XLVIII (1974), 73–94.

849 NIGRO, Felix A. "The Lilienthal Case." *S W Soc Sci Q,* XL (1959), 147–158.

850 OSGOOD, Robert E. *Limited War.* See 299.

851 PAPPAS, George S. *Prudens Futuri: The US Army War College, 1901–1967.* Carlisle Barracks, Pa., 1967.

852 PARRISH, Noel F. "Behind the Sheltering Bomb: Military Indecision from Alamogordo to Korea." Doctoral dissertation, Rice University, 1968.

853 RANSOM, Harry Howe. *The Intelligence Establishment.* Cambridge, Mass., 1970.

854 RAPPAPORT, Armin. *The Navy League of the United States.* Detroit, Mich., 1962.

855 RICE, Berkeley. *The C-5A Scandal: An Inside Story of the Military-Industrial Complex.* Boston, 1971.

856 RIDGWAY, Matthew B., and Harold H. MARTIN. *Soldier: The Memoirs of Matthew B. Ridgway.* New York, 1956.

857 ROGOW, Arnold A. *James Forrestal: A Study of Personality, Politics and Policy.* New York, 1963.

858 ROHERTY, James M. *Decisions of Robert S. McNamara: A Study of the Role of the Secretary of Defense.* Miami, Fla., 1970.

859 SANDER, Alfred D. "Truman and the National Security Council: 1945-1947." *J Am Hist,* LIX (1972), 369-388

860 SCHAFFER, Ronald. "The 1940 *Small Wars Manual* and the 'Lessons of History'." *Mil Aff,* XXXVI (1972), 46-51.

861 SCHWARZ, Urs. *American Strategy: A New Perspective.* Garden City, N.Y., 1966.

862 SCHWIEBERT, Ernest G., *et al. A History of the U.S. Air Force Ballistic Missiles.* New York, 1965.

863 SMITH, Bruce L. R. *The RAND Corporation: Case Study of a Nonprofit Advisory Corporation.* Cambridge, Mass., 1966.

864 SMITH, Louis. *American Democracy and Military Power: A Study of Civil Control of the Military Power in the United States.* Chicago, 1951.

865 SMITH, Perry McCoy. *The Air Force Plans for Peace 1943-1945.* Baltimore, 1970.

866 STEIN, Harold, ed. *American Civil-Military Decisions: A Book of Case Studies.* University, Ala., 1963.

867 STRAUSS, Lewis L. *Men and Decisions.* Garden City, N.Y., 1962. Autobiography.

868 TAYLOR, Maxwell D. *Swords and Plowshares.* New York, 1972. Autobiography.

869 TREWHITT, H. L. *McNamara: His Ordeal in the Pentagon.* New York, 1971.

870 TWINING, Nathan F. *Neither Liberty Nor Safety: A Hard Look at U.S. Military Policy and Strategy.* New York, 1966.

871 TYLER, Lyon G. "Civil Defense: The Impact of the Planning Years, 1945-1950." Doctoral dissertation, Duke University, 1967.

872 VAN DYKE, Vernon, and Edward LANE. "Senator Taft and American Security." See 350.

873 WEIGLEY, Russell F. *History of the United States Army.* New York, 1967.

874 WHITNEY, Courtney. *MacArthur: His Rendevous with History.* New York, 1956.

875 WILLOUGHBY, Charles A., and John CHAMBERLAIN. *MacArthur, 1941-1951.* New York, 1954.

876 YARMOLINSKY, Adam. *The Military Establishment: Its Impacts on American Society.* New York, 1971.†

877 YARMOLINSKY, Adam. "Picking up the Pieces: The Impact of Vietnam on the Military Establishment." *Yale Rev,* LXI (1972), 481–495.

B. World War II

878 ABBAZIA, Patrick. "Mr. Roosevelt's Navy: The Little War of the United States Atlantic Fleet, 1939–1942." Doctoral dissertation, Columbia University, 1972.

879 AMBROSE, Stephen E. *Eisenhower and Berlin, 1945: The Decision to Halt at the Elbe.* New York, 1967.†

880 AMBROSE, Stephen E. *The Supreme Commander: The War Years of General Dwight D. Eisenhower.* Garden City, N.Y., 1970.

881 AMRINE, Michael. *The Great Decision: The Secret History of the Atomic Bomb.* New York, 1959.

882 ANDERS, Leslie. *The Ledo Road: General Joseph W. Stilwell's Highway to China.* Norman, Okla., 1965.

883 ARNOLD, H. H. *Global Mission.* New York, 1949. U.S. Army Air Force.

884 ARRINGTON, Leonard J., and Thomas G. ALEXANDER. "Utah's Small Arms Ammunition Plant during World War II." *Pac Hist Rev,* XXXIV (1965), 185–196.

885 BALLANTINE, Duncan. *U.S. Naval Logistics in the Second World War.* Princeton, N.J., 1947.

886 BARBEY, Daniel E. *MacArthur's Amphibious Navy: Seventh Amphibious Force Operations, 1943–1945.* Annapolis, Md., 1969.

887 BATCHELDER, Robert C. *The Irreversible Decision, 1939–1950.* Boston, 1962. Atomic bomb.

888 BAXTER, James P., III. *Scientists against Time.* Cambridge, Mass., 1968.† Science and government in World War II.

889 BLUM, Albert A. *Drafted or Deferred: Practices Past and Present.* Ann Arbor, Mich., 1967.

890 BLUM, Albert A. "The Farmer, the Army and the Draft." *Ag Hist,* XXXVIII (1964), 34–42.

891 BLUM, Albert A. "The Fight for a Young Army." *Mil Aff,* XVIII (1954), 81–85.

892 BLUM, Albert A. "Sailor or Worker: A Manpower Dilemma during the Second World War." *Lab Hist,* VI (1965), 232–243.

893 BLUM, Albert A. "Work or Fight: The Use of the Draft as a Manpower Sanction during the Second World War." *Indust Lab Rel Rev,* XVI (1963), 366–380.

894 BLUMENSON, Martin. "The Bombing of Monte Cassino." *Am Her,* XIX (August 1968), 18–23, 84–89.

895 BOYLAN, Bernard L. "The Search for a Long Range Escort Plane, 1919–1945." *Mil Aff,* XXX (1966), 57–67.

896 BRADLEY, Omar. *A Soldier's Story.* New York, 1951.†

897 BROWN, Frederic J. *Chemical Warfare: A Study in Restraints.* Princeton, N.J., 1968.

898 BUCHANAN, A. Russell. *The United States and World War II.†* See 39.

899 BUNKER, John Gorley. *Liberty Ships: The Ugly Ducklings of World War II.* Annapolis, Md., 1972.

900 BUSCO, Ralph A., and Douglas D. ADLER. "German and Italian Prisoners of War in Utah and Idaho." *Utah Hist Q,* XXXIX (1971), 55–72.

901 BUSH, Vannevar. *Pieces of the Action.* New York, 1970.† Wartime science.

902 BUTLER, Joseph T., Jr. "Prisoner of War Labor in the Sugar Cane Fields of Lafourche Parish, Louisiana: 1943–1944." *La Hist,* XIV (1973), 283–296.

903 CATTON, Bruce. *The War Lords of Washington.* New York, 1948. Wartime economic mobilization.

904 CHANDLER, Alfred D., Jr., ed. *The Papers of Dwight David Eisenhower: The War Years.* 5 Vols. Baltimore, 1970.

905 CHRISTMAN, Calvin L. "Donald Nelson and the Army: Personality as a Factor in Civil-Military Relations during World War II." *Mil Aff,* XXXVII (1973), 81–83.

906 CHRISTMAN, Calvin Lee. "Ferdinand Eberstadt and Economic Mobilization for War, 1941–1943." Doctoral dissertation, Ohio State University, 1971.

907 CLARK, Mark. *Calculated Risk.* New York, 1950.

908 CLEVELAND, Reginald M. *Air Transport at War.* New York, 1946.

909 COLEMAN, John M. *The Development of Tactical Services in the Army Air Forces.* New York, 1950.

910 CONNERY, Robert H. *The Navy and the Industrial Mobilization in World War II.* Princeton, N.J., 1951.

911 COOLING, B. Franklin. "U.S. Army Support of Civil Defense: The Formative Years." *Mil Aff,* XXXV (1971), 7–11.

912 CRAVEN, Wesley Frank, and James Lea CATE, et al. *The Army Air Forces in World War II.* 7 Vols. Chicago, 1948–1958.

913 CURRENT, Richard N. *Secretary Stimson: A Study in Statecraft.* New Brunswick, N.J., 1954.

914 DAVIS, Kenneth S. *Experience of War: The United States in World War II.* Garden City, N.Y., 1965.

915 DULLES, Allen. *The Secret Surrender.* New York, 1966. Re the German army in Italy.

916 DYER, George Carroll. *The Amphibians Came to Conquer: The Story of Admiral Richmond Kelly Turner.* 2 Vols., Washington, 1972.

917 EDMONDS, Walter D. *They Fought with What They Had: The Story of the Army Air Forces in the Southwest Pacific, 1941–1942.* Boston, 1951.

918 EISENHOWER, Dwight D. *Crusade in Europe.* Garden City, N.Y., 1948.

919 EISENHOWER, John D. S. *The Bitter Woods.* New York, 1969.† The German Ardennes offensive.

920 Eisenhower Foundation. *D-Day: The Normandy Invasion in Retrospect.* Lawrence, Kans., 1971.†

921 EMERSON, William. "Franklin Roosevelt as Commander-in-Chief in World War II." *Mil Aff,* XXII (1958), 181–207.

922 FALK, Stanley L. *Decision at Leyte.* New York, 1966.

923 FESLER, James W., *et al. Industrial Mobilization for War: A History of the War Production Board and Predecessor Agencies, 1940–1945.* Washington, 1947.

924 FORD, Corey. *Donovan of OSS.* Boston, 1970.

925 FORRESTEL, E. P. *Admiral Raymond A. Spruance, USN: A Study in Command.* Washington, 1966.

926 FUNK, Arthur L. "American Contacts with the Resistance in France, 1940–1943." *Mil Aff,* XXXIV (1970), 15–21.

927 FUNK, Arthur L. "Eisenhower, Giraud, and the Command of 'TORCH.' " *Mil Aff,* XXXV (1971), 103–108.

928 FURER, Julius Augustus. *Administration of the Navy Department in World War II.* Washington, 1959.

929 GIOVANNITTI, Len, and Fred FREED. *The Decision to Drop the Bomb.* New York, 1965.

930 GREENFIELD, Kent Roberts. *American Strategy in World War II: A Reconsideration.* Baltimore, 1963.[†]

931 GREENFIELD, Kent Roberts, ed. *Command Decisions.* Washington, 1960.

932 GREENFIELD, Kent Roberts. "Forging the United States Army in World War II into a Combined Arms Team." *Miss Val Hist Rev,* XXXIV (1947), 443–452.

933 GRIFFITH, Samuel B. *The Battle for Guadalcanal.* Philadelphia, 1963.

934 GROUEFF, Stephane. *Manhattan Project: The Untold Story of the Making of the Atomic Bomb.* Boston, 1967.

935 GROVES, Leslie R. *Now It Can Be Told: The Story of the Manhattan Project.* New York, 1962.

936 HALSEY, William F., and J. BRYAN, III. *Admiral Halsey's Story.* New York, 1947.

937 HANSELL, Haywood S., Jr. *The Air Plan That Defeated Hitler.* Atlanta, Ga., 1972.

938 HEWITT, H. Kent. "Planning Operation ANVIL-DRAGOON." *USN Inst Proc,* LXXX (1954), 731–745.

939 HIGGINS, Trumbull. *Soft Underbelly: The Anglo-American Controversy over the Italian Campaign, 1939–1945.* New York, 1968.

940 *History of U.S. Marine Corps Operations in World War II.* 5 Vols. Washington, 1958–1968.

941 HOBBS, Joseph P., ed. *Dear General: Eisenhower's Wartime Letters to Marshall.* Baltimore, 1971.

942 HOOLE, W. Stanley. "Alabama's World War II Prisoner of War Camps." *Ala Rev,* XX (1967), 83–114.

943 HOUGH, Frank. *The Island War: The United States Marine Corps in The Pacific.* Philadelphia, 1947.

944 HUSTON, James A. *Out of the Blue: U.S. Army Airborne Operations in World War II.* West Lafayette, Ind., 1972.

945 ISELY, Jeter A., and Philip A. CROWL. *The U.S. Marines and Amphibious War: Its Theory, and Its Practice in the Pacific.* Princeton, N.J., 1951.

946 ISRAEL, Fred L. "Military Justice in Hawaii 1941–1944." *Pac Hist R,* XXXVI (1967), 243–267.

947 JANEWAY, Eliot. *The Struggle for Survival: A Chronicle of Economic Mobilization in World War II.* New Haven, Conn., 1951.

948 JOHNSON, Ann R. "The WASP of World War II." *Aero Hist,* XVII (1970), 76–82.

949 KARIG, Walter, *et al.,* eds. *Battle Report.* 5 Vols. New York, 1944–1949.

950 KING, Ernest J., and Walter Muir WHITEHILL. *Fleet Admiral King: A Naval Record.* New York, 1952.

951 KING, Spencer Bidwell. *Selective Service in North Carolina in World War II.* Chapel Hill, N.C., 1949.

952 LAFARGE, Oliver. *The Eagle in the Egg.* Boston, 1949. U.S. Army Air Force.

953 LAMONT, Lansing. *Day of Trinity.* New York, 1965. Atomic bomb.

954 LANE, Frederic C., *et al. Ships for Victory: A History of Shipbuilding under the U.S. Maritime Commission in World War II.* Baltimore, 1951.

955 LAURENCE, William L. *Dawn over Zero: The Story of the Atomic Bomb.* New York, 1946.

956 LEAHY, William D. *I Was There: The Personal Story of the Chief of Staff to Presidents Roosevelt and Truman.* New York, 1950.

957 LECKIE, Robert. *Strong Men Armed: The U.S. Marines Against Japan.* New York, 1962.

958 LEIGHTON, Richard M. "The American Arsenal Policy in World War II: A Retrospective View." *Some Pathways in Twentieth-Century History.* Ed. Daniel R. Beaver. Detroit, Mich., 1969.

959 LEIGHTON, Richard M. "Overlord Revisited: An Interpretation of American Strategy in the European War, 1942–1944." *Am Hist Rev,* LXVIII (1963), 919–937.

960 LERNER, Daniel. *Psychological Warfare against Nazi Germany: The Sykewar Campaign, D-Day to VE-Day.* Cambridge Mass., 1971.†

961 LIANG, Chin-tung. *General Stilwell in China, 1942–1944.* See 465.

962 LOBDELL, George H., Jr. "A Biography of Frank Knox." Doctoral dissertation, University of Illinois, 1954.

963 LUKAS, Richard C. *Eagles East: The Army Air Forces and the Soviet Union, 1941–1945.* Tallahassee, Fla., 1970.

964 LUKAS, Richard C. "The Middle East—Corridor to Russia: Lend-Lease Aircraft to the Russians, 1941–1942." *Airpower Hist,* XII (1965), 78–84.

965 LUKAS, Richard C. "The *Velvet* Project: Hope and Frustration." *Mil Aff,* XXVIII (1964), 145–162.

966 LUVAAS, Jay, ed. *Dear Miss Em: General Eichelberger's War in the Pacific, 1942–1945.* Westport, Conn., 1972.

967 MACDONALD, Charles B. *The Mighty Endeavor: American Armed Forces in the European Theater in World War II.* New York, 1969.

968 MCILVENNA, Don E. "Prelude to D-Day: American Strategy and the Second Front Issue." Doctoral dissertation, Stanford University, 1966.

969 MACISAAC, David. "The United States Strategic Bombing Survey, 1944–1947." Doctoral dissertation, Duke University, 1970.

970 MAGINNIS, John J. *Military Government Journal: Normandy to Berlin.* Ed. Robert A. Hart. Amherst, Mass., 1971.

971 *Marine Corps Monographs.* 15 Vols. Washington, 1947–1955.

972 MARTIN, Ralph G. *The GI War, 1941–1945.* Boston, 1967.[†]

973 MATLOFF, Maurice. "Was the Invasion of Southern France a Blunder?" *USN Inst Proc,* LXXXIV (July 1958), 35–45.

974 MORISON, Elting E. *Turmoil and Tradition: A Study of the Life and Times of Henry L. Stimson.* Boston, 1960.[†]

975 MORISON, Samuel E. *The Two-Ocean War.* Boston, 1963.[†]

976 MORISON, Samuel Eliot. *History of United States Naval Operations in World War II.* 15 Vols. Boston, 1947–1962.

977 NELSON, Donald M. *Arsenal of Democracy: The Story of American War Production.* New York, 1946.

978 NORMAN, Albert. *Operation Overlord: Design and Reality, The Allied Invasion of Western Europe.* Harrisburg, Pa., 1952.

979 O'BRIEN, Charles F. "The Canol Project: A Study in Emergency Military Planning." *Pac N W Q,* LXI (1970), 101–108.

980 O'SULLIVAN, John Joseph. "From Voluntarism to Conscription: Congress and Selective Service, 1940–1945." Doctoral dissertation, Columbia University, 1971.

981 PLUTH, Edward J. "The Administration and Operation of German Prisoner of War Camps in the United States during World War II." Doctoral dissertation, Ball State University, 1970.

982 POGUE, Forrest C. *George C. Marshall: Ordeal and Hope, 1939–1942.* New York, 1966.

983 POGUE, Forrest C. *George C. Marshall: Organizer of Victory, 1943–1945.* New York, 1973.

984 PRANGE, Gordon W. "The Battle of Midway: A Study in Command." Doctoral dissertation, University of Maryland, 1971.

985 PRATT, Fletcher. *War for the World: A Chronicle of Our Fighting Forces in World War II.* New Haven, Conn., 1950.

986 QUESTER, George H. *Deterrence before Hiroshima: The Air-Power Background of Modern Strategy.* New York, 1966.

987 REYNOLDS, Clark G. *The Fast Carriers: The Forging of an Air Navy.* New York, 1968.

988 REYNOLDS, Clark G. "Submarine Attacks on the Pacific Coast, 1942." *Pac Hist Rev,* XXXIII (1964), 183–193.

989 RIDDLE, Donald H. *The Truman Committee: A Study in Congressional Responsibility.* New Brunswick, N.J., 1964.

990 ROSE, Joseph R. *American Wartime Transportation.* New York, 1953.

991 RUNDELL, Walter. *Black Market Money: The Collapse of U.S. Military Currency Control in World War II.* Baton Rouge, La., 1964.

992 SCHILLING, Warner R. "The H-Bomb Decision: How to Decide without Actually Choosing." *Pol Sci Q*, LXXVI (1961), 24–46.

993 SCHLEGEL, Marvin Wilson. *Virginia on Guard: Civilian Defense and the State Militia in the Second World War.* Richmond, Va., 1949.

994 SCHOENBERGER, Walter Smith. *Decision of Destiny.* Athens, Ohio, 1969. Atomic bomb.

995 SHANDROFF, Gary Joseph. "The Evolution of Area Bombing in American Doctrine and Practice." Doctoral dissertation, New York University, 1972.

996 SHEEHAN, Fred. *Anzio: Epic of Bravery.* Norman, Okla., 1964.

997 SHERROD, Robert. *History of Marine Corps Aviation in World War II.* Washington, 1952.

998 SMITH, R. Harris. *OSS: The Secret History of America's First Central Intelligence Agency.* Berkeley, Cal., 1972.†

999 SMITH, S. E., ed. *The United States Marine Corps in World War II.* New York, 1969.†

1000 SMITH, S. E., ed. *The United States Navy in World War II.* New York, 1966.

1001 SOMERS, H. M. *Presidential Agency: OWMR. The Office of War Mobilization and Reconversion.* Cambridge, Mass., 1950.

1002 STAGG, J. M. *Forecast for Overlord: June 6, 1944.* New York, 1971.

1003 STEELE, Richard W. *The First Offensive, 1942: Roosevelt, Marshall, and the Making of American Strategy.* Bloomington, Ind., 1973.

1004 STEELE, Richard W. "Political Aspects of American Military Planning, 1941–1942." *Mil Aff.* XXV (1971), 68–74.

1005 STIMSON, Henry L., and McGeorge BUNDY. *On Active Service in Peace and War.* New York, 1948.

1006 STOLER, Mark Alan. "The Politics of the Second Front: American Military Planning and Diplomacy 1941–44." See 487.

1007 STOUFFER, Samuel A., *et al. The American Soldier.* 2 Vols. Princeton, N.J., 1949.

1008 TUCHMAN, Barbara W. *Stilwell and the American Experience in China, 1911–1945.*† See 491.

1009 TUTTLE, William M., Jr. "James B. Conant, Pressure Groups, and the National Defense, 1933–1945." See 348.

1010 *United States Army in World War II.* Washington, 1947–   80 Vols. to date.

1011 VANDEGRIFT, A. A., as told to Robert B. ASPREY. *Once a Marine: The Memoirs of General A. A. Vandegrift.* New York, 1964.

1012 VERRIER, Anthony. *The Bomber Offensive.* New York, 1969.

1013 WALLIN, Homer N. *Pearl Harbor: Why, How, Fleet Salvage and Final Appraisal.* Washington, 1968.

1014 WENDT, Paul. "The Control of Rubber in World War II." *S Eco J*, XIII (1947), 203–227.

1015 WERRELL, Kenneth P. "The Tactical Development of the Eighth Air Force in World War II." Doctoral dissertation, Duke University, 1969.

1016 WILLSON, Roger E. "The Truman Committee." Doctoral dissertation, Harvard University, 1966.

1017 WOHLSTETTER, Roberta. *Pearl Harbor: Warning and Decision.* Stanford, Cal., 1962.[†]

1018 WOODWARD, C. Vann. *The Battle for Leyte Gulf.* New York, 1947.

C. The Korean War

1019 BACCHUS, Wilfred A. "The Relationship between Combat and Peace Negotiations: Fighting while Talking in Korea, 1951–1953." *Orbis,* XVII (1973), 545–574.

1020 BERGER, Carl. *The Korea Knot.* See 621.

1021 BIDERMAN, Albert D. *March to Calumny: The Story of American POW's in the Korean War.* New York, 1963.

1022 BLANCHARD, Carroll H., Jr. ed. *Korean War Bibliography and Maps of Korea.* See 3.

1023 CAGLE, Malcolm W., and Frank A. MANSON. *The Sea War in Korea.* Annapolis, Md., 1957.

1024 CARIDI, Ronald J. *The Korean War and American Politics.* See 629.

1025 CARIDI, Ronald James. "The GOP and the Korean War." See 630.

1026 CLARK, Mark Wayne. *From the Danube to the Yalu.* New York, 1954.

1027 COLLINS, J. Lawton. *War in Peacetime: The History and Lessons of Korea.* Boston, 1969.

1028 CROFTS, Alfred. "The Start of the Korean War Reconsidered." *Rocky Mt Soc Sci J,* VII (April 1970), 109–117.

1029 FEHRENBACH, T. R. *This Kind of War: A Study in Unpreparedness.* New York, 1967.

1030 FIELD, James A., Jr. *History of United States Naval Operations: Korea.* Washington, 1962.

1031 FUTRELL, Robert Frank. *The United States Air Force in Korea, 1950–1953.* New York, 1961.

1032 GOODRICH, Leland M. *Korea.* See 653.

1033 HALPERIN, Morton H. "The Limiting Process in the Korean War." *Pol Sci Q,* LXXVIII (1963), 13–39.

1034 HEINL, Robert Debs, Jr. *Victory at High Tide: The Inchon-Seoul Campaign.* Philadelphia, 1968.

1035 HIGGINS, Trumbull. *Korea and the Fall of MacArthur: A Précis in Limited War.* New York, 1960.

1036 KARIG, Walter, *et al.,* eds. *Battle Report: The War in Korea.* New York, 1952.

1037 LECKIE, Robert. *Conflict: The History of the Korean War, 1950–1953.* New York, 1962.

1038 LOFGREN, Charles A. "Congress and the Korean Conflict." See 687.

1039 LOFGREN, Charles A. "Mr. Truman's War: A Debate and Its Aftermath." See 688.

1040 LYONS, Gene. *Military Policy and Economic Aid.* See 690.

1041 MCLELLAN, David S. "Dean Acheson and the Korean War." See 691.

1042 MANTELL, Matthew Edwin. "Opposition to the Korean War: A Study in American Dissent." See 692.

1043 MIDDLETON, Harry J. *The Compact History of the Korean War.* New York, 1965.

1044 MUELLER, John E. "Trends in Popular Support for the Wars in Korea and Vietnam." See 698.

1045 NORMAN, John. "MacArthur's Blockade Proposals against Red China." *Pac Hist Rev,* XXVI (1957), 161–174.

1046 PAIGE, Glenn D. *The Korean Decision: June 24–30, 1950.* New York, 1968.†

1047 POATS, Rutherford M. *Decision in Korea: An Authentic History of the Korean War.* New York, 1954.

1048 REES, David. *Korea: The Limited War.* New York, 1964.†

1049 RIDGWAY, Matthew B. *The Korean War: How We Met the Challenge.* Garden City, N.Y., 1967.†

1050 RIGGS, James Richard. "Congress and the Conduct of the Korean War." See 708.

1051 ROVERE, Richard H., and Arthur SCHLESINGER, Jr. *The MacArthur Controversy and American Foreign Policy.* New York, 1965.

1052 RUETTEN, Richard T. "General Douglas MacArthur's 'Reconnaissance in Force': The Rationalization of a Defeat in Korea." *Pac Hist Rev,* XXXVI (1967), 79–93.

1053 SAWYER, Robert K. *Military Advisors in Korea.* See 710.

1054 SHELDON, Walt. *Hell or High Water: MacArthur's Landing at Inchon.* New York, 1968.†

1055 SPANIER, John W. *The Truman-MacArthur Controversy and the Korean War.* Cambridge, Mass., 1959.†

1056 *United States Army in the Korean War.* Washington, 1961– 3 Vols. to date.

1057 *U.S. Marine Operations in Korea 1950–1953.* 5 Vols. Washington, 1954–1972.

1058 WUBBEN, H. H. "American Prisoners of War in Korea: A Second Look at the 'Something New in History' Theme." *Am Q,* XXII (1970), 3–19.

D. The Vietnam War

1059 AUSTIN, Anthony. *The President's War.* See 618.

1060 BOYLE, Richard. *The Flower of the Dragon: The Breakdown of the U.S. Army in Vietnam.* San Franscisco, 1972.†

1061 BRANDON, Henry. *Anatomy of Error.* See 626.

1062 BROUGHTON, Jack. *Thud Ridge.* Philadelphia, 1969.†

1063 CLIFFORD, Clark. "A Viet Nam Reappraisal: The Personal History of One Man's View and How It Evolved." See 631.

1064 COOPER, Chester L. *The Lost Crusade.*† See 634.

1065 DIBACCO, Thomas V. "The Business Press and Vietnam: Ectasy or Agony?" See 635.

1066 DRAPER, Theodore. *Abuse of Power.*† See 637.

1067 FALK, Richard A., ed. *The Vietnam War and International Law.*† See 642.

1068 FITZGERALD, Frances. *Fire in the Lake.*† See 648.

1069 FULTON, William B. *Vietnam Studies: Riverine Operations, 1966–1969.* Washington, 1973.

1070 GALLOWAY, John. *The Gulf of Tonkin Resolution.* See 650.

1071 GRAFF, Henry F. *The Tuesday Cabinet.* See 655.

1072 GREENHALGH, William H., Jr. "AOK Airpower over Khe Sanh." *Aero Hist,* XIX (1972), 2–9.

1073 HALBERSTAM, David. *The Best and the Brightest.*† See 658.

1074 HOOPER, Edwin Bickford. *Mobility, Support, Endurance: A Story of Naval Operational Logistics in the Vietnam War 1965–1968.* Washington, 1972.

1075 HOOPES, Townsend. *The Limits of Intervention.*† See 665.

1076 KAHIN, George M., and John W. LEWIS. *The United States in Vietnam.*† See 673.

1077 KAIL, F. M. *What Washington Said.* See 675.

1078 KALB, Marvin, and Elie ABEL. *Roots of Involvement.* See 676.

1079 LITTAUER, Raphael, and Norman UPHOFF, eds. *The Air War in Indochina.* Boston, 1972.†

1080 MARSHALL, S. L. A. *Ambush.* New York, 1969.

1081 MARSHALL, S. L. A. *Battles in the Monsoon: Campaigning in the Central Highlands Vietnam, Summer 1966.* New York, 1967.†

1082 MARSHALL, S. L. A. *The Fields of Bamboo.* New York, 1971.

1083 MOORE, John Norton. *Law and the Indo-China War.*† See 697.

1084 MUELLER, John E. "Trends in Popular Support for the Wars in Korea and Vietnam." See 698.

1085 MULLIGAN, Hugh A. *No Place to Die: The Agony of Viet Nam.* New York, 1967.

1086 NEEL, Spurgeon. *Vietnam Studies: Medical Support of the U.S. Army in Vietnam, 1965–1970.* Washington, 1973.

1087 *The Pentagon Papers as Published by the "New York Times."*† See 703.

1088 *The Pentagon Papers.* The Gravel edn.† See 704.

V. Politics and Government

A. National Politics and Government

1089 ADER, Emile B. "Why the Dixiecrats Failed." *J Pol,* XV (1953), 356–369.

1090 ALBRIGHT, Joseph. *What Makes Spiro Run: The Life and Times of Spiro Agnew.* New York, 1972.†

1091 AMLUND, Curtis Arthur. "Executive-Legislative Imbalance: Truman to Kennedy?" *W Pol Q,* XVIII (1965), 640–645.

1092 ANDERSON, Clinton P., with Milton VIORST. *Outsider in the Senate: Senator Clinton Anderson's Memoirs.* New York, 1970.

1093 APPLEBY, Paul H. "Roosevelt's Third-Term Decision." *Am Pol Sci Rev,* XLVI (1952), 745–765.

1094 ARNOLD, Delbert D. "The C.I.O.'s Role in American Politics, 1936–1948." Doctoral dissertation, University of Maryland, 1953.

1095 AXELROD, Robert. "Where the Votes Came from: An Analysis of Electoral Coalitions, 1952–1968." *Am Pol Sci Rev,* LXVI (1972), 11–20.

1096 BAILEY, Stephen Kemp. *Congress Makes a Law: The Story behind the Employment Act of 1946.* New York, 1950.

1097 BANKS, James G. "Strom Thurmond and the Revolt against Modernity." Doctoral dissertation, Kent State University, 1970.

1098 BARKLEY, Alben W. *That Reminds Me—.* Garden City, N.Y., 1954. Autobiography.

1099 BARNARD, Ellsworth. *Wendell Willkie: Fighter for Freedom.* Marquette, Mich., 1966.†

1100 BARTO, Harold Emery. "Clark Clifford and the Presidential Election of 1948." Doctoral dissertation, Rutgers University, 1970.

1101 BARUCH, Bernard. *Baruch: The Public Years.* New York, 1960.

1102 BATEMAN, Herman E. "The Election of 1944 and Foreign Policy." See 180.

1103 BERNSTEIN, Carl, and Robert WOODWARD. *All the President's Men.* New York, 1974.† The Watergate scandals.

1104 BLACKORBY, Edward C. *Prairie Rebel: The Public Life of William Lemke.* Lincoln, Neb., 1963.

1105 BLAKE, I. George. *Paul V. McNutt: Portrait of a Hoosier Statesman.* Indianapolis, Ind., 1966.

1106 BLOOM, Lynn Z. *Doctor Spock: Biography of a Conservative Radical.* Indianapolis, Ind., 1972.

1107 BLUM, Albert A., and J. Douglas SMYTH. "National Citizens Political Action Committee: An Example of Liberal-Labor Cooperation." *Societas,* I (1971), 187–206.

1108 BOWLES, Chester. *Promises to Keep.*† See 625.

49

1109 BRANYAN, Robert L., and R. Alton LEE. "Lyndon B. Johnson and the Art of the Possible." *S W Soc Sci Q*, XLV (1964), 213–225.

1110 BROCK, Clifton. *Americans for Democratic Action.* Washington, 1962.

1111 BRODER, David S. *The Party's Over: The Failure of Politics in America.* New York, 1972.†

1112 BROWN, Stuart Gerry. *Conscience in Politics: Adlai E. Stevenson in the 1950's.* Syracuse, N.Y. 1962.

1113 BROWN, Stuart Gerry. *The Presidency on Trial: Robert Kennedy's 1968 Campaign and Afterwards.* Honolulu, Hawaii, 1972.

1114 BULLOCK, Paul. " 'Rabbits and Radicals:' Richard Nixon's 1946 Campaign against Jerry Voorhis." *S Calif Q*, LV (1973), 319–359.

1115 BURNS, James MacGregor. *John Kennedy: A Political Profile.* New York, 1960.

1116 BYRNES, James F. *All in One Lifetime.* See 508.

1117 CALKINS, Fay. *The CIO and the Democratic Party.* Chicago, 1952.

1118 CARIDI, Ronald J. *The Korean War and American Politics.* See 629.

1119 CARIDI, Ronald James. "The GOP and the Korean War." See 630.

1120 CARLETON, William G. "The Revolution in the Presidential Nominating Convention." *Pol Sci Q*, LXXII (1957), 224–240.

1121 CATER, Douglass. *Power in Washington.* New York, 1964.†

1122 CHESTEEN, Richard D. " 'Mississippi Is Gone Home': A Study of the 1948 States' Right Bolt." *J Miss Hist*, XXXII (1970), 43–59.

1123 CHESTER, Edward W. *Radio, Television and American Politics.* New York, 1969.†

1124 CHESTER, Lewis, et al. *An American Melodrama: The Presidential Campaign of 1968.* New York, 1969.

1125 CLINCH, Nancy Gager. *The Kennedy Neurosis.* New York, 1973.

1126 COCHRAN, Bert. *Adlai Stevenson: Patrician among the Politicians.* New York, 1969.

1127 COHEN, Richard M., and Jules WITCOVER. *A Heartbeat Away: The Investigation and Resignation of Vice President Spiro T. Agnew.* New York, 1974.

1128 COIT, Margaret L. *Mr. Baruch.* Boston, 1957.

1129 CONNALLY, Tom, as told to Alfred STEINBERG. *My Name is Tom Connally.* See 197.

1130 CONVERSE, Philip E., et al. "Continuity and Change in American Politics: Parties and Issues in the 1968 Election." *Am Pol Sci Rev*, LXII (1969), 1083–1105.

1131 CONVERSE, Philip E., et al. "Stability and Change in 1960: A Reinstating Campaign." *Am Pol Sci Rev*, LV (1961), 269–280.

1132 COODE, Thomas H. "The Presidential Election of 1940 as Reflected in the Tennessee Metropolitan Press." *E Tenn Hist Soc Pub* No. 40 (1968), 83–100.

1133 CORNWELL, Elmer E., Jr. *Presidential Leadership of Public Opinion.* Bloomington, Ind., 1965.

1134 COSER, Lewis and Irving HOWE. *The American Communist Party: A Critical History.* New York, 1962.

1135 COSMAN, Bernard. "Presidential Republicanism in the South, 1960." *J Pol,* XXIV (1962), 303–322.

1136 COSMAN, Bernard. "Republicanism in the South: Goldwater's Impact upon Voting Alignments in Congressional, Gubernatorial, and Senatorial Races." *S W Soc Sci Q,* XLVIII (1967), 13–23.

1137 COX, Edward Franklin. *State and National Voting in Federal Elections, 1910–1970.* Hamden, Conn., 1972.

1138 CRESPI, Irving. "The Structural Basis for Right-wing Conservatism: The Goldwater Case." *Pub Opin Q,* XXIX (1965–66), 523–543.

1139 CUMMINGS, Milton C., Jr., ed. *The National Election of 1964.* Washington, 1966.

1140 CURRY, Lawrence Hopkins. "Southern Senators and Their Roll-Call Votes in Congress, 1941–1944." Doctoral dissertation, Duke University, 1971.

1141 DALFIUME, Richard M., ed. *American Politics since 1945.* Chicago, 1969.†

1142 DARILEK, Richard E. "A Loyal Opposition in Time of War: The Republican Party and the Politics of Foreign Policy from Pearl Harbor to Yalta." See 202.

1143 DAVIS, Kenneth S. *The Politics of Honor: A Biography of Adlai E. Stevenson.* New York, 1967.

1144 DAVIS, Polly Ann. "Alben W. Barkley: Senate Majority Leader and Vice President." Doctoral dissertation, University of Kentucky, 1963.

1145 DEAKIN, James. *The Lobbyists.* Washington, 1966.

1146 DESANTIS, Vincent P. "The Presidential Election of 1952." *Rev Pol,* XV (1953), 131–150.

1147 DILLON, Mary Earhart. *Wendell Willkie, 1892–1944.* Philadelphia, 1952.

1148 DIVINE, Robert A. "The Cold War and The Election of 1948." See 210.

1149 DIVINE, Robert A. *Foreign Policy and U.S. Presidential Elections 1940–1960.*† See 211.

1150 DONAHOE, Bernard F. *Private Plans and Public Dangers: The Story of FDR's Third Nomination.* Notre Dame, Ind., 1965.

1151 DOROUGH, C. Dwight. *Mr. Sam.* New York, 1962. Sam Rayburn.

1152 DOUGHERTY, Richard. *Goodbye, Mr. Christian.* Garden City, N.Y., 1973. The 1972 McGovern presidential campaign.

1153 DOUGLAS, Paul H. *In the Fullness of Time: The Memoirs of Paul H. Douglas.* New York, 1972.

1154 EISELE, Albert. *Almost to the Presidency: A Biography of Two American Politicians.* Blue Earth, Minn., 1972. Hubert H. Humphrey and Eugene J. McCarthy.

1155 EMERY, Edwin. "Press Support for Johnson and Goldwater." *Jour Q,* XLI (1964), 485–488.

1156 EPSTEIN, Leon D., and Austin RANNEY. "Who Voted for Goldwater: The Wisconsin Case." *Pol Sci Q,* LXXXI (1966), 82–94.

1157 ETHRIDGE, Richard Calvin. "Mississippi's Role in the Dixiecratic Movement." Doctoral dissertation, Mississippi State University, 1971.

1158 EULAU, Heinz. *Class and Party in the Eisenhower Years.* New York, 1962.

1159 EVJEN, Henry O. "An Analysis of Some of the Propaganda Features of the Campaign of 1940." *S W Soc Sci Q*, XXVII (1946), 235–261.

1160 EVJEN, Henry O. "The Willkie Campaign: An Unfortunate Chapter in Republican Leadership." *J Pol*, XIV (1952), 241–256.

1161 FARLEY, James A. *Jim Farley's Story: The Roosevelt Years.* New York, 1948.

1162 FEREJOHN, John A. *Pork Barrel Politics: Rivers and Harbors Legislation, 1947–1968.* Stanford, Cal., 1974.

1163 FLEISCHMAN, Harry. *Norman Thomas: A Biography.* New York, 1964.

1164 FLYNN, Edward J. *You're the Boss.* New York, 1947. Democratic Party politics.

1165 FORSYTHE, James L. "Postmortem on the Election of 1948: An Evaluation of Cong. Clifford R. Hope's Views." *Kan Hist Q*, XXXVIII (1972), 338–359.

1166 FOSTER, James C. "1954: A CIO Victory?" *Lab Hist*, XII (1971), 392–408.

1167 FOSTER, James Caldwell. "The Union Politic: The CIO Political Action Committee." Doctoral dissertation, Cornell University, 1972.

1168 FUCHS, Lawrence H. "American Jews and the Presidential Vote." *Am Pol Sci Rev*, XLIX (1955), 385–401.

1169 FUCHS, Lawrence H. *The Political Behavior of American Jews.* Glencoe, Ill., 1956.

1170 GARSON, Robert A. "The Alienation of the South: A Crisis for Harry S. Truman and the Democratic Party, 1945–1948." *Mo Hist Rev*, LXIV (1970), 448–471.

1171 GARSON, Robert A. *The Democratic Party and the Politics of Sectionalism, 1941–1948.* Baton Rouge, La., 1974.

1172 GERSON, Louis L. *The Hyphenate in Recent American Politics and Diplomacy.* See 234.

1173 GILBERT, Robert E. *Television and Presidential Politics.* North Quincy, Mass., 1972.

1174 GORMAN, Joseph Bruce. *Kefauver: A Political Biography.* New York, 1971.

1175 Graebner, Norman A. "American Nominating Politics and the Failure of Consensus: 1968." *Aust J Pol Hist*, XIV (1968), 393–408.

1176 GRANT, Philip A., Jr. "Editorial Reaction to the 1952 Presidential Candidacy of Richard B. Russell." *Ga Hist Q*, LVII (1973), 167–178.

1177 GRANT, Philip A., Jr. "Kefauver and the New Hampshire Presidential Primary." *Tenn Hist Q*, XXXI (1972), 372–380.

1178 GRANT, Philip A., Jr. "The 1952 New Hampshire Presidential Primary: A Press Reaction." *Hist N H*, XXVII (1972), 210–223.

1179 GREENSTONE, J. David. *Labor in American Politics.* New York, 1969.†

1180 GRUENING, Ernest. *The Battle for Alaska Statehood.* Seattle, Wash., 1967.

1181 GRUENING, Ernest. *Many Battles: The Autobiography of Ernest Gruening.* New York, 1973.

1182 HAGENS, William J. "The Moss Committee and Freedom of Information." *Mich Acad*, IV (1971), 205–216.

1183 HAMBY, Alonzo L. *Beyond the New Deal: Harry S. Truman and American Liberalism.* New York, 1973.

1184 HAREVEN, Tamara K. *Eleanor Roosevelt: An American Conscience.* Chicago, 1968.

1185 HART, Gary Warren. *Right from the Start: A Chronicle of the McGovern Campaign.* New York, 1973.

1186 HARTMANN, Susan M. *Truman and the 80th Congress.* See 86.

1187 HASTING, Ann Celeste. "Intraparty Struggle: Harry S. Truman—1945–1948." Doctoral dissertation, St. Louis University, 1972.

1188 HATTERY, John W. "The Presidential Election Campaigns of 1928 and 1960: A Comparison of *The Christian Century* and *America.*" *J Ch State,* IX (1967), 36–50.

1189 HENDERSON, Cary S. "Congressman John Tabor of Auburn: Politics and Federal Appropriations, 1923–1962." Doctoral dissertation, Duke University, 1964.

1190 HENDERSON, Richard B. *Maury Maverick: A Political Biography.* Austin, Tex., 1970.

1191 HERSH, Burton. *The Education of Edward Kennedy: A Family Biography.* New York, 1972.

1192 HERZOG, Arthur. *McCarthy for President.* New York, 1969.

1193 HINCHEY, Mary H. "The Frustration of the New Deal Revival, 1944–1946." Doctoral dissertation, University of Missouri, 1965.

1194 HUGHES, Emmet John. *The Living Presidency.* New York, 1973.

1195 HUTHMACHER, J. Joseph. *Senator Robert F. Wagner and the Rise of Urban Liberalism.* New York, 1968.†

1196 HYMAN, Sidney. *The Lives of William Benton.* Chicago, 1970.

1197 HYMAN, Sidney. *Youth in Politics: Expectations and Realities.* New York, 1972.

1198 IRONS, Peter Hanlon. "America's Cold War Crusade: Domestic Politics and Foreign Policy, 1942–1948." See 546.

1199 JAFFE, Philip J. "The Rise and Fall of Earl Browder." *Survey,* XVIII (1972), 14–65.

1200 JOHNPOLL, Bernard K. *Pacifist's Progress: Norman Thomas and the Decline of American Socialism.* Chicago, 1970.

1201 JOHNSON, Donald Bruce. *The Republican Party and Wendell Willkie.* Urbana, Ill., 1960.†

1202 JOHNSON, Walter. *How We Drafted Adlai Stevenson.* New York, 1955.

1203 JOHNSON, Walter. *1600 Pennsylvania Avenue.†* See 94.

1204 JONES, Charles O. *Party and Policy-Making: The House Republican Policy Committee.* New Brunswick, N.J., 1964.

1205 KAMMERER, Gladys M. *Impact of War on Federal Personnel Administration, 1939–1945.* Lexington, Ky., 1951.

1206 KATCHER, Leo. *Earl Warren: A Political Biography.* New York, 1967.

1207 KEY, V. O., Jr. *The Responsible Electorate: Rationality in Presidential Voting, 1936–1960.* Cambridge, Mass., 1966.†

1208 KIMBALL, Penn. *Bobby Kennedy and the New Politics.* Englewood Cliffs, N.J., 1968.

1209 KIMBALL, Penn T. *The Disconnected.* New York, 1972.† Poor people and voting.

1210 KOLODZIEJ, Edward A. "Joe Clark (Reformer, Pa.): Profile of a New Senatorial Style." *Ant Rev,* XXIII (1963–1964), 463–476.

1211 KRUEGER, Thomas A. *And Promises to Keep: The Southern Conference for Human Welfare, 1938–1948.* Nashville, Tenn., 1967.

1212 LACHMAN, Seymour P. "Barry Goldwater and the 1964 Religious Issue." *J Ch State,* X (1968), 389–404.

1213 LAGUMINA, Salvatore John. *Vito Marcantonio: The People's Politician.* Dubuque, Ia., 1969.

1214 LANG, Kurt, and Gladys Engel LANG. *Politics and Television.* Chicago, 1968.†

1215 LAPOMARDA, Vincent A. "A Jesuit Runs for Congress: The Rev. Robert F. Drinan, S. J. and His 1970 Campaign." *J Ch State,* XV (1973), 205–222.

1216 LARSEN, Lawrence H. "William Langer: A Maverick in the Senate." *Wis Mag Hist,* XLIV (1961), 189–198.

1217 LASH, Joseph P. *Eleanor.*† See 99.

1218 LASH, Joseph P. *Eleanor and Franklin.*† See 100.

1219 LASKY, Victor. *JFK: The Man and the Myth.* New York, 1963.

1220 LASKY, Victor. *Robert F. Kennedy: The Myth and the Man.* New York, 1968.†

1221 LEARY, William M., Jr. "Smith of New Jersey: A Biography of H. Alexander Smith, United States Senator from New Jersey, 1944–1959." Doctoral dissertation, Princeton University, 1966.

1222 LEE, R. Alton. "The Turnip Session of the Do-Nothing Congress: Presidential Campaign Strategy." *S W Soc Sci Q,* XLIV (1963), 256–267.

1223 LEVIN, Murray B. *Kennedy Campaigning: The System and Style as Practiced by Senator Edward Kennedy.* Boston, 1966.

1224 LEVINE, Erwin L. *Theodore Francis Green: The Washington Years, 1937–1960.* Providence, R. I., 1971.

1225 LIEBERMAN, Joseph I. *The Power Broker: A Biography of John M. Bailey, Modern Political Boss.* Boston, 1966.

1226 LINCOLN, Evelyn. *Kennedy and Johnson.* See 101.

1227 LINCOLN, Evelyn. *My Twelve Years with John F. Kennedy.* See 102.

1228 LIPPMAN, Theo, Jr. *Spiro Agnew's America.* New York, 1972.

1229 LITTLE, Dwayne L. "The Political Leadership of Speaker Sam Rayburn, 1940–1961." Doctoral dissertation, University of Cincinnati, 1970.

1230 LODGE, Henry Cabot. *The Storm Has Many Faces.* See 280.

1231 LONGLEY, Lawrence D., and Alan G. BRAUN. *The Politics of Electoral College Reform.* New Haven, Conn., 1972.†

1232 LORD, Russell. *The Wallaces of Iowa.* Boston, 1947.

1233 LORENZ, A. L., Jr. "Truman and the Press Conference." *Jour Q,* XLIII (1966), 671–679.

1234 LUBELL, Samuel. *The Future of American Politics.* Garden City, N.Y., 1956.†

1235 LUBELL, Samuel. *The Hidden Crisis in American Politics.* New York, 1970.†

1236 LUBELL, Samuel. *Revolt of the Moderates.* New York, 1956.

1237 LUCAS, Jim G. *Agnew: Profile in Conflict.* New York, 1970.†

1238 LYNN, Naomi B., and Arthur F. MCCLURE. *The Fulbright Premise: Senator J. William Fulbright's Views on Presidential Power.* Lewisburg, Pa., 1973.

1239 MCCARTHY, Eugene J. *The Year of the People.* Garden City, N.Y., 1969.

1240 MCCLURE, Arthur F., and Donna COSTIGAN. "The Truman Vice Presidency: Constructive Apprenticeship or Brief Interlude?" *Mo Hist R,* LXV (1971), 318–341.

1241 MCCORD, James W., Jr. *A Piece of Tape—The Watergate Story: Fact and Fiction.* Rockville, Md., 1974.†

1242 MCCOY, Donald R. *Landon of Kansas.* Lincoln, Neb., 1966.

1243 MCCOY, Donald R. "Republican Opposition during Wartime, 1941–1945." *Mid Am,* XLIX (1967), 174–189.

1244 MACDOUGALL, Curtis D. *Gideon's Army.* 3 Vols. New York, 1965. Henry A. Wallace and the 1948 Progressive Party.

1245 MCLAURIN, Ann Mathison, "The Role of the Dixiecrats in the 1948 Election." Doctoral dissertation, University of Oklahoma, 1972.

1246 MACNEIL, Neil. *Dirksen: Portrait of a Public Man.* New York, 1970.

1247 MADISON, Charles A. *Leaders and Liberals in 20th Century America.* New York, 1961.

1248 MAGRUDER, Jeb Stuart. *An American Life: One Man's Road to Watergate.* New York, 1974.

1249 MANLEY, John F. "Wilbur D. Mills: A Study in Congressional Influence." *Am Pol Sci Rev,* LXIII (1969), 442–464.

1250 MARKOWITZ, Norman D. *The Rise and Fall of the People's Century: Henry A. Wallace and American Liberalism, 1941–1948.* New York, 1973.

1251 MARTIN, Joe, as told to Robert J. DONOVAN. *My First Fifty Years in Politics.* New York, 1960.

1252 MAYER, George H. *The Republican Party 1854–1966.* New York, 1967.

1253 MAYHEW, David R. *Party Loyalty among Congressmen: The Difference between Democrats and Republicans, 1947–1962.* Cambridge, Mass., 1966.

1254 MAZLISH, Bruce. *In Search of Nixon: A Psychohistorical Inquiry.* New York, 1972.†

1255 MAZLISH, Bruce. "Toward a Psychohistorical Inquiry: The 'Real' Richard Nixon." *J Interdis Hist,* I (1970), 49–105.

1256 MAZO, Earl. *Richard Nixon: A Political and Personal Portrait.* New York, 1959.

1257 MICKELSON, Sig. *The Electric Mirror: Politics in an Age of Television.* New York, 1972.

1258 MILLER, William J. *Henry Cabot Lodge.* See 287.

1259 MOORE, John Robert. "The Conservative Coalition in the United States Senate, 1942–1945." *J S Hist,* XXXIII (1967), 368–376.

1260 MOORE, John Robert. *Senator Josiah William Bailey of North Carolina.* Durham, N.C., 1968.

1261 MOORE, William Howard. *The Kefauver Committee and the Politics of Crime.* Columbia, Mo., 1974.

1262 MOOS, Malcolm. *Politics, Presidents, and Coattails.* Baltimore, 1952.

1263 MORRISON, Joseph L. *Governor O. Max Gardner: A Power in North Carolina and New Deal Washington.* Chapel Hill, N.C., 1971.

1264 MOSCOW, Warren. *Roosevelt and Willkie.* Englewood Cliffs, N.J., 1968.

1265 MULLEN, Jay Carlton. "West Virginia's Image: The 1960 Presidential Primary and the National Press." *West Va Hist,* XXXII (1971), 215–223.

1266 MULLER, Herbert J. *Adlai Stevenson: A Study in Values.* New York, 1967.

1267 NESS, Gary Clifford. "The State's Rights Democratic Movement of 1948." Doctoral dissertation, Duke University, 1972.

1268 NEUSTADT, Richard E. "Approaches to Staffing the Presidency: Notes on FDR and JKF." *Am Pol Sci Rev,* CVII (1963), 855–862.

1269 NEUSTADT, Richard E. "Congress and the Fair Deal: A Legislative Balance Sheet." See 105.

1270 NEUSTADT, Richard E. *Presidential Power: The Politics of Leadership.* New York, 1960.[†]

1271 NEVINS, Allan. *Herbert H. Lehman and His Era.* New York, 1963.

1272 *New York Times,* ed. *The Watergate Hearings.* New York, 1973.[†]

1273 NEWFIELD, Jack. *Robert Kennedy: A Memoir.* New York, 1969.

1274 NOVAK, Robert D. *The Agony of the G.O.P., 1964.* New York, 1965.

1275 PATTERSON, James T. *Mr. Republican: A Biography of Robert A. Taft.* Boston, 1972.

1276 PAUL, Justus F. "The Political Career of Senator Hugh Butler, 1940–1954." Doctoral dissertation, University of Nebraska, 1966.

1277 PETERSON, F. Ross. "Fighting the Drive toward War: Glen H. Taylor, the 1948 Progressives, and the Draft." *Pac N W Q,* LXI (1970), 41–45.

1278 PETERSON, F. Ross. *Prophet without Honor: Glen Taylor and the Fight for American Liberalism.* Lexington, Ky., 1974.

1279 PETERSON, Frank Ross. "Harry S. Truman and His Critics: The 1948 Progressives and the Origins of the Cold War." See 579.

1280 PHILIPOSE, Thomas. "The 'Loyal Opposition': Republican Leaders and Foreign Policy, 1943–1946." See 308.

1281 PHILLIPS, Kevin. *The Emerging Republican Majority.* New Rochelle, N.Y., 1969.[†]

1282 POLLARD, James E. "The Kennedy Administration and the Press." *Jour Q,* XLI (1964), 3–14.

1283 POLLARD, James E. *The Presidents and the Press: Truman to Johnson.* Washington, 1964.

1284 POMPER, Gerald. "The Nomination of Hubert Humphrey for Vice-President." *J Pol,* XXVIII (1966), 639–659.

1285 POMPER, Gerald M. "From Confusion to Clarity: Issues and American Voters, 1956–1968." *Am Pol Sci Rev,* LXVI (1972), 415–428.

1286 PORTER, Kirk H., and Donald Bruce JOHNSON, eds. *National Party Platforms, 1840–1968.* Urbana, Ill., 1970.†

1287 PRATT, William C. "Glen H. Taylor: Public Image and Reality." *Pac N W Q,* LX (1969), 10–16.

1288 PRITCHARD, Robert L. "Southern Politics in the Truman Administration: Georgia as a Test Case." Doctoral dissertation, University of California at Los Angeles, 1970.

1289 REDDING, Jack. *Inside the Democratic Party.* Indianapolis, Ind., 1958.

1290 REICHARD, Gary Warren. "The Reaffirmation of Republicanism: Dwight Eisenhower and the Eighty-Third Congress." See 113.

1291 RIKER, William H. "The CIO in Politics, 1936–1946." Doctoral dissertation, Harvard University, 1948.

1292 ROBINSON, Edgar Eugene. *They Voted for Roosevelt.* Stanford, Cal., 1947.

1293 ROBINSON, George W. "Alben Barkley and the 1944 Tax Veto." *Reg Ky Hist Soc,* LXVII (1969), 197–210.

1294 ROGIN, Michael. "Wallace and the Middle Class: The White Backlash in Wisconsin." *Pub Opin Q,* XXX (1966), 98–108.

1295 ROPER, Elmo. *You and Your Leaders: Their Actions and Your Reactions, 1936–1956.* New York, 1957.

1296 ROSEBOOM, Eugene H. *A History of Presidential Elections: From George Washington to Richard M. Nixon.* New York, 1970.

1297 ROSS, Hugh. "Roosevelt's Third-Term Nomination." *Mid Am,* XLIV (1962), 80–94.

1298 ROSS, Hugh. "Was the Nomination of Wendell Willkie a Political Miracle?" *Ind Mag Hist,* LVIII (1962), 79–100.

1299 ROSS, Irwin. *The Loneliest Campaign: The Truman Victory of 1948.* New York, 1968.

1300 ROVERE, Richard H. *The Goldwater Caper.* New York, 1965.

1301 SAPOSS, David J. *Communism in American Politics.* Washington, 1960.

1302 SCAMMON, Richard M., and Ben J. WATTENBERG. *The Real Majority.* New York, 1970.†

1303 SCHAFFER, Alan. *Vito Marcantonio: Radical in Congress.* Syracuse, N.Y., 1966.

1304 SCHAPSMEIER, Edward L., and Frederick H. SCHAPSMEIER. *Prophet in Politics: Henry A. Wallace and the War Years, 1940–1965.* Ames, Ia., 1970.

1305 SCHEELE, Henry Z. *Charlie Halleck: A Political Biography.* New York, 1966.

1306 SCHLESINGER, Arthur M., Jr., gen. ed. *History of U.S. Political Parties.* Vols. 3 & 4. New York, 1973.

1307 SCHLESINGER, Arthur M., Jr., and Fred L. ISRAEL, eds. *History of American Presidential Elections.* Vol. 4. New York, 1971.

1308 SCHMIDT, Karl M. *Henry A. Wallace: Quixotic Crusade 1948.* Syracuse, N.Y., 1960.

1309 SCHONBERGER, Howard B. "The General and the Presidency: Douglas MacArthur and the Election of 1948." *Wis Mag Hist,* LVII (1974), 201–219.

1310 SEIDLER, Murray B. *Norman Thomas: Respectable Rebel.* Syracuse, N.Y., 1967.

1311 SHANNON, David A. *The Decline of American Communism: A History of the Communist Party of the United States since 1945.* New York, 1959.

1312 SHANNON, William V. *The Heir Apparent: Robert Kennedy and the Struggle for Power.* New York, 1967.

1313 SHELTON, James Hill. "The Tax Scandals of the 1950's." Doctoral dissertation, American University, 1971.

1314 SHOGAN, Robert. "1948 Election." *Am Her,* XIX (June 1968), 22–31, 104–111.

1315 SIEVERS, Rodney Merle. "Adlai E. Stevenson: An Intellectual Portrait." Doctoral dissertation, University of Virginia, 1971.

1316 SILLARS, Malcolm O. "The Premises of the Candidates." *Ant Rev,* XVI (1956), 319–331.

1317 SMALLWOOD, James. "Sam Rayburn and the Rules Committee Change of 1961." *E Tex Hist J,* XI (1973), 51–56.

1318 SMITH, A. Robert. *The Tiger in the Senate: A Biography of Wayne Morse.* Garden City, N.Y., 1962.

1319 SNETSINGER, John. *Truman, the Jewish Vote, and the Creation of Israel.* See 716.

1320 SPRITZER, Donald E. "B. K. Wheeler and Jim Murray: Senators in Conflict." *Mont Mag W Hist,* XXIII (1973), 16–33.

1321 STAROBIN, Joseph R. *American Communism in Crisis, 1943–1957.* Cambridge, Mass., 1972.

1322 STEIN, Jean. *American Journey: The Times of Robert Kennedy.* New York, 1970.†

1323 STEINBERG, Alfred. *Sam Johnson's Boy.* See 127.

1324 STOESEN, Alexander R. "The Senatorial Career of Claude D. Pepper." Doctoral dissertation, University of North Carolina, 1965.

1325 STROMER, Marvin E. *The Making of a Political Leader: Kenneth S. Wherry and the United States Senate.* Lincoln, Neb., 1969.

1326 STRONG, Donald S. "The Presidential Election in the South, 1952." *J Pol,* XVII (1955), 343–389.

1327 *Submission of Recorded Presidential Conversations to the Committee on the Judiciary of the House of Representatives by President Richard Nixon.* Washington, 1974.†

1328 SZULC, Tad. *Compulsive Spy: The Strange Career of E. Howard Hunt.* New York, 1974.

1329 THEOHARIS, Athan. "The Republican Party and Yalta: Partisan Exploitation of the Polish American Concern over the Conference, 1945–1960." See 341.

1330 THEOHARIS, Athan G. *The Yalta Myths.* See 342.

1331 THOMSON, Charles, and Frances SHATTUCK. *The 1956 Presidential Campaign.* Washington, 1960.

1332 TILLET, Paul, et al. *The National Election of 1964.* Washington, 1966.

1333 TIMMISCH, Nick, and William JOHNSON. *Robert Kennedy at 40.* New York, 1965.

1334 TOMPKINS, C. David. *Senator Arthur H. Vandenberg.* See 343.

1335 VANDEN HEUVEL, William, and Milton GWIRTZMAN. *On His Own: Robert F. Kennedy, 1964–1968.* Garden City, N.Y., 1970.

1336 VASILEW, Eugene. "The New Style in Political Campaigns: Lodge in New Hampshire, 1964." *Rev Pol,* XXX (1968), 131–152.

1337 VOIGHT, Barton R. "Joseph C. O'Mahoney and the 1952 Senate Election in Wyoming." *Ann Wyo,* XLV (1973), 177–224.

1338 VOORHIS, Jerry. *Confessions of a Congressman.* Garden City, N.Y., 1947.

1339 WAGNON, William O., Jr. "John Roy Steelman: Native Son to Presidential Advisor." *Ark Hist Q,* XXVII (1968), 205–225.

1340 WALLACE, Harold L. "The Campaign of 1948." Doctoral dissertation, Indiana University, 1970.

1341 WANN, A. J. *The President as Chief Administrator: A Study of Franklin D. Roosevelt.* Washington, 1968.

1342 WATSON, Richard A. "Religion and Politics in Mid-America: Presidential Voting in Missouri, 1928 and 1960." *Midcon Am Stud J,* V (Spring 1964), 33–55.

1343 WEAVER, John D. *Warren: The Man, the Court, the Era.* Boston, 1967.

1344 WEIL, Gordon L. *The Long Shot: George McGovern Runs for President.* New York, 1973.

1345 WESTERFIELD, H. Bradford. *Foreign Policy and Party Politics.* See 356.

1346 WHITE, F. Clifton. *Suite 3505: The Story of the Draft Goldwater Movement.* New York, 1967.

1347 WHITE, Theodore H. *The Making of the President 1960.* New York, 1961.[†]

1348 WHITE, Theodore H. *The Making of the President 1964.* New York, 1965.[†]

1349 WHITE, Theodore H. *The Making of the President 1968.* New York, 1969.

1350 WHITE, Theodore H. *The Making of the President 1972.* New York, 1973.[†]

1351 WHITE, William S. *The Taft Story.* New York, 1954.

1352 WILDAVSKY, Aaron. "The Goldwater Phenomenon: Purists, Politicians, and the Two-Party System." *Rev Pol,* XXVII (1965), 386–413.

1353 WILLIAMS, Oliver P. "The Commodity Credit Corporation and the 1948 Presidential Election." *M W J Pol Sci,* I (1957), 111–124.

1354 WILLS, Garry. *Nixon Agonistes: The Crisis of the Self-Made Man.* Boston, 1970.[†]

1355 WITCOVER, Jules. *85 Days: The Last Campaign of Robert Kennedy.* New York, 1969.[†]

1356 WITCOVER, Jules. *The Resurrection of Richard Nixon.* New York, 1970.

1357 WITCOVER, Jules. *White Knight: The Rise of Spiro Agnew.* New York, 1972.

1358 YARNELL, Allen. *Democrats and Progressives: The 1948 Presidential Election as a Test of Postwar Liberalism.* Berkeley, Cal., 1974.

1359 YOUNG, Roland. *Congressional Politics in the Second World War.* New York, 1956.

B. Regional, State, and Local Politics

1360 ADAMS, Harreld S. "The Dingell-Lesinski 1964 Primary Race." *W Pol Q*, XIX (1966), 688–696.

1361 AKERMAN, Robert H. "The Triumph of Moderation in Florida Thought and Politics: A Study of the Race Issue from 1954 to 1960." Doctoral dissertation, American University, 1967.

1362 BARNARD, William Dean. "Southern Liberalism in Triumph and Frustration: Alabama Politics, 1946–1950." Doctoral dissertation, University of Virginia, 1971.

1363 BARTHOLOMEW, Paul C. *The Indiana Third Congressional District: A Political History.* Notre Dame, Ind., 1970.

1364 BARTLEY, Numan V. *From Thurmond to Wallace: Political Tendencies in Georgia, 1948–1968.* Baltimore, 1970.†

1365 BLACK, Earl. "Southern Governors and Political Change: Campaign Stances on Racial Segregation and Economic Development, 1950–69." *J Pol*, XXXIII (1971), 703–734.

1366 BOLLENS, John C., and Grant B. GEYER. *Yorty: Politics of a Constant Candidate.* Pacific Palisades, Cal., 1973.

1367 BOWLES, Chester. *Promises to Keep.*† See 625.

1368 BUNI, Andrew. *The Negro in Virginia Politics, 1902–1965.* Charlottesville, Va., 1967.

1369 BURKE, Robert E. *Olson's New Deal for California.* Berkeley, Cal., 1953.

1370 BURNHAM, Walter Dean. "The Alabama Senatorial Election of 1962: Return of Inter-Party Competition." *J. Pol*, XXVI (1964), 798–829.

1371 BURTON, Robert E. *Democrats of Oregon: The Pattern of Minority Politics, 1900–1956.* Eugene, Ore., 1970.

1372 CARLETON, William G., and Hugh Douglas PRICE. "America's Newest Voters: A Florida Case Study." *Ant Rev*, XIV (1954), 441–457.

1373 CASDORPH, Paul. *A History of the Republican Party in Texas 1865–1965.* Austin, Tex., 1965.

1374 CHERNY, Robert W. "Isolationist Voting in 1940: A Statistical Analysis." See 376.

1375 COFFMAN, Tom. *Catch a Wave: A Case Study of Hawaii's New Politics.* Honolulu, Hawaii, 1973.†

1376 COOKE, Edward F. "Patterns of Voting in Pennsylvania Counties, 1944–1958." *Pa Hist*, XXVII (1960), 69–87.

1377 COSMAN, Bernard. "Religion and Race in Louisiana Presidential Politics, 1960." *S W Soc Sci Q*, XLIII (1962), 235–241.

1378 DAVIDSON, Chandler. *Biracial Politics: Conflict and Coalition in the Metropolitan South.* Baton Rouge, La., 1972.

1379 DELMATIER, Royce D., et al., eds. *The Rumble of California Politics, 1848–1970.* New York, 1970.†

1380 EPSTEIN, Leon D. *Politics in Wisconsin.* Madison, Wis., 1958.

1381 ERSHKOWITZ, Miriam, and Joseph ZIKMUND, II. *Black Politics in Philadelphia.* New York, 1973.

1382 FAIR, Daryl R. "The Reaction of Pennsylvania Voters to Catholic Candidates." *Pa Hist,* XXXII (1965), 305–315.

1383 FARRIS, Charles D. "The Re-Enfranchisement of Negroes in Florida." *J Neg Hist,* XXXIX (1954), 259–283.

1384 FEAGIN, Joe R., and Harlan HAHN. "The Second Reconstruction: Black Political Strength in the South." *Soc Sci Q,* LI (1970), 42–56.

1385 FINCH, Glenn. "The Election of United States Senators in Kentucky: The Cooper Period." *Fil C Hist Q,* XLVI (1972), 161–178.

1386 FINK, Joseph Richard. "Reform in Philadelphia: 1946–1951." Doctoral dissertation, Rutgers University, 1971.

1387 GARRETT, Charles. *The La Guardia Years: Machine and Reform Politics in New York City.* New Brunswick, N.J., 1961.

1388 GRANTHAM, Dewey W., Jr. "The South and the Reconstruction of American Politics." *J Am Hist,* LIII (1966), 227–246.

1389 GREEN, George N. "The Far Right Wing in Texas Politics, 1930's–1960's." Doctoral dissertation, Florida State University, 1966.

1390 GRELE, Ronald John. "The Structural Development of Urban Liberalism in the Democratic Party of the Fourth Congressional District of New Jersey, 1930–1960." Doctoral dissertation, Rutgers University, 1971.

1391 HAAS, Edward F. *The Illusion of Reform: De Lesseps S. Morrison and New Orleans Politics, 1946–1961.* Baton Rouge, La., 1974.

1392 HANEY, Richard C. "A History of the Democratic Party of Wisconsin since World War Two." Doctoral dissertation, University of Wisconsin, 1970.

1393 HARVEY, Richard B. *Earl Warren: Governor of California.* Jericho, N.Y., 1969.

1394 HARVEY, Richard B. "Governor Earl Warren of California: A Study in 'Non-Partisan' Republican Politics." *Calif Hist Soc Q,* XLVI (1967), 33–51.

1395 HAVARD, William C., ed. *The Changing Politics of the South.* Baton Rouge, La., 1972.

1396 HAVARD, William C., et al. *The Louisiana Elections of 1960.* Baton Rouge, La., 1963.

1397 HEARD, Alexander. *A Two-Party South?* Chapel Hill, N.C. 1952.

1398 HENDERSON, Lloyd R. "Earl Warren and California Politics." Doctoral dissertation, University of California at Berkeley, 1965.

1399 HENRIQUES, Peter Ros. "John S. Battle and Virginia Politics: 1948–1953." Doctoral dissertation, University of Virginia, 1971.

1400 HOLLINGSWORTH, Harold M., ed. *Essays on Recent Southern Politics.* Austin, Tex., 1970.

1401 HOLMES, Jack E. *Politics in New Mexico.* Albuquerque, N. Mex., 1967.

1402 HOWARD, Perry H. *Political Tendencies in Louisiana.* Baton Rouge, La., 1971.

1403 JEANSONNE, Glen. "de Lesseps Morrison: Why He Couldn't Become Governor of Louisiana." *La Hist,* XIV (1973), 255–269.

1404 JEANSONNE, Glen. "Racism and Longism in Louisiana: The 1959–60 Gubernatorial Elections." *La Hist,* XI (1970), 259–270.

1405 JEFFRIES, John Worthington. "Testing the Roosevelt Coalition: Connecticut Society and Politics." Doctoral dissertation, Yale University, 1973.

1406 JOHNSON, Roger T. *Robert M. La Follette, Jr. and the Decline of the Progressive Party in Wisconsin.* Madison, Wis., 1964.

1407 JOHNSON, Walter, ed. *The Papers of Adlai E. Stevenson: Governor of Illinois, 1949–1953.* Boston, 1973.

1408 JOHNSON, Walter, ed. *The Papers of Adlai E. Stevenson: Washington to Springfield, 1941–1948.* See 263.

1409 KEY, V. O., Jr. *American State Politics.* New York, 1966.

1410 KEY, V. O., Jr. *Southern Politics in State and Nation.* New York, 1949.†

1411 KURTZ, Michael L. "Earl Long's Political Relations with the City of New Orleans: 1948–1960." *La Hist,* X (1969), 241–254.

1412 KURTZ, Michael Louis. "The 'Demagogue and the Liberal': A Study of the Political Rivalry of Earl Long and deLesseps Morrison." Doctoral dissertation, Tulane University, 1971.

1413 LADD, Everett C. *Negro Political Leadership in the South.* Ithaca, N.Y., 1966.†

1414 LAGUMINA, Salvatore J. "Ethnic Groups in the New York Elections of 1970." *N Y Hist,* LIII (1972), 55–71.

1415 LAPOMARDA, Vincent A. "Maurice Joseph Tobin: The Decline of Bossism in Boston." *N Eng Q,* XLIII (1970), 355–381.

1416 LEBEDOFF, David. *The Twenty-First Ballot: A Political Party Struggle in Minnesota.* Minneapolis, Minn., 1969.

1417 LEGGETT, John C. "Class Consciousness and Politics in Detroit: A Study in Change." *Mich Hist,* XLII (1964), 289–314.

1418 LIEBERMAN, Joseph I. *The Power Broker.* See 1225.

1419 LITT, Edgar. *The Political Cultures of Massachusetts.* Cambridge, Mass., 1965.

1420 LOCKARD, Duane. *New England State Politics.* Princeton, N.J., 1959.†

1421 MCKAY, S. S. "O'Daniel, Roosevelt, and the Texas Republican Counties." *S W Soc Sci Q,* XXVI (1945), 1–21.

1422 MCKENNA, William J. "The Influence of Religion in the Pennsylvania Elections of 1958 and 1960." *Pa Hist,* XXIX (1962), 407–419.

1423 MCKENNA, William J. "The Negro Vote in Philadelphia Elections." *Pa Hist,* XXXII (1965), 406–415.

1424 MCPHAIL, I. R. "The Vote for Mayor of Los Angeles in 1969." *Ann Assoc Am Geog,* LXI (1971), 744–758.

1425 MAJORS, William R. "Gordon Browning and Tennessee Politics, 1949–1953." *Tenn Hist Q,* XXVIII (1969), 166–181.

1426 MATTHEWS, Donald R., and James W. PROTHRO. *Negroes and the New Southern Politics.* New York, 1966.

1427 MELLON, Carlotta Herman. "The Rise and Fall of Grass Roots Politics: The California Democratic Council, 1953–1966." Doctoral dissertation, Claremont Graduate School, 1973.

1428 MILLER, William D. *Mr. Crump of Memphis.* Baton Rouge, La., 1964.

1429 MITAU, G. Theodore. "The Democratic–Farmer–Labor Party Schism of 1948." *Minn Hist,* XXXIV (1955), 187–194.

1430 MITAU, G. Theodore. *Politics in Minnesota.* Minneapolis, Minn., 1970.†

1431 MOSCOW, Warren. *The Last of the Big-Time Bosses: The Life and Times of Carmine DeSapio and the Rise and Fall of Tammany Hall.* New York, 1971.

1432 MOSCOW, Warren. *Politics in the Empire State.* New York, 1948.

1433 MOSCOW, Warren. *What Have You Done for Me Lately? The Ins and Outs of New York City Politics.* Englewood Cliffs, N.J., 1967.

1434 O'BRIEN, Michael. "The Anti-McCarthy Campaign in Wisconsin, 1951–1952." *Wis Mag Hist,* LVI (1972–73), 91–108.

1435 O'BRIEN, Michael James. "Senator Joseph McCarthy and Wisconsin: 1946–1957." Doctoral dissertation, University of Wisconsin, 1971.

1436 OSHINSKY, David M. "Wisconsin Labor and the Campaign of 1952." *Wis Mag Hist,* LVI (1972–73), 109–118.

1437 PARKER, Joseph B. *The Morrison Era: Reform Politics in New Orleans.* Gretna, La., 1974.

1438 PARKS, Norman L. "Tennessee Politics since Kefauver and Reece: A 'Generalist' View." *J Pol,* XXVIII (1966), 144–168.

1439 PEDERSEN, James F., and Kenneth D. WALD. *Shall the People Rule? A History of the Democratic Party in Nebraska Politics, 1854–1972.* Lincoln, Neb., 1972.

1440 PETTIGREW, Thomas F., and Ernest Q. CAMPBELL. "Faubus and Segregation: An Analysis of Arkansas Voting." *Pub Opin Q,* XXIV (1960), 436–447.

1441 PRICE, Hugh D. *The Negro and Southern Politics: A Chapter of Florida History.* New York, 1957.

1442 PRICE, Hugh Douglas. "The Negro and Florida Politics, 1944–1954." *J Pol,* XVII (1955), 198–220.

1443 PUTNAM, Jackson K. *Old-Age Politics in California: From Richardson to Reagan.* Stanford, Cal., 1970.

1444 ROGIN, Michael Paul, and John L. SHOVER. *Political Change in California: Critical Elections and Social Movements, 1890–1966.* Westport, Conn., 1970.†

1445 SALAMON, Lester M. "Leadership and Modernization: The Emerging Black Political Elite in the American South." *J Pol,* XXXV (1973), 615–646.

1446 SARASOHN, Stephen B., and Vera H. SARASOHN. *Political Party Patterns in Michigan.* Detroit, Mich., 1957.

1447 SCOTT, George William. "Arthur B. Langlie: Republican Governor in a Democratic Age." Doctoral dissertation, University of Washington, 1971.

1448 SINDLER, Allan P. *Huey Long's Louisiana: State Politics, 1920–1952.* Baltimore, 1956.†

1449 SMITH, Carl O., and Stephen B. SARASOHN. "Hate Propaganda in Detroit." *Pub Opin Q,* X (1946), 24–52.

1450 SMITH, Frank E. *Look Away from Dixie.* Baton Rouge, La., 1965.[†]

1451 STARR, J. Barton. "Birmingham and the 'Dixiecrat' Convention of 1948." *Ala Hist Q,* XXXII (1970), 23–50.

1452 STRONG, Donald S. "The Rise of Negro Voting in Texas." *Am Pol Sci Rev,* XLII (1948), 510–522.

1453 TAFT, Philip. *Labor Politics American Style: The California State Federation of Labor.* Cambridge, Mass., 1968.

1454 TAYLOR, Quintard. "The Chicago Political Machine and Black-Ethnic Conflict and Accommodation." *Pol Am Stud,* XXIX (1972), 40–66.

1455 THELEN, David P., and Esther S. THELEN. "Joe Must Go: The Movement to Recall Senator Joseph R. McCarthy." *Wis Mag Hist,* XLIX (1966), 185–209.

1456 TINDALL, George Brown. *The Disruption of the Solid South.* Athens, Ga., 1972.[†]

1457 WATTERS, Pat, and Reese CLEGHORN. *Climbing Jacob's Ladder: The Arrival of Negroes in Southern Politics.* New York, 1967.[†]

1458 WEEKS, O. Douglas. "The White Primary: 1944–1948." *Am Pol Sci Rev,* XLII (1948), 500–509.

1459 WILKINSON, J. Harvie, III. *Harry Byrd and the Changing Face of Virginia Politics, 1945–1966.* Charlottesville, Va., 1968.

1460 YARNELL, Allen. "Pension Politics in Washington State, 1948." *Pac N W Q,* LXI (1970), 147–155.

C. Civil Liberties and McCarthyism

1461 BACHER, Robert F. "Robert Oppenheimer (1904–1967)." *Proc Am Philos Soc,* CXVI (1972), 279–293.

1462 BARRETT, Edward L., Jr. *The Tenney Committee: Legislative Investigation of Subversive Activities in California.* Ithaca, N.Y., 1951.

1463 BECK, Carl. *Contempt of Congress: A Study of the Prosecutions Initiated by the Committee on Un-American Activites, 1945–1957.* New Orleans, La., 1959.

1464 BENTLEY, Eric. *Are You Now or Have You Ever Been: The Investigation of Show Business by the Un-American Activities Committee 1947–1958.* New York, 1972.[†]

1465 BENTLEY, Eric, ed. *Thirty Years of Treason: Excerpts from Hearings before the House Committee on Un-American Activities, 1938–1968.* New York, 1971.[†]

1466 BOLNER, James. "Mr. Chief Justice Vinson and the Communist Controversy: A Reassessment." *Reg Ky Hist Soc,* LXVI (1968), 378–391.

1467 BONTECOU, Eleanor. *The Federal Loyalty and Security Program.* Ithaca, N.Y., 1953.

1468 BROWN, Stuart Gerry. "Eisenhower and Stevenson in the McCarthy Era: A Study in Leadership." *Ethics,* LXIX (1959), 233–254.

1469 BUCKLEY, William, Jr., and L. Brent BOZELL. *McCarthy and His Enemies.* Chicago, 1954.

1470 CARLSON, Lewis H. "J. Parnell Thomas and the House Committee on Un-American Activities, 1938–1948." Doctoral dissertation, Michigan State University, 1967.

1471 CARR, Robert. *The House Committee on Un-American Activities, 1945–1950.* Ithaca, N.Y., 1952.

1472 CAUGHEY, John W. *In Clear and Present Danger: The Crucial State of Our Freedom.* Chicago, 1958.

1473 CHAMBERS, Whittaker. *Witness.* New York, 1952.† Memoirs of the chief accuser of Alger Hiss.

1474 CHASE, Harold. *Security and Liberty: The Problem of Native Communists, 1947–55.* Garden City, N.Y., 1955.

1475 CHEVALIER, Haakon. *Oppenheimer: The Story of a Friendship.* New York, 1965.

1476 COHN, Roy. *McCarthy.* New York, 1968.

1477 COOK, Fred J. *The Nightmare Decade: The Life and Times of Senator Joe McCarthy.* New York, 1971.

1478 COOKE, Alistair. *A Generation on Trial.* New York, 1952.

1479 COTTER, Cornelius P., and J. Malcolm SMITH. "An American Paradox: The Emergency Detention Act of 1950." *J Pol,* XIX (1957), 20–33.

1480 CURTIS, Charles P. *The Oppenheimer Case: The Trial of a Security System.* New York, 1955.

1481 DESANTIS, Vincent P. "American Catholics and McCarthyism." *Cath Hist Rev,* LI (1965), 1–30.

1482 FREELAND, Richard M. *The Truman Doctrine and the Origins of McCarthyism: Foreign Policy, Domestic Politics, and Internal Security, 1946–1948.* New York, 1972.†

1483 GARDNER, David P. *The California Oath Controversy.* Berkeley, Cal., 1967.

1484 GELLERMANN, William. *Martin Dies.* New York, 1944.

1485 GOODMAN, Walter. *The Committee: The Extraordinary Career of the House Committee on Un-American Activities.* New York, 1968.

1486 GRIFFITH, Robert. "The General and the Senator: Republican Politics and the 1952 Campaign in Wisconsin." *Wis Mag Hist,* LIV (1970), 23–29.

1487 GRIFFITH, Robert. "The Political Context of McCarthyism." *Rev Pol,* XXXIII (1971), 24–35.

1488 GRIFFITH, Robert. *The Politics of Fear: Joseph R. McCarthy and the Senate.* Lexington, Ky., 1970.†

1489 GRIFFITH, Robert. "Ralph Flanders and the Censure of Senator Joseph R. McCarthy." *Vt Hist,* XXXIX (1971), 5–20.

1490 GRIFFITH, Robert, and Athan THEOHARIS, eds. *The Specter: Original Essays on the Cold War and the Origins of McCarthyism.* New York, 1974.†

1491 HALTOM, John F. "National Security and Civil Liberty: Governmental Techniques Employed to Combat Subversive Activities, 1938–1953." Doctoral dissertation, University of Texas, 1954.

1492 HARPER, Alan D. *The Politics of Loyalty: The White House and the Communist Issue, 1946–1952.* Westport, Conn., 1969.

1493 HICKS, Granville. *Where We Came Out.* New York, 1954. Views of an ex-Communist.

1494 HISS, Alger. *In the Court of Public Opinion.* New York, 1957.†

1495 KANFER, Stefan. *A Journal of the Plague Years.* New York, 1973.

1496 KEMPER, Donald J. *Decade of Fear: Senator Hennings and Civil Liberties.* Columbia, Mo., 1965.

1497 KONVITZ, Milton R. *Expanding Liberties: Freedom's Gains in Postwar America.* New York, 1966.

1498 LATHAM, Earl. *The Communist Controversy in Washington: From the New Deal to McCarthy.* Cambridge, Mass., 1966.†

1499 MCAULIFFE, Mary Sperling. "The Red Scare and the Crisis in American Liberalism, 1947–1954." Doctoral dissertation, University of Maryland, 1972.

1500 MAJOR, John. *The Oppenheimer Hearing.* New York, 1971.

1501 MARKER, Jeffrey M. "The Jewish Community and the Case of Julius and Ethel Rosenberg." *Md Hist,* III (1972). 105–121.

1502 O'BRIEN, Michael. "The Anti-McCarthy Campaign in Wisconsin, 1951–1952." See 1434.

1503 O'BRIEN, Michael. "Robert Fleming, Senator McCarthy and the Myth of the Marine Hero." *Jour Q,* L (1973), 48–53.

1504 O'BRIEN, Michael James. "Senator Joseph McCarthy and Wisconsin: 1946–1957." See 1435.

1505 OSHINSKY, David M. "Senator Joseph McCarthy and the American Labor Movement." Doctoral dissertation, Brandeis University, 1971.

1506 PARMELEE, K. Stephen. "The Presbyterian Letter against McCarthyism." *J Presby Hist,* XLI (1963), 210–223.

1507 POTTER, Charles E. *Days of Shame.* New York, 1965. A senatorial view of the McCarthy era.

1508 PRITCHARD, Robert L. "California Un-American Activities Investigations: Subversion on the Right?" *Calif Hist Soc Q,* XLIX (1970), 309–327.

1509 REES, David. *Harry Dexter White.* See 315.

1510 REEVES, Thomas C. "The Foundation and Freedoms: An Inquiry into the Origins of the Fund for the Republic." *Pac Hist Rev,* XXXIV (1965), 197–218.

1511 REEVES, Thomas C. *Freedom and the Foundation: The Fund for the Republic in the Era of McCarthyism.* New York, 1969.

1512 ROCHE, John P. *The Quest for the Dream: The Development of Civil Rights and Human Relations in Modern America.* New York, 1963.

1513 ROGIN, Michael Paul. *The Intellectuals and McCarthy: The Radical Specter.* Cambridge, Mass., 1967.†

1514 ROVERE, Richard H. *Senator Joe McCarthy.* New York, 1959. †

1515 SCOBIE, Ingrid W. "Jack B. Tenney: Molder of Anti-Communist Legislation in California, 1940–1949." Doctoral dissertation, University of Wisconsin, 1970.

1516 SCOBIE, Ingrid Winther. "Jack B. Tenney and the 'Parasitic Menace': Anti-Communist Legislation in California, 1940–1949." *Pac Hist Rev,* XLIII (1974), 188–211.

1517 SHATTUCK, Henry L. "The Loyalty Review Board of the U. S. Civil Service Commission, 1947–1953." *Proc Mass Hist Soc,* LXXVIII (1966), 63–80.

1518 SIMMONS, Jerold Lee. "Operation Abolition: The Campaign to Abolish the House Un-American Activities Committee, 1938–1965." Doctoral dissertation, University of Minnesota, 1971.

1519 SMYLIE, James H. "Mackay and McCarthyism, 1953–1954." *J Ch State,* VI (1964), 352–365.

1520 STERN, Philip M., and Harold P. GREEN. *The Oppenheimer Case: Security on Trial.* New York, 1969.

1521 TANNER, William Randolph. "The Passage of the Internal Security Act of 1950." Doctoral dissertation, University of Kansas, 1971.

1522 THELEN, David P., and Esther S. THELEN. "Joe Must Go: The Movement to Recall Senator Joseph R. McCarthy." See 1455.

1523 THEOHARIS, Athan. "The Escalation of the Loyalty Program." *Politics and Policies of the Truman Administration.* Ed. Barton J. Bernstein. Chicago, 1970.†

1524 THEOHARIS, Athan. "The Rhetoric of Politics: Foreign Policy, Internal Security, and Domestic Politics in the Truman Era, 1945–1950." *Politics and Policies of the Truman Administration.* Ed. Barton J. Bernstein. Chicago, 1970.†

1525 THEOHARIS, Athan. *Seeds of Repression: Harry S. Truman and the Origins of McCarthyism.* Chicago, 1971.

1526 THEOHARIS, Athan. "The Threat to Civil Liberties." *Cold War Critics: Alternatives to American Foreign Policy in the Truman Years.* Ed. Thomas G. Paterson. Chicago, 1971.†

1527 THOMAS, John N. *The Institute of Pacific Relations.* See 717.

1528 THOMPSON, Francis H. "Truman and Congress: The Issue of Loyalty, 1946–1952." Doctoral dissertation, Texas Tech University, 1970.

1529 TROW, Martin. "Small Businessmen, Political Tolerance, and Support for McCarthy." *Am J Soc,* LXIV (1958), 270–281.

1530 VAUGHN, Robert. *Only Victims: A Study of Show Business Blacklisting.* New York, 1972.

1531 WEINSTEIN, Allen. "The Symbolism of Subversion: Notes on Some Cold War Icons." *J Am Stud,* VI (1972), 165–179.

1532 WILSON, Thomas W., Jr. *The Great Weapons Heresy.* Boston, 1970. Re the Oppenheimer case.

1533 ZELIGS, Meyer A. *Friendship and Fratricide: An Analysis of Whittaker Chambers and Alger Hiss.* New York, 1967.

D. The Legal System

1534 ABRAHAM, Henry J. *Freedom and the Court: Civil Rights and Liberties in the United States.* New York, 1972.†

1535 BAKER, Liva. *Felix Frankfurter.* New York, 1969.

1536 BARKER, Lucius J. "The Supreme Court as Policy Maker: The Tidelands Oil Controversy." *J Pol,* XXIV (1962), 350–366.

1537 BARTLEY, Ernest R. *The Tidelands Oil Controversy: A Legal and Historical Analysis.* Austin, Tex., 1953.

1538 BELZ, Herman. "Changing Conceptions of Constitutionalism in the Era of World War II and the Cold War." *J Am Hist,* LIX (1972), 640–669.

1539 BENSON, Paul R., Jr. *The Supreme Court and the Commerce Clause, 1937–1970.* New York, 1970.

1540 BICKEL, Alexander M. *Politics and the Warren Court.* New York, 1965.

1541 BICKEL, Alexander M. *The Supreme Court and the Idea of Progress.* New York, 1970.†

1542 BIDDLE, Francis B. *In Brief Authority.* Garden City, N.Y., 1962. Autobiography.

1543 BLAND, Randall W. *Private Pressure on Public Law: The Legal Career of Justice Thurgood Marshall.* Port Washington, N.Y., 1973.†

1544 CORTNER, Richard C. *The Apportionment Cases.* Knoxville, Tenn., 1970.

1545 COX, Archibald. *The Warren Court: Constitutional Decision as an Instrument of Reform.* Cambridge, Mass., 1968.†

1546 FINE, Sidney. "Frank Murphy, the Thornhill Decision, and Picketing as Free Speech." *Lab Hist,* VI (1965), 99–120.

1547 FINE, Sidney. "Mr. Justice Murphy and the Hirabayashi Case." *Pac Hist Rev,* XXXIII (1964), 195–209.

1548 FINE, Sidney. "Mr. Justice Murphy in World War II." *J Am Hist,* LIII (1966), 90–106.

1549 FISH, Peter Graham. *The Politics of Federal Judicial Administration.* Princeton, N.J., 1973.

1550 FRANK, John P. *Mr. Justice Black.* New York, 1949.

1551 FRIEDMAN, Leon, and Fred L. ISRAEL, eds. *The Justices of the United States Supreme Court 1789–1969: Their Lives and Major Opinions.* Vols. 3 & 4. New York, 1969.

1552 GERHART, Eugene C. *America's Advocate: Robert H. Jackson.* Indianapolis, Ind., 1958.

1553 GRIFFITH, Kathryn. *Judge Learned Hand and the Role of the Federal Judiciary.* Norman, Okla., 1973.

1554 HOWARD, J. Woodford. *Mr. Justice Murphy: A Political Biography.* Princeton, N.J., 1968.

1555 KATCHER, Leo. *Earl Warren.* See 1206.

1556 KELLEY, Alfred H., and Winfred A. HARBISON. *The American Constitution: Its Origins and Development.* New York, 1970.

1557 KOHLMEIER, Louis M., Jr. *'God Save This Honorable Court!'* New York, 1972.

1558 KURLAND, Philip B. *Mr. Justice Frankfurter and the Constitution.* Chicago, 1971.

1559 KURLAND, Philip B. *Politics, the Constitution, and the Warren Court.* Chicago, 1970.†

1560 LEVY, Leonard W., ed. *The Supreme Court under Earl Warren.* Chicago, 1972.†

1561 LEWIS, Anthony. *Gideon's Trumpet.* New York, 1964.† The right of a defendant to legal counsel.

1562 LYTLE, Clifford M. *The Warren Court and Its Critics.* Tucson, Ariz., 1968.

1563 MCCLOSKEY, Robert G. *The American Supreme Court.* Chicago, 1960.†

1564 MCCLOSKEY, Robert G. *The Modern Supreme Court.* Cambridge, Mass., 1972.†

1565 MCCUNE, Wesley. *The Nine Young Men.* New York, 1947.

1566 MANWARING, David R. *Render unto Caesar: The Flag-Salute Controversy.* Chicago, 1962.

1567 MASON, Alpheus Thomas. "The Burger Court in Historical Perspective." *Pol Sci Q,* LXXXIX (1974), 27–45.

1568 MASON, Alpheus Thomas. *Harlan Fiske Stone: Pillar of the Law.* New York, 1956.

1569 MASON, Alpheus Thomas. *The Supreme Court from Taft to Warren.* Baton Rouge, La., 1968.†

1570 MASON, Alpheus Thomas. "Understanding the Warren Court: Judicial Self-Restraint and Judicial Duty." *Pol Sci Q,* LXXXI (1966), 523–563.

1571 MENDELSON, Wallace. "From Warren to Burger: The Rise and Decline of Substantive Equal Protection." *Am Pol Sci Rev,* LXVI (1972), 1226–1233.

1572 MENDELSON, Wallace. "Hugo Black and Judicial Discretion." *Pol Sci Q,* LXXXV (1970), 17–39.

1573 MENDELSON, Wallace. *Justices Black and Frankfurter: Conflict in the Court.* Chicago, 1961.

1574 MITAU, G. T. *Decade of Decision: The Supreme Court and the Constitutional Revolution 1954–64.* New York, 1967.

1575 MURPHY, Paul L. *The Constitution in Crisis Times, 1918–1969.* New York, 1972.†

1576 NAVASKY, Victor S. *Kennedy Justice.* New York, 1971. Attorney General Robert F. Kennedy.

1577 PRITCHETT, C. Herman. *Civil Liberties and the Vinson Court.* Chicago, 1954.

1578 PRITCHETT, C. Herman. *Congress versus the Supreme Court, 1957–1960.* Minneapolis, Minn., 1961.

1579 PRITCHETT, C. Herman. *The Roosevelt Court: A Study in Judicial Politics and Values, 1937–1947.* New York, 1948.†

1580 ROSTOW, Eugene V. "The Japanese American Cases—A Disaster." *Yale Law J,* LIV (1945), 489–533.

1581 SCHICK, Marvin. *Learned Hand's Court.* Baltimore, 1970.

1582 SCHMIDHAUSER, John R., and Larry L. BERG. *The Supreme Court and Congress: Conflict and Interaction, 1945–1968.* New York, 1972.†

1583 SCHUBERT, Glendon A. *The Judicial Mind: The Attitudes and Ideologies of Supreme Court Justices, 1946–1963.* Evanston, Ill., 1965.

1584 SHOGAN, Robert. *A Question of Judgment: The Fortas Case and the Struggle for the Supreme Court.* Indianapolis, Ind., 1972.

1585 SIMON, James F. *In His Own Image: The Supreme Court in Richard Nixon's America.* New York, 1973.†

1586 SWINDLER, William F. *Court and Constitution in the Twentieth Century: The New Legality, 1932–1968.* Indianapolis, Ind., 1970.

1587 SWISHER, Carl Brent. *The Supreme Court in Modern Role.* New York, 1965.†

1588 TEN BROEK, Jacobus, et al. *Prejudice, War and the Constitution.* Berkeley, Cal., 1968.†

1589 THOMAS, Helen Shirley. *Felix Frankfurter: Scholar on the Bench.* Baltimore, 1960.

1590 THOMPSON, Dennis L. "The Kennedy Court: Left and Right of Center." *W Pol Q,* XXVI (1973), 263–279.

1591 WEAVER, John D. *Warren.* See 1343.

1592 WILBER, Leon A. "Development of Criminal Law in the Supreme Court 1966 to 1971." *South Q,* XI (1973), 121–145.

1593 WILLIAMS, Charlotte. *Hugo L. Black: A Study in the Judicial Process.* Baltimore, 1950.

VI. Economic Life

A. *Economic Conditions and Policies*

1594 AFROS, John L. "Labor Participation in the Office of Price Administration." *Am Pol Sci Rev,* XL (1946), 458–484.

1595 AHEARN, Daniel S. *Federal Reserve Policy Reappraised, 1951–1959.* New York, 1963.

1596 BAILEY, Stephen Kemp. *Congress Makes a Law.* See 1096.

1597 BECKER, Joseph. "Twenty-Five Years of Unemployment Insurance: An Experiment in Competitive Collectivism." *Pol Sci Q,* LXXV (1960), 481–499.

1598 BERLE, Adolf A. *The American Economic Republic.* New York, 1963.†

1599 BERLE, Adolf A., Jr. *Power without Property: A New Development in American Political Economy.* New York, 1959.†

1600 BERNSTEIN, Barton J. "Charting a Course between Inflation and Depression: Secretary of the Treasury Fred Vinson and the Truman Administration's Bill." *Reg Ky Hist Soc,* LXVI (1968), 53–64.

1601 BERNSTEIN, Barton J. "The Debate on Industrial Reconversion: The Protection of Oligopoly and Military Control of the War Economy." *Am J Econ Socio,* XXVI (1967), 159–172.

1602 BERNSTEIN, Barton J. "Economic Policies." *The Truman Period as a Research Field.* Ed. Richard S. Kirkendall. Columbia, Mo., 1967.

1603 BERNSTEIN, Barton J. "The Removal of War Production Board Controls on Business, 1944–1946." *Bus Hist Rev,* XXXIX (1965), 243–260.

1604 BERNSTEIN, Barton J. "The Truman Administration and Its Reconversion Wage Policy." *Lab Hist,* VI (1965), 214–231.

1605 BERNSTEIN, Barton J. "The Truman Administration and the Politics of Inflation." Doctoral dissertation, Harvard University, 1964.

1606 BLUM, John Morton. *From the Morgenthau Diaries: Years of Urgency, 1938–1941.* See 371.

1607 BLUM, John Morton, *From the Morgenthau Diaries: Years of War, 1941–1945.* See 427.

1608 BLYTH, Conrad A. *American Business Cycles, 1945–50.* New York, 1969.

1609 BRANYAN, Robert L. "The Antimonopoly Activities during the Truman Administration." Doctoral dissertation, University of Oklahoma, 1961.

1610 BREIT, William, and Roger L. RANSOM. *The Academic Scribblers: American Economists in Collision.* New York, 1971.†

1611 BUCKHORN, Robert F. *Nader: The People's Lawyer.* Englewood Cliffs, N.J., 1972.

1612 CAGAN, Phillip, et al. *Economic Policy and Inflation in the Sixties.* Washington, 1972.†

1613 CANTERBERY, E. Ray. *The President's Council of Economic Advisers: A Study of Its Functions and Its Influence on the Chief Executive's Decisions.* New York, 1961.

1614 CARSON, Robert B. "Changes in Federal Fiscal Policy and Public Attitudes since the Employment Act of 1946." *Soc Stud,* LVIII (1967), 308–314.

1615 CHANDLER, Lester V. *Inflation in the United States, 1940–48.* New York, 1951.

1616 CLAYTON, James L. "The Fiscal Cost of the Cold War to the United States: The First 25 Years, 1947–1971." *W Pol Q,* XXV (1972), 375–395.

1617 CLAYTON, James L. "The Impact of the Cold War on the Economies of California and Utah, 1946–1965." *Pac Hist Rev,* XXXVI (1967), 449–473.

1618 CLAYTON, James L. "An Unhallowed Gathering: The Impact of Defense Spending on Utah's Population Growth, 1940–1964." *Utah Hist Q,* XXXIV (1966), 227–242.

1619 COLBERG, Marshall R. *Human Capital in Southern Development, 1939–1963.* Chapel Hill, N.C., 1965.

1620 DALE, Edwin L., Jr. *Conservatives in Power: A Study in Frustration.* Garden City, N.Y., 1960.

1621 DOBNEY, Frederick J. "The Evolution of a Reconversion Policy: World War II and Surplus War Property Disposal." *Hist,* XXXVI (1974), 498–519.

1622 ECCLES, Marriner S. *Beckoning Frontiers: Public and Personal Recollections.* New York, 1951.

1623 EDWARDS, Rhoda D. K. "The Seventy-Eighth Congress on the Home Front: Domestic Economic Legislation, 1943–1944." Doctoral dissertation, Rutgers University, 1967.

1624 FLASH, Edward S., Jr. *Economic Advice and Presidential Leadership: The Council of Economic Advisers.* New York, 1965.

1625 FRIEDMAN, Bernard. *The Financial Role of Indiana in World War II.* Bloomington, Ind., 1965.

1626 FRIEDMAN, Milton, and Anna Jacobson SCHWARTZ. *A Monetary History of the United States, 1867–1960.* Princeton, N.J., 1963.†

1627 GALBRAITH, John Kenneth. *The New Industrial State.* Boston, 1967.†

1628 GILMARTIN, Jeanine. "An Historical Analysis of the Growth of the National Consumer Movement in the United States from 1947 to 1967." Doctoral dissertation, Georgetown University, 1970.

1629 GRAYSON, C. Jackson, Jr., and Louis NEEB. *Confessions of a Price Controller.* Homewood, Ill., 1974.

1630 GROSS, Bertram M., and John P. LEWIS. "The President's Economic Staff during the Truman Administration." *Am Pol Sci Rev,* XLVIII (1954), 114–130.

1631 HAMBY, Alonzo L. "The Vital Center, the Fair Deal, and the Quest for a Liberal Political Economy." *Am Hist Rev,* LXXVII (1972), 653–678.

1632 HANSEN, Alvin H. *The Postwar American Economy: Performance and Problems.* New York, 1964.†

1633 HARRIS, Seymour E. *Economics of the Kennedy Years and a Look Ahead.* New York, 1964.

1634 HARRIS, Seymour E. *The Economics of the Political Parties.* New York, 1962.

1635 HEATH, Jim F. "American War Mobilization and the Use of Small Manufacturers, 1939–1943." *Bus Hist Rev,* XLVI (1972), 295–319.

1636 HEATH, Jim F. *John F. Kennedy and the Business Community.* Chicago, 1969.

1637 HICKMAN, Bert G. *Growth and Stability of the Postwar Economy.* Washington, 1960.

1638 HOLMANS, A. E. *United States Fiscal Policy, 1945–1959.* New York, 1961.

1639 HOOPES, Roy. *The Steel Crisis.* New York, 1963.

1640 HOOVER, Calvin. *Memoirs of Capitalism, Communism, and Socialism.* Durham, N.C., 1965.

1641 HOWARD, Nathaniel R., ed. *The Basic Papers of George M. Humphrey as Secretary of the Treasury, 1953–1957.* Cleveland, Ohio, 1965.

1642 JONES, E. Terrence. "Congressional Voting on Keynesian Legislation, 1945–1964." *W Pol Q,* XXI (1968), 240–251.

1643 JONES, Jesse H. *Fifty Billion Dollars.* New York, 1951. The Reconstruction Finance Corporation.

1644 KENDRICK, John W. *Postwar Productivity Trends in the United States, 1948–1969.* New York, 1973.

1645 KENDRICK, John W. *Productivity Trends in the United States.* Princeton, N.J., 1961.

1646 KLEIN, Lawrence R. "The Role of War in the Maintenance of American Economic Prosperity." *Proc Am Philos Soc,* LXV (1971), 507–516.

1647 KNIPE, James L. *The Federal Reserve and the American Dollar: Problems and Policies, 1946–1964.* Chapel Hill, N.C., 1965.

1648 LAMMIE, Wayne David. "Unemployment in the Truman Administration: Political, Economic and Social Aspects." Doctoral dissertation, Ohio State University, 1973.

1649 LAMPMAN, Robert J. "Recent Changes in Income Inequality Reconsidered." *Am Econ Rev,* XLIV (1954), 251–268.

1650 LEE, R. Alton. "Federal Assistance in Depressed Areas in the Postwar Recessions." *W Econ J,* II (Fall 1963), 1–23.

1651 LEE, R. Alton. *A History of Regulatory Taxation.* Lexington, Ky., 1973.

1652 LEE, R. Alton. "The Truman–80th Congress Struggle over Tax Policy." *Hist,* XXXIII (1970), 68–82.

1653 LEKACHMAN, Robert. *The Age of Keynes.* New York, 1966.†

1654 LEWIS, Wilfred. *Federal Fiscal Policy in the Postwar Recessions.* Washington, 1962.†

1655 MCCARRY, Charles. *Citizen Nader.* New York, 1972.†

1656 MCCONNELL, Grant. *Steel and the Presidency, 1962.* New York, 1963.†

1657 MANSFIELD, Harvey C., et al. *A Short History of O.P.A.,* Washington, 1948.

1658 MOORE, Harry E. "War Boom, Texas Style." *S W Soc Sci Q,* XXIV (1943), 214–229.

1659 MYERS, Margaret G. *A Financial History of the United States.* New York, 1970.†

1660 PAUL, Randolph E. *Taxation in the United States.* Boston, 1954.

1661 PERLO, Victor, "People's Capitalism and Stock Ownership." *Am Econ Rev,* XLVIII (1958), 333–347.

1662 RATNER, Sidney. *Taxation and Democracy.* New York, 1967.

1663 ROSENOF, Theodore. "The Economic Ideas of Henry A. Wallace, 1933–1948." *Ag Hist,* XLI (1967), 143–153.

1664 ROWEN, Hobart. *The Free Enterprisers: Kennedy, Johnson, and the Business Establishment.* New York, 1964.

1665 SALANT, Walter S. "Some Intellectual Contributions of the Truman Council of Economic Advisers to Policy-Making." *Hist Pol Econ,* V (1973), 36–49.

1666 SAWYER, Charles. *Concerns of a Conservative Democrat.* Carbondale, Ill., 1968.

1667 SCHRIFTGIESSER, Karl. *Business and Public Policy: The Role of the Committee for Economic Development, 1942–1967.* Englewood Cliffs, N.J., 1967.

1668 SOULE, George. *Planning U.S.A.* New York, 1967.

1669 STEBBINS, Philip E. "Truman and the Seizure of Steel: A Failure in Communication." *Hist,* XXXIV (1971), 1–21.

1670 STEIN, Bruno. "Labor's Role in Government Agencies during World War II." *J Econ Hist,* XVII (1957), 389–408.

1671 STEIN, Bruno. "Wage Stabilization in the Korean War Period: The Role of the Subsidiary Wage Boards." *Lab Hist,* IV (1963), 161–177.

1672 STEIN, Herbert. *The Fiscal Revolution in America.* Chicago, 1969.†

1673 STEINMEYER, George W. "Disposition of Surplus War Property: An Administrative History, 1944–1949." Doctoral dissertation, University of Oklahoma, 1969.

1674 VATTER, Harold G. *The U.S. Economy in the 1950's.* New York, 1963.

1675 WAGNON, William O., Jr. "The Politics of Economic Growth: The Truman Administration and the 1949 Recession." Doctoral dissertation, University of Missouri, 1970.

1676 WHITE, Gerald T. "Financing Industrial Expansion for War: The Origin of the Defense Plant Corporation Leases." *J Econ Hist,* IX (1949), 156–183.

1677 WILSON, Richard B. "The Eisenhower Antitrust Policy: Progressivism or Conservatism?" *Rocky Mt Law Rev,* XXXII (1960), 179–203.

B. Business and Industry

1678 ALLEN, James B. "The Changing Impact of Mining on the Economy of Twentieth Century Utah." *Utah Hist Q,* XXXVIII (1970), 240–255.

1679 ANDERSON, Donald Norton. "The Decline of the Woolen and Worsted Industry of New England, 1947–1958; A Regional Economic History." Doctoral dissertation, New York University, 1971.

1680 ARRINGTON, Leonard J. *Beet Sugar in the West: A History of the Utah-Idaho Sugar Company, 1891–1966.* Seattle, Wash., 1966.

1681 ARRINGTON, Leonard J., and Jon G. PERRY. "Utah's Spectacular Missiles Industry: Its History and Impact." *Utah Hist Q,* XXX (1962), 3–39.

1682 BABCOCK, Glenn D. *History of the United States Rubber Company: A Case Study in Corporation Management.* Bloomington, Ind., 1966.

1683 BAILEY, Kenneth R. "Development of Surface Mine Legislation, 1939–1967." *West Va Hist,* XXX (1969), 525–529.

1684 BARITZ, Loren. *The Servants of Power: A History of the Use of Social Science in American Industry.* Middletown, Conn., 1960.

1685 BARLOON, Marvin J. "Institutional Foundations of Pricing Policy in the Steel Industry." *Bus Hist Rev,* XXVIII (1954), 214–235.

1686 BEATON, Kendall. *Enterprise in Oil: A History of Shell in the United States.* New York, 1957.

1687 BERNSTEIN, Barton J. "The Automobile Industry and the Coming of the Second World War." *S W Soc Sci Q,* XLVII (1966), 22–33.

1688 BIRR, Kendall. *Pioneering in Industrial Research: The Story of the General Electric Research Laboratory.* Washington, 1957.

1689 BRANYAN, Robert L. "From Monopoly to Oligopoly: The Aluminum Industry after World War II." *S W Soc Sci Q,* XLIII (1962), 242–252.

1690 BULEY, Roscoe Carlyle. *The Equitable Life Assurance Society of the United States, 1859–1964.* 2 Vols. New York, 1967.

1691 BUNZEL, John H. "The General Ideology of American Small Business." *Pol Sci Q,* LXX (1955), 87–102.

1692 CALDWELL, Edwin L. "Highlights of the Development of Manufacturing in Texas, 1900–1960." *S W Hist Q,* LXVIII (1965), 405–431.

1693 CAROSSO, Vincent P. *Investment Banking in America: A History.* Cambridge, Mass., 1970.

1694 CARSON, Robert B. *Main Line to Oblivion: The Disintegration of New York Railroads in the Twentieth Century.* Port Washington, N.Y., 1971.

1695 CHANDLER, Alfred D., Jr. "Management Decentralization: An Historical Analysis." *Bus Hist Rev,* XXX (1956), 111–174.

1696 CHANDLER, Alfred D., Jr. "The Structure of American Industry in the Twentieth Century: A Historical Overview." *Bus Hist Rev,* XLIII (1969), 255–298.

1697 CHAPMAN, Herman H. *The Iron and Steel Industries of the South.* University, Ala., 1953.

1698 COCHRAN, Thomas C. *American Business in the Twentieth Century.* Cambridge, Mass., 1972.

1699 COTTON, Frank E., Jr. "Recent Trends in Manufacturing Employment in Mississippi, 1940–1960." *J Miss Hist,* XXIX (1967), 28–42.

1700 DIBACCO, Thomas V. "American Business and Foreign Aid: The Eisenhower Years." See 206.

1701 DIBACCO, Thomas V. " 'Draft the Strikers (1946) and Seize the Mills (1952)': The Business Reaction." *Duquesne R,* XIII (1968), 63–75.

1702 DIBACCO, Thomas V. "Return to Dollar Diplomacy? American Business Reaction to the Eisenhower Foreign Aid Program, 1953–1961." See 207.

1703 DIDRICHSEN, Jon. "The Development of Diversified and Conglomerate Firms in the United States, 1920–1970." *Bus Hist Rev,* XLVI (1972), 202–219.

1704 EDWARDS, Charles E. *Dynamics of the United States Automobile Industry.* Columbia, S.C., 1965.

1705 ELDREDGE, David S. "The Gloucester Fishing Industry in World War II." *Am Nep,* XXVII (1967), 202–210.

1706 ELLIS, L. Ethan. *Newsprint: Producers, Publishers, Political Pressures.* New Brunswick, N.J., 1960.

1707 ENGLER, Robert. *The Politics of Oil: A Study of Private Power and Democratic Directions.* New York, 1961.†

1708 ESTALL, R. C. *New England: A Study in Industrial Adjustment.* New York, 1966.

1709 EWING, John S., and Nancy P. NORTON. *Broadlooms and Businessmen: A History of the Bigelow-Sanford Carpet Company.* Cambridge, Mass., 1955.

1710 FITE, Gilbert C. *Farm to Factory: A History of the Consumers Cooperative Association.* Columbia, Mo., 1965.

1711 FITZGERALD, Richard. "Land Use Planning in Southern California: In the Matter of Sears, Roebuck & Co. and the City of Riverside." *S Calif Q,* LII (1970), 383–403.

1712 GELBER, Steven M. *Black Men and Businessmen: The Growing Awareness of a Social Responsibility.* Port Washington, N.Y., 1974.

1713 GIDDENS, Paul H. *Standard Oil Company (Indiana), Oil Pioneer of the Middle West.* New York, 1955.

1714 GORTER, Wytze, and George H. HILDEBRAND. *The Pacific Coast Maritime Shipping Industry, 1930–1948.* 2 Vols. Berkeley, Cal., 1952–1954.

1715 GRAY, James. *Business without Boundary: The Story of General Mills.* Minneapolis, Minn., 1954.

1716 HEALD, Morrell. *The Social Responsibilities of Business: Company and Community, 1900–1960.* Cleveland, Ohio, 1970.

1717 HILL, Frank Ernest, and Mira WILKINS. *American Business Abroad: Ford on Six Continents.* Detroit, Mich., 1964.

1718 HOOPES, Roy. *The Steel Crisis.* See 1639.

1719 HUTCHINS, John G. B. "The American Shipping Industry since 1914." *Bus Hist Rev,* XXVIII (1954), 105–127.

1720 JOHNSON, Arthur M. *Petroleum Pipelines and Public Policy, 1906–1959.* Cambridge, Mass., 1967.

1721 LANG, Herbert H. "Uranium Mining and the AEC: The Birth Pangs of a New Industry." *Bus Hist Rev,* XXXVI (1962), 325–353.

1722 LARSON, Henrietta M., and Kenneth Wiggins PORTER. *History of Humble Oil and Refining Company: A Study in Industrial Growth.* New York, 1959.

1723 LARSON, Henrietta M., *et al. History of Standard Oil Company (New Jersey): New Horizons, 1927–1950.* New York, 1971.

1724 LOOS, John L. *Oil on Stream! A History of Interstate Oil Pipe Line Company, 1909–1959.* Baton Rouge, La., 1959.

1725 MCCONNELL, Grant. *Steel and the Presidency, 1962.*† See 1656.

1726 MCDONALD, Stephen L. "Some Factors in the Recent Economic Development of the Southwest." *S W Soc Sci Q,* XLV (1965), 329–339.

1727 MCLELLAN, David S., and Charles E. WOODHOUSE. "The Business Elite and Foreign Policy." See 283.

1728 MADISON, Charles A. *Book Publishing in America.* New York, 1966.

1729 MAHOOD, H. R. "The St. Lawrence Seaway Bill of 1954: A Case Study of Pressure Groups in Conflict." *S W Soc Sci Q,* XLVII (1966), 141–149.

1730 MARTIN, David Dale. *Mergers and the Clayton Act.* Berkeley, Cal., 1959.

1731 MILLER, Raymond C. *The Force of Energy: A Business History of the Detroit Edison Company.* East Lansing, Mich., 1971.

1732 MOODY, J. Carroll, and Gilbert C. FITE. *The Credit Union Movement: Origins and Development 1850–1970.* Lincoln, Neb., 1971.†

1733 MROZEK, Donald J. "The Truman Administration and the Enlistment of the Aviation Industry in Postwar Defense." See 848.

1734 MUNN, Robert F. "The First Fifty Years of Strip Mining in West Virginia, 1916–1965." *West Va Hist,* XXXV (1973), 66–74.

1735 NASH, Gerald D. *United States Oil Policy, 1890–1964: Business and Government in Twentieth Century America.* Pittsburgh, Pa., 1968.

1736 NELSON, R. L. *Merger Movements in American Industry, 1895–1956.* Pittsburgh, Pa., 1959.

1737 NEVINS, Allan, and Frank Ernest HILL. *Ford: Decline and Rebirth, 1933–1962.* New York, 1963.

1738 NORRIS, James D. *AZn: A History of the American Zinc Company.* Madison, Wis., 1968.

1739 NUTTER, G. W., and H. A. EINHORN. *Enterprise Monopoly in the United States, 1899–1958.* New York, 1969.

1740 O'NEIL, John Tettemer. *Policy Formation in Railroad Finance: Refinancing the Burlington, 1936–1945.* Cambridge, Mass., 1956.

1741 PECK, Merton J. *Competition in the Aluminum Industry, 1945–1958.* Cambridge, Mass., 1961.

1742 PORTER, David. "Representative Lindsay Warren, the Water Bloc, and the Transportation Act of 1940." *N C Hist Rev,* L (1973), 273–288.

1743 PUTH, Robert C. "Supreme Life: The History of a Negro Life Insurance Company, 1919–1962." *Bus Hist Rev,* XLIII (1969), 1–20.

1744 RAE, John B. *The American Automobile: A Brief History.* Chicago, 1965.†

1745 RAE, John B. *Climb to Greatness: The American Aircraft Industry, 1920–1960.* Cambridge, Mass., 1968.

1746 ROBOCK, Stefan H. "Industrialization and Economic Progress in the Southeast." *S Eco J,* XX (1954), 307–327.

1747 RODGERS, William. *Think: A Biography of the Watsons and I.B.M.* New York, 1969.

1748 ROSE, Joseph R. *American Wartime Transportation.* See 990.

1749 ROSS, W. D., and W. H. BAUGHN. "Changes in the Manufacturing Economy of the Southwest between 1939 and 1947." *S W Soc Sci Q,* XXXI (1950), 79–92.

1750 SAUNDERS, Richard Leroy. "Railroad Consolidation in the Eastern United States, 1940–1964." Doctoral dissertation, University of Illinois, 1971.

1751 SCHARY, Philip B. "The Civil Aeronautics Board and the All-Cargo Airlines: The Early Years." *Bus Hist Rev,* XLI (1967), 272–284.

1752 SCHRIFTGIESSER, Karl. *Business and Public Policy.* See 1667.

1753 SIMONSON, G. R. "The Demand for Aircraft and the Aircraft Industry, 1907–1958." *J Econ Hist,* XX (1960), 361–382.

1754 SIMONSON, G. R., ed. *The History of the American Aircraft Industry: An Anthology.* Cambridge, Mass., 1968.

1755 SIMONSON, G. R. "Missiles and Creative Destruction in the American Aircraft Industry, 1956–1961." *Bus Hist Rev,* XXXVIII (1964), 302–314.

1756 SOBEL, Robert. *The Age of Giant Corporations: A Microeconomic History of American Business, 1914–1970.* Westport, Conn., 1972.

1757 SOBEL, Robert. *Amex: A History of the American Stock Exchange, 1921–1971.* New York, 1972.

1758 SOBEL, Robert. *The Big Board: A History of the New York Stock Market.* New York, 1965.†

1759 STEKLER, Herman O. *The Structure and Performance of the Aerospace Industry.* Berkeley, Cal., 1965.

1760 STOVER, John F. *The Life and Decline of the American Railroad.* New York, 1970.

1761 TRESCOTT, Paul B. *Financing American Enterprise: The Story of Commercial Banking.* New York, 1963.

1762 WAGONER, Harless D. *The U.S. Machine Tool Industry from 1900 to 1950.* Cambridge, Mass., 1968.

1763 WHITE, Lawrence J. *The Automobile Industry since 1945.* Cambridge, Mass., 1971.

1764 WHITNAH, Donald R. *Safer Skyways: Federal Control of Aviation, 1926–1966.* Ames, Ia., 1966.

1765 WILBURN, James Richard. "Social and Economic Aspects of the Aircraft Industry in Metropolitan Los Angeles during World War II." Doctoral dissertation, University of California at Los Angeles, 1971.

1766 WILLIAMSON, Harold F., *et al. The American Petroleum Industry: The Age of Energy, 1899–1959.* Evanston, Ill., 1963.

1767 WILLIAMSON, Harold F., and Kenneth H. MYERS. *Designed for Digging: The First 75 Years of Bucyrus-Erie Company.* Evanston, Ill., 1955.

1768 WILLIAMSON, Harold F., and Orange A. SMALLEY. *Northwestern Mutual Life: A Century of Trusteeship.* Evanston, Ill., 1957.

C. Labor

1769 AARON, Benjamin. "Amending the Taft-Hartley Act: A Decade of Frustration." *Indust Lab Rel Rev,* XI (1958), 327–338.

1770 AFROS, John L. "Labor Participation in the Office of Price Administration." See 1594.

1771 ALINSKY, Saul D. *John L. Lewis: An Unauthorized Biography.* New York, 1949.[†]

1772 ANDERSON, Jervis. *A. Philip Randolph: A Biographical Portrait.* New York, 1973.[†]

1773 ARNOLD, Delbert D. "The C.I.O.'s Role in American Politics, 1936–1948." See 1094.

1774 BAKER, Elizabeth F. *Printers and Technology: A History of the International Printing Pressmen and Assistants' Union.* New York, 1957.

1775 BARBASH, Jack, ed. "David Dubinsky, the I.L.G.W.U., and the American Labor Movement." *Lab Hist,* IX (Special Supplement 1968), 3–126.

1776 BERGER, Henry W. "Union Diplomacy: American Labor's Foreign Policy in Latin America, 1932–1955." See 730.

1777 BERNSTEIN, Barton J. "The Truman Administration and the Steel Strike of 1946." *J Am Hist,* LII (1966), 791–803.

1778 BERNSTEIN, Barton J. "Walter Reuther and the General Motors Strike of 1945–1946." *Mich Hist,* XLIX (1965), 260–277.

1779 BERNSTEIN, Irving. "The Growth of American Unions, 1945–1960." *Lab Hist,* II (1961), 131–157.

1780 BLACKMAN, John L., Jr. *Presidential Seizure in Labor Disputes.* Cambridge, Mass., 1967.

1781 BLUM, Albert A., and J. Douglas SMYTH. "National Citizens Political Action Committee: An Example of Liberal-Labor Cooperation." See 1107.

1782 BRODY, David. *The Butcher Workmen: A Study of Unionization.* Cambridge, Mass., 1964.

1783 BROOKS, Thomas R. *Picket Lines and Bargaining Tables: Organized Labor Comes of Age, 1935–1955.* New York, 1968.

1784 BROPHY, Jacqueline. "The Merger of the AFL and the CIO in Michigan." *Mich Hist,* L (1966), 139–157.

1785 CALKINS, Fay. *The CIO and the Democratic Party.* See 1117.

1786 CARPENTER, Jesse Thomas. *Competition and Collective Bargaining in the Needle Trades, 1910–1967.* Ithaca, N.Y., 1972.

1787 CORMIER, Frank, and William J. EATON. *Reuther.* Englewood Cliffs, N.J., 1970.

1788 DANISH, Max D. *The World of David Dubinsky.* Cleveland, Ohio, 1957.

1789 DUBOFSKY, Melvyn, ed. *American Labor since the New Deal.* Chicago, 1971.

1790 DULLES, Foster Rhea. *Labor in America: A History.* New York, 1966.†

1791 DUNNE, John Gregory. *Delano: The Story of the California Grape Strike.* New York, 1967.†

1792 EMSPAK, Frank. "The Break-Up of the Congress of Industrial Organizations (CIO), 1945–1950." Doctoral dissertation, University of Wisconsin, 1972.

1793 FONER, Philip S. *Organized Labor and the Black Worker 1619–1973.* New York, 1974.

1794 FOSTER, Jack R. "The Coal Strike of 1943." *Conn Rev,* VI (October 1972), 57–69.

1795 FOSTER, James C. "1954: A CIO Victory?" See 1166.

1796 FOSTER, James Caldwell. "The Union Politic: The CIO Political Action Committee." See 1167.

1797 GOLDBERG, Joseph P. *The Maritime Story: A Study in Labor-Management Relations.* Cambridge, Mass., 1958.

1798 GORDON, Gerald R. "The Coming of the Cold War: The American Labor Movement and the Problem of Peace, 1945–1946." See 535.

1799 GOULD, Jean, and Lorena HICKOK. *Walter Reuther: Labor's Rugged Individualist.* New York, 1972.

1800 GOULDEN, Joseph C. *Meany.* New York, 1972.

1801 GRAHAM, Harry Edward. *The Paper Rebellion: Development and Upheaval in Pulp and Paper Unionism.* Iowa City, Ia., 1970.

1802 GREENSTONE, J. David. *Labor in American Politics.*† See 1179.

1803 GREGORY, George W. "The Problem of Labor during World War II: The Employment of Women in Defense Production." Doctoral Dissertation, Ohio State University, 1969.

1804 HARBISON, Frederick H., and Robert C. SPENCER. "The Politics of Collective Bargaining: The Postwar Record in Steel." *Am Pol Sci Rev,* XLVIII (1954), 705–720.

1805 HARTMAN, Paul T. *Collective Bargaining and Productivity: The Longshore Mechanization Agreement.* Berkeley, Cal., 1969.

1806 HOWE, Irving, and B. J. WIDICK. *The UAW and Walter Reuther.* New York, 1949.

1807 HUTCHINSON, John. *The Imperfect Union: A History of Corruption in American Trade Unions.* New York, 1970.†

1808 JAMES, Ralph C., and Estelle Dinerstein JAMES. *Hoffa and the Teamsters: A Study of Union Power.* Princeton, N.J., 1965.

1809 JENSEN, Vernon H. *Nonferrous Metals Industry Unionism, 1932–1954: A History of Leadership Controversy,* Ithaca, N.Y., 1954.

1810 JENSEN, Vernon H. *Strife on the Waterfront: The Port of New York since 1945.* Ithaca, N.Y., 1974.

1811 JOSEPHSON, Matthew. *Sidney Hillman: Statesman of American Labor.* Garden City, N.Y., 1952.

1812 KAMPELMAN, Max M. *The Communist Party vs. the C.I.O.* New York, 1957.

1813 KOISTINEN, Paul A. C. "Mobilizing the World War II Economy: Labor and the Industrial-Military Alliance." *Pac Hist Rev,* XLII (1973), 443–478.

1814 KRISLOV, Joseph. "Organizing, Union Growth, and the Cycle, 1949–1966." *Lab Hist,* XI (1970), 212–222.

1815 LEE, R. Alton. *Truman and Taft-Hartley: A Question of Mandate.* Lexington, Ky., 1966.

1816 LEVENSTEIN, Harvey A. *Labor Organizations in the United States and Mexico.* See 754.

1817 LIBERTELLA, Anthony Frank. "The Steel Strike of 1959: Labor, Management, and Government Relations." Doctoral dissertation, Ohio State University, 1972.

1818 MCCLURE, Arthur F. *The Truman Administration and the Problems of Postwar Labor, 1945–1948.* Rutherford, N.J., 1969.

1819 MCLAUGHLIN, Doris B. *Michigan Labor: A Brief History from 1818 to the Present.* Ann Arbor, Mich., 1970.†

1820 MADISON, Charles A. *American Labor Leaders: Personalities and Forces in the Labor Movement.* New York, 1962.

1821 MANGUM, Garth L. *The Operating Engineers: The Economic History of a Trade Union.* Cambridge, Mass., 1964.

1822 MARSHALL, F. Ray. *Labor in the South.* Cambridge, Mass., 1967.

1823 MASON, Lucy Randolph. *To Win These Rights: A Personal Story of the CIO in the South.* New York, 1952.

1824 MATTHIESSEN, Peter. *Sal Si Puedes: Cesar Chavez and the New American Revolution.* New York, 1973.†

1825 MILLER, Glenn W., and Stephen B. WARE. "Organized Labor in the Political Process: A Case Study of the Right-to-Work Campaign in Ohio." *Lab Hist,* IV (1963), 51–67.

1826 MILLIS, H. A., and E. E. BROWN. *From the Wagner Act to Taft-Hartley.* Chicago, 1950.

1827 MOORE, Michael A. "A Community's Crisis: Hillsdale and the Essex Wire Strike." *Ind Mag Hist,* LXVI (1970), 238–262.

1828 O'BRIEN, F. S. "The 'Communist-Dominated' Unions in the United States since 1950." *Lab Hist,* IX (1968), 184–209.

1829 OSHINSKY, David M. "Senator Joseph McCarthy and the American Labor Movement." See 1505.

1830 OSHINSKY, David M. "Wisconsin Labor and the Campaign of 1952." See 1436.

1831 PERLMAN, Mark. *The Machinists: A New Study in American Trade Unionism.* Cambridge, Mass., 1961.

1832 PIERSON, Frank. *Unions in Postwar America: An Economic Assessment.* New York, 1967.†

1833 POMPER, Gerald. "Labor and Congress: The Repeal of Taft-Hartley." *Lab Hist,* II (1961), 323–343.

1834 POMPER, Gerald. "Labor Legislation: The Revision of Taft-Hartley in 1953–1954." *Lab Hist,* VI (1965), 143–158.

1835 PRICKETT, James R. "Communism and Factionalism in the United States Automobile Workers, 1939–1947." *Sci Soc,* XXXII (1968), 257–277.

1836 PRICKETT, James R. "Some Aspects of the Communist Controversy in the CIO." *Sci Soc,* XXXIII (1969), 299–321.

1837 RADOSH, Ronald. *American Labor and Foreign Policy.*† See 313.

1838 RAYBACK, Joseph G. *A History of American Labor.* New York, 1966.†

1839 REES, Albert. "Postwar Wage Determination in the Basic Steel Industry." *Am Econ Rev,* XLI (1951), 389–404.

1840 REILLY, Gerard D. "The Legislative History of the Taft-Hartley Act." *Geo Wash Law Rev,* XXIX (1960), 285–300.

1841 RICHARDSON, Reed C. *The Locomotive Engineer, 1863–1963: A Century of Railway Labor Relations and Work Rules.* Ann Arbor, Mich., 1963.

1842 RIKER, William H. "The CIO in Politics, 1936–1946." See 1291.

1843 SANDON, Leo, Jr. "When Kansas Said Yes to 'Right-to-Work'." *Mid W Q,* IV (1963), 269–281.

1844 SAPOSS, David J. *Communism in American Unions.* New York, 1959.

1845 SCHER, Seymour. "Regulatory Agency Control through Appointment: The Case of the Eisenhower Administration and the NLRB." *J Pol,* XXIII (1961), 667–688.

1846 SCHRAMM, Leroy H. "Union Rivalry in Detroit in World War II." *Mich Hist,* LIV (1970), 201–215.

1847 SEIDMAN, Joel. *American Labor from Defense to Reconversion.* Chicago, 1953.

1848 SEIDMAN, Joel. "Efforts toward Merger, 1935–1955." *Indust Lab Rel Rev,* IX (1956), 353–370.

1849 SEIDMAN, Joel. "Labor Policy of the Communist Party during World War II." *Indust Lab Rel Rev,* IV (1950), 55–69

1850 SHERIDAN, Walter. *The Fall and Rise of Jimmy Hoffa.* New York, 1972.

1851 SHISTER, Joseph. "The Direction of Unionism 1947–1962: Thrust or Drift?" *Indust Lab Rel Rev,* XX (1967), 578–601.

1852 SLACK, Walter H. "Walter Reuther: A Study of Ideas." Doctoral dissertation, State University of Iowa, 1965.

1853 SPERRY, J. R. "Rebellion within the Ranks: Pennsylvania Anthracite, John L. Lewis, and the Coal Strikes of 1943." *Pa Hist,* XL (1973), 293–312.

1854 STEIN, Bruno. "Labor's Role in Government Agencies during World War II." See 1670.

1855 STRAUB, Eleanor F. "United States Government Policy toward Civilian Women during World War II." *Prol,* V (1973), 240–254.

1856 TAFT, Philip. *The A. F. of L. from the Death of Gompers to the Merger.* New York, 1959.

1857 TAFT, Philip. *Labor Politics American Style.* See 1453.

1858 TATE, Juanita D. "Philip Murray as a Labor Leader." Doctoral dissertation, New York University, 1961.

1859 TROY, Leo. "The Growth of Union Membership in the South, 1939–1953." *S Eco J,* XXIV (1958), 407–420.

1860 TYLER, Robert L. *Walter Reuther.* Grand Rapids, Mich., 1973.†

1861 UPHOFF, Walter H. *Kohler on Strike: Thirty Years of Conflict.* Boston, 1966.

1862 WHITTEMORE, L. H. *The Man Who Ran the Subways: The Story of Mike Quill.* New York, 1968.†

1863 WIDICK, B. J. *Labor Today: The Triumphs and Failures of Unionism in the United States.* Boston, 1964.

1864 WINDMULLER, John P. "The Foreign Policy Conflict in American Labor." See 361.

1865 WINKLER, Allan M. "The Philadelphia Transit Strike of 1944." *J Am Hist,* LIX (1972), 73–89.

1866 ZITRON, Celia Lewis. *The New York City Teachers Union 1916–1964.* New York, 1968.

D. Agriculture

1867 ALBERTSON, Dean. *Roosevelt's Farmer: Claude R. Wickard in the New Deal.* New York, 1961.

1868 BALDWIN, Sidney. *Poverty and Politics: The Rise and Decline of the Farm Security Administration.* Chapel Hill, N.C., 1968.

1869 BENEDICT, Murray R. *Farm Policies of the United States, 1790–1950: A Study of Their Origins and Development.* New York, 1953.

1870 BENEDICT, Murray R., and Oscar C. STINE. *The Agricultural Commodity Programs: Two Decades of Experience.* New York, 1956.

1871 BENSON, Ezra Taft. *Cross Fire: The Eight Years with Eisenhower.* Garden City, N.Y., 1962.

1872 BERNSTEIN, Barton J. "Clash of Interests: The Postwar Battle between the Office of Price Administration and the Department of Agriculture." *Ag Hist,* XLI (1967), 45–57.

1873 BERNSTEIN, Barton J. "The Postwar Famine and Price Control, 1946." *Ag Hist,* XXXVIII (1964), 235–240.

1874 BLOCK, William J. *The Separation of the Farm Bureau and the Extension Service: Political Issue in a Federal System.* Urbana, Ill., 1960.

1875 CHRISTENSON, Reo M. *The Brannan Plan: Farm Politics and Policy.* Ann Arbor, Mich., 1959.

1876 COALSON, George O. "Mexican Contract Labor in American Agriculture." *S W Soc Sci Q,* XXXIII (1952), 228–238.

1877 CRAIG, Richard B. *The Bracero Program.* See 738.

1878 FITE, Gilbert C. *Farm to Factory.* See 1710.

1879 FORSYTHE, James Lee. "Clinton P. Anderson: Politician and Businessman as Truman's Secretary of Agriculture." Doctoral dissertation, University of New Mexico, 1970.

1880 GOLD, Bela. *Wartime Economic Planning in Agriculture: A Study in the Allocation of Resources.* New York, 1949.

1881 HADWIGER, Don F. "The Freeman Administration and the Poor." *Ag Hist,* XLV (1971), 21–32.

1882 HALL, Tom G. "The Aiken Bill, Price Supports and the Wheat Farmer in 1948." *N D Hist,* XXXIX (1972), 13–22, 47.

1883 HARDIN, Charles M. *The Politics of Agriculture: Soil Conservation and the Struggle for Power in Rural America.* Glencoe, Ill., 1951.

1884 HAWLEY, Ellis W. "The Politics of the Mexican Labor Issue, 1950–1965." *Ag Hist,* XL (1966), 157–176.

1885 HIGBEE, Edward. *Farms and Farmers in an Urban Age.* New York, 1963.†

1886 HILLIARD, Sam B. "The Dynamics of Power: Recent Trends in Mechanization on the American Farm." *Tech Cult,* XIII (1972), 1–24.

1887 KIRKENDALL, Richard S. "Social Science in the Central Valley of California: An Episode." *Calif Hist Soc Q,* XLIII (1964), 195–218.

1888 KIRKENDALL, Richard S. *Social Scientists and Farm Politics in the Age of Roosevelt.* Columbia, Mo., 1966.

1889 LISS, Samuel. "The Concept and Determination of Prevailing Wages in Agriculture during World War II." *Ag Hist,* XXIV (1950), 4–18.

1890 LISS, Samuel. "Farm Wage Boards under the Cooperative Extension Service during World War II." *Ag Hist,* XXVII (1953), 103–108.

1891 LISS, Samuel. "Farm Wage Boards under the Wage Stabilization Program during World War II." *Ag Hist,* XXX (1956), 128–137.

1892 MCCONNELL, Grant. *The Decline of Agrarian Democracy.* Berkeley, Cal., 1953.†

1893 MATUSOW, Allen J. *Farm Policies and Politics in the Truman Years.* Cambridge, Mass., 1967.†

1894 MORGAN, Robert J. *Governing Soil Conservation: Thirty Years of the New Decentralization.* Baltimore, 1966.

1895 PRICE, David E. "The Politics of Sugar." *Rev Pol,* XXXIII (1971), 212–232.

1896 RASMUSSEN, Wayne D. "Advances in American Agriculture: The Mechanical Tomato Harvester as a Case Study." *Tech Cult,* IX (1968), 531–543.

1897 RAUP, Philip. "Corporate Farming in the United States." *J Econ Hist,* XXXIII (1973), 274–290.

1898 SALOUTOS, Theodore. "The American Farm Bureau Federation and Farm Policy: 1933–1945." *S W Soc Sci Q,* XXVIII (1948), 313–333.

1899 SCHAPSMEIER, Edward L., and Frederick H. SCHAPSMEIER. "Eisenhower and Ezra Taft Benson: Farm Policy in the 1950s." *Ag Hist,* XLIV (1970), 369–378.

1900 SCHLEBECKER, John T. *Cattle Raising on the Plains, 1900–1961.* Lincoln, Neb., 1963.

1901   SCHLEBECKER, John T. "The Great Holding Action: The NFO in September, 1962." *Ag Hist,* XXXIX (1965), 204–213.

1902   SCRUGGS, Otey M. "The Bracero Program under the Farm Security Administration, 1942–1943." *Lab Hist,* III (1962), 149–168.

1903   SCRUGGS, Otey M. "Texas and the Bracero Program, 1942–1947." *Pac Hist Rev,* XXXII (1963), 251–264.

1904   SUMMONS, Terry G. "Animal Feed Additives, 1940–1966." *Ag Hist,* XLII (1968), 305–313.

1905   TAYLOR, Fred R. "North Dakota Agriculture since World War II." *N D Hist,* XXXIV (1967), 47–61.

1906   TUCKER, William P. "The Farmers Union: The Social Thought of a Current Agrarian Movement." *S W Soc Sci Q,* XXVII (1946), 45–53.

1907   TWEETEN, Luther. *Foundations of Farm Policy.* Lincoln, Neb., 1970.

1908   WILCOX, Walter W. *The Farmer in the Second World War.* Ames, Ia., 1947.

1909   WILSON, James A. "The Arizona Cattle Industry: Its Political and Public Image, 1950–1963." *Ariz West,* VIII (1966), 339–348.

1910   WILSON, Theodore A., and Richard D. MCKINZIE. "The Food Crusade of 1947." *Prol,* III (1971), 136–152.

E. Public Power and Conservation

1911   BENINCASA, Frederick A. "An Analysis of the Historical Development of the Tennessee Valley Authority from 1933 to 1961." Doctoral dissertation, St. John's University, 1961.

1912   BROWN, Deward Clayton. "Rural Electrification in the South, 1920–1955." Doctoral dissertation, University of California at Los Angeles, 1970.

1913   CLAPP, Gordon R. *The TVA: An Approach to the Development of a Region.* Chicago, 1955.

1914   DINNERSTEIN, Leonard. "The Senate's Rejection of Aubrey Williams as Rural Electrification Administrator." *Ala Rev,* XXI (1968), 133–143.

1915   ELLIS, Clyde T. *A Giant Step.* New York, 1966. The Rural Electrification Administration.

1916   ESTALL, R. C. "Population Growth and Environment: Some Aspects of the Problem in the United States and the Response." *J Am Stud,* VI (1972), 55–68.

1917   FINKLE, Jason L. *The President Makes a Decision: A Study of Dixon-Yates.* Ann Arbor, Mich., 1960.

1918   FLEMING, Donald. "Roots of the New Conservation Movement." *Pers Am Hist,* VI (1972), 7–91.

1919   HARRIS, Joseph P. "The Senatorial Rejection of Leland Olds: A Case Study." *Am Pol Sci Rev,* XLV (1951), 674–692.

1920   LEUCHTENBURG, William E. *Flood Control Politics: The Connecticut River Valley Problem, 1927–1950.* Cambridge, Mass., 1953.

1921   LILIENTHAL, David E. *The Journals of David E. Lilienthal: The TVA Years, 1939–1945.* New York, 1964.

1922 LILIENTHAL, David E. *TVA: Democracy on the March.* New York, 1953.

1923 MCCLOSKEY, Michael. "Wilderness Movement at the Crossroads, 1945–1970." *Pac Hist Rev,* XLI (1972), 346–361.

1924 MAHAR, Franklyn D. "Douglas McKay and the Issues of Power Development in Oregon, 1953–1956." Doctoral dissertation, University of Oregon, 1968.

1925 O'RIORDAN, Timothy. "The Third American Conservation Movement: New Implications for Public Policy." *J Am Stud,* V (1971), 155–171.

1926 RICHARDSON, Elmo. *Dams, Parks and Politics: Resource Development and Preservation in the Truman-Eisenhower Era.* Lexington, Ky., 1973.

1927 RICHARDSON, Elmo. "The Interior Secretary as Conservation Villain: The Notorious Case of Douglas 'Giveaway' McKay." *Pac Hist Rev,* XLI (1972), 333–345.

1928 SELZNICK, Philip. *TVA and the Grass Roots: A Study in the Sociology of Formal Organization.* Berkeley, Cal., 1949.†

1929 SWANSON, Bert E., and Deborah ROSENFIELD. "The Coon-Neuberger Debates of 1955: 'Ten Dam Nights in Oregon'." *Pac N W Q,* LV (1964), 55–66.

1930 TALBOT, Allan R. *Power along the Hudson: The Storm King Case and the Birth of Environmentalism.* New York, 1972.

1931 WALTRIP, John R. "Public Power during the Truman Administration." Doctoral dissertation, University of Missouri, 1965.

1932 WILDAVSKY, Aaron. *Dixon-Yates: A Study in Power Politics.* New Haven, Conn., 1962.

VII. Race, Ethnicity, Minority Groups

A. Black-White Relations: Civil Rights, Desegregation, Discrimination, and Confrontation

1933 AKERMAN, Robert H. "The Triumph of Moderation in Florida Thought and Politics: A Study of the Race Issue from 1954 to 1960." See 1361.

1934 ANDERSON, J. W. *Eisenhower, Brownell, and the Congress: The Tangled Origins of the Civil Rights Bill of 1956–1957.* University, Ala., 1964.

1935 BAKER, Liva. "With All Deliberate Speed." *Am Her,* XXIV (February 1973), 42–48.

1936 BARRETT, Russell H. *Integration at Ole Miss.* Chicago, 1965.

1937 BARTLEY, N. V. "Looking Back at Little Rock." *Ark Hist Q,* XXV (1966), 101–116.

1938 BARTLEY, Numan V. *The Rise of Massive Resistance: Race and Politics in the South during the 1950's.* Baton Rouge, La., 1969.

1939   BATES, Daisy. *The Long Shadow of Little Rock: A Memoir.* New York, 1962.

1940   BERGER, Morroe. *Equality by Statute: The Revolution in Civil Rights.* Garden City, N.Y., 1968.

1941   BERMAN, Daniel M. *A Bill Becomes a Law: The Civil Rights Act of 1960.* New York, 1962.†

1942   BERMAN, William C. *The Politics of Civil Rights in the Truman Administration.* Columbus, Ohio, 1970.

1943   BERNSTEIN, Barton J. "The Ambiguous Legacy: The Truman Administration and Civil Rights." *Politics and Policies of the Truman Administration.* Ed. Barton J. Bernstein. Chicago, 1970.†

1944   BILLINGTON, Monroe. "Civil Rights, President Truman and the South." *J Neg Hist,* LVIII (1973), 127–139.

1945   BILLINGTON, Monroe. "Freedom to Serve: The President's Committee on Equality of Treatment and Opportunity in the Armed Forces, 1949–1950." *J Neg Hist,* LI (1966), 262–274.

1946   BILLINGTON, Monroe. "Public School Integration in Missouri, 1954–64." *J Neg Edu,* XXXV (1966), 252–262.

1947   BILLINGTON, Monroe. "Public School Integration in Oklahoma, 1954–1963." *Hist,* XXVI (1964), 521–537.

1948   BLACK, Isabella. "Race and Unreason: Anti-Negro Opinion in Professional and Scientific Literature since 1954." *Phylon,* XXVI (1965), 65–79.

1949   BLAUSTEIN, Albert P., and Clarence Clyde FERGUSON, Jr. *Desegregation and the Law: The Meaning and Effect of the School Segregation Cases.* New Brunswick, N.J., 1962.

1950   BOESEL, David, and Peter H. ROSSI, eds. *Cities under Siege: An Anatomy of the Ghetto Riots, 1964–1968.* New York, 1971.

1951   BOLNER, James. "Mr. Chief Justice Fred M. Vinson and Racial Discrimination." *Reg Ky Hist Soc,* LXIV (1966), 29–43.

1952   BOSKIN, Joseph. "Violence in the Ghettos: A Consensus of Attitudes." *New Mex Q,* XXXVII (1968), 317–334.

1953   BRINK, William, and Louis HARRIS. *The Negro Revolution in America.* New York, 1964.†

1954   BROWN, Stuart Gerry. "Civil Rights and National Leadership: Eisenhower and Stevenson in the 1950's." *Ethics,* LXX (1960), 118–134.

1955   BUNI, Andrew. *The Negro in Virginia Politics.* See 1368.

1956   CAMPBELL, Ernest, and Thomas F. PETTIGREW. *Christians in Racial Crisis: A Study of Little Rock's Ministry.* Washington, 1959.

1957   CAUGHEY, John. *To Kill a Child's Spirit: The Tragedy of School Segregation in Los Angeles.* Itasca, Ill., 1973.†

1958   CELARIER, Michelle. "A Study of Public Opinion on Desegregation in Oklahoma Higher Education." *Chron Okla,* XLVII (1969), 268–281.

1959   CHALMERS, David M. *Hooded Americanism: The History of the Ku Klux Klan.* Garden City, N.Y., 1965.†

1960   COLLE, Royal D. "Negro Image in the Mass Media: A Case Study in Social Change." *Jour Q,* XLV (1968), 55–60.

1961 CONNERY, Robert H., ed. "Urban Riots: Violence and Social Change." *Proc Acad Pol Sci,* XXIX (1968), 1–190.

1962 CONOT, Robert. *Rivers of Blood, Years of Darkness.* New York, 1968.† The Watts Riot.

1963 CRIPPS, Thomas R. "The Death of Rastus: Negroes in American Films since 1945." *Phylon,* XXVIII (1967), 267–275.

1964 DALFIUME, Richard M. *Desegregation of the U.S. Armed Forces: Fighting on Two Fronts, 1939–1953.* Columbia, Mo., 1969.

1965 DALFIUME, Richard M. "The Fahy Committee and Desegregation of the Armed Forces." *Hist,* XXXI (1968), 1–20.

1966 DAVIDSON, Chandler. *Biracial Politics.* See 1378.

1967 DEWING, Rolland L. "Teacher Organizations and Desegregation, 1954–1964." Doctoral dissertation, Ball State University, 1967.

1968 DINNERSTEIN, Leonard. "Southern Jewry and the Desegregation Crisis, 1954–1970." *Am Jew Hist Q,* LXII (1973), 231–241.

1969 DINNERSTEIN, Leonard, and Mary Dale PALSSON, eds. *Jews in the South.* Baton Rouge, La., 1973.

1970 DULLES, Foster Rhea. *The Civil Rights Commission: 1957–1965.* East Lansing, Mich., 1968.

1971 DYKEMAN, Wilma, and James STOKELY. *Seeds of Southern Change: The Life of Will Alexander.* Chicago, 1962.

1972 ELLIFF, John T. "Aspects of Federal Civil Rights Enforcement: The Justice Department and the F.B.I., 1939–1964." *Pers Am Hist,* V (1971), 605–673.

1973 ELY, James W., Jr. "The Crisis of Conservative Virginia: The Decline and Fall of Massive Resistance, 1957–1965." Doctoral dissertation, University of Virginia, 1971.

1974 FARRIS, Charles D. "The Re-Enfranchisement of Negroes in Florida." See 1383.

1975 FEAGIN, Joe R., and Harlan HAHN. *Ghetto Riots: The Politics of Violence in American Cities.* New York, 1973.

1976 FEAGIN, Joe R., and Harlan HAHN. "The Second Reconstruction: Black Political Strength in the South." See 1384.

1977 FISH, John Hall. *Black Power/White Control: The Struggle of the Woodlawn Organization in Chicago.* Princeton, N.J., 1973.

1978 FOGELSON, Robert M. "From Resentment to Confrontation: The Police, the Negroes, and the Outbreak of the Nineteen-Sixties Riots." *Pol Sci Q,* LXXXIII (1968), 217–247.

1979 FONER, Philip S. *Organized Labor and the Black Worker 1619–1973.* See 1793.

1980 FUSFELD, Daniel R. "The Basic Economics of the Urban and Racial Crisis." *Mich Acad,* II (Winter 1970), 3–34.

1981 GARFINKEL, Herbert. "Social Science Evidence and the School Segregation Cases." *J Pol,* XXI (1959), 37–59.

1982 GATES, Robbins L. *The Making of Massive Resistance: Virginia's Politics of Public School Desegregation, 1954–1956.* Chapel Hill, N.C., 1964.

1983 GELBER, Steven M. *Black Men and Businessmen.* See 1712.

1984 Governor's Select Commission on Civil Disorder, State of New Jersey. *Report for Action: An Investigation into the Causes and Events of the 1967 Newark Race Riots.* New York, 1972.

1985 GRAHAM, Hugh Davis. *Crisis in Print: Desegregation and the Press in Tennessee.* Nashville, Tenn., 1967.

1986 GRAHAM, Hugh Davis. "Desegregation in Nashville: The Dynamics of Compliance." *Tenn Hist Q,* XXV (1966), 135–154.

1987 GRAY, Gibson Hendrix. *The Lobbying Game: A Study of the 1953 Campaign of the State Council for a Pennsylvania Fair Employment Practice Commission.* Tyler, Tex., 1970.

1988 GREEN, Constance McLaughlin. *The Secret City: A History of Race Relations in the Nation's Capital.* Princeton, N.J., 1967.[†]

1989 GREENBERG, Jack, ed. "Blacks and the Law." *Ann Am Acad Pol Soc Sci,* CCCCVII (1973), 1–178.

1990 GRUNDMAN, Adolph H. "Public School Desegregation in Virginia from 1954 to the Present." Doctoral dissertation, Wayne State University, 1972.

1991 HARRELL, David Edwin, Jr. *White Sects and Black Men in the Recent South.* Nashville, Tenn., 1971.

1992 HAYS, Brooks. *A Southern Moderate Speaks.* Chapel Hill, N.C., 1959.

1993 HEIN, Virginia H. "The Image of 'A City Too Busy to Hate': Atlanta in the 1960's." *Phylon,* XXXIII (1972), 205–221.

1994 HOUGH, Joseph C., Jr. *Black Power and White Protestants: A Christian Response to the New Negro Pluralism.* New York, 1968.[†]

1995 HUBBELL, John T. "The Desegregation of the University of Oklahoma, 1946–1950." *J Neg Hist,* LVII (1972), 370–384.

1996 HUBBELL, John T. "Some Reactions to the Desegregation of the University of Oklahoma, 1946–1950." *Phylon,* XXIV (1973), 187–196.

1997 INGER, Morton. *Politics and Reality in an American City: The New Orleans School Crisis of 1960.* New York, 1969.

1998 JIRRAN, Raymond J. "Cleveland and the Negro Following World War II." Doctoral dissertation, Kent State University, 1972.

1999 Keesing's Research Report. *Race Relations in the USA, 1954–68.* New York, 1970.

2000 KELLOGG, Peter John. "Northern Liberals and Black America: A History of White Attitudes, 1936–1952." Doctoral dissertation, Northwestern University, 1971.

2001 KELLY, Thomas James. "White Press/Black Man. An Analysis of the Editorial Opinion of the Four Chicago Daily Newspapers toward the Race Problem: 1954–1968." Doctoral dissertation, University of Illinois, 1971.

2002 KESSELMAN, Louis. *The Social Politics of FEPC.* Chapel Hill, N.C., 1948.

2003 KLIBANER, Irwin. "The Southern Conference Educational Fund: A History." Doctoral dissertation, University of Wisconsin, 1971.

2004 KRAUSE, P. Allen. "Rabbis and Negro Rights in the South, 1954–1967." *Am Jew Arch,* XXI (1969), 20–47.

2005 KRISLOV, Samuel. *The Negro in Federal Employment: The Quest for Equal Opportunity.* Minneapolis, Minn., 1967.

2006 KUSHNICK, Louis. "Race, Class and Power: The New York Decentralization Controversy." *J Am Stud,* III (1969), 201–219.

2007 LEVY, Frank. *Northern Schools and Civil Rights: The Racial Imbalance Act of Massachusetts.* Chicago, 1971.

2008 LEWIS, Anthony, et al. *Portrait of a Decade: The Second American Revolution.* New York, 1964.

2009 LICHTMAN, Allan. "The Federal Assault against Voting Discrimination in the Deep South, 1957–1967." *J Neg Hist,* LIV (1969), 346–367.

2010 LOCKE, Hubert G. *The Detroit Riot of 1967.* Detroit, Mich., 1969.

2011 LUBELL, Samuel. *White and Black: Test of a Nation.* New York, 1964.†

2012 LYTLE, Clifford M. "The History of the Civil Rights Bill of 1964." *J Neg Hist,* LI (1966), 275–296.

2013 MCBETH, Leon. "Southern Baptists and Race since 1947." *Bapt Hist Her,* VII (1972), 155–169.

2014 MCCAIN, R. Ray. "Reactions to the United States Supreme Court Segregation Decision of 1954." *Ga Hist Q,* LII (1968), 371–387.

2015 MCCORD, John H., ed. *With All Deliberate Speed: Civil Rights Theory and Reality.* Urbana, Ill., 1969.

2016 MCCOY, Donald R., and Richard T. RUETTEN. "The Civil Rights Movement, 1940–1954." *Mid W Q,* XI (1969), 11–34.

2017 MCCOY, Donald R., and Richard T. RUETTEN. *Quest and Response: Minority Rights and the Truman Administration.* Lawrence, Kans., 1973.

2018 MCMILLEN, Neil R. *The Citizens' Council: Organized Resistance to the Second Reconstruction, 1954–64.* Urbana, Ill., 1971.

2019 MCMILLEN, Neil R. "Organized Resistance to School Desegregation in Tennessee." *Tenn Hist Q,* XXX (1971), 315–328.

2020 MCMILLEN, Neil R. "White Citizens' Council and Resistance to School Desegregation in Arkansas." *Ark Hist Q,* XXX (1971), 95–122.

2021 MACK, Raymond W., ed. *Our Children's Burden: Studies of Desegregation in Nine American Communities.* New York, 1968.

2022 MATTHEWS, Donald R., and James W. PROTHRO. *Negroes and the New Southern Politics.* See 1426.

2023 MEREDITH, James. *Three Years in Mississippi.* Bloomington, Ind., 1966. Integrating the University of Mississippi.

2024 MIDDLETON, Russell. "The Civil Rights Issue and Presidential Voting among Southern Negroes and Whites." *Soc Forces,* XL (1962), 209–214.

2025 MILLER, Loren. *The Petitioners: The Story of the Supreme Court of the United States and the Negro.* New York, 1966.

2026 MORROW, E. Frederic. *Black Man in the White House.* New York, 1963. The Eisenhower Administration.

2027 MOUNGER, Dwyn M. "Racial Attitudes in the Presbyterian Church in the United States, 1944–1954." *J Presby Hist,* XLVIII (1970), 38–68.

2028 MURPHY, Walter F. "The South Counterattacks: The Anti-NAACP Laws." *W Pol Q*, XII (1959), 371–390.

2029 MURRELL, Glen. "The Desegregation of Paducah Junior College." *Reg Ky Hist Soc*, LXVII (1969), 63–79.

2030 MUSE, Benjamin. *Ten Years of Prelude: The Story of Integration since the Supreme Court's 1954 Decision.* New York, 1964.

2031 MUSE, Benjamin. *Virginia's Massive Resistance.* Bloomington, Ind., 1961.

2032 MYRDAL, Gunnar. *An America Dilemma: The Negro Problem and Modern Democracy.* New York, 1944.[†]

2033 NEWBY, I. A. *Challenge to the Court: Social Scientists and the Defense of Segregation, 1954–1966.* Baton Rouge, La., 1969.

2034 NICHOLS, Guerdon D. "Breaking the Color Line at the University of Arkansas." *Ark Hist Q*, XXVII (1968), 3–21.

2035 ORFIELD, Gary. *The Reconstruction of Southern Education: The Schools and the 1964 Civil Rights Act.* New York, 1969.

2036 ORSER, W. Edward. "Racial Attitudes in Wartime: The Protestant Churches during the Second World War." *Church Hist*, XLI (1972), 337–353.

2037 OSBORNE, William A. *The Segregated Covenant: Race Relations and American Catholics.* New York, 1967.

2038 PANETTA, Leon E., and Peter GALL. *Bring Us Together: The Nixon Team and the Civil Rights Retreat.* Philadelphia, 1971.

2039 PARKS, Robert J. "The Development of Segregation in U.S. Army Hospitals, 1940–1942." *Mil Aff*, XXXVII (1973), 145–150.

2040 PELTASON, J. W. *Fifty-Eight Lonely Men: Southern Federal Judges and School Desegregation.* New York, 1961.[†]

2041 PRICE, Hugh D. *The Negro and Southern Politics.* See 1441.

2042 PRICE, Hugh Douglas. "The Negro and Florida Politics, 1944–1954." See 1442.

2043 QUINT, Howard H. *Profile in Black and White: A Frank Portrait of South Carolina.* Washington, 1958.

2044 RECORD, Wilson. *The Negro and the Communist Party.* Chapel Hill, N.C., 1951.[†]

2045 REDDICK, L. D. "The Negro Policy of the American Army since World War II." *J Neg Hist*, XXXVIII (1953), 194–215.

2046 REIMERS, David M. *White Protestantism and the Negro.* New York, 1965.

2047 ROBINSON, Jackie, and Carl T. ROWAN. *Wait Till Next Year: The Life Story of Jackie Robinson.* New York, 1960.

2048 RODGERS, Harrell, R., Jr., and Charles S. BULLOCK, III. "School Desegregation: A Policy Analysis." *J Black Stud*, II (1972), 409–437.

2049 RUBIN, Lillian B. *Busing and Backlash: White against White in a California School District.* Berkeley, Cal., 1972.[†]

2050 RUCHAMES, Louis. *Race, Jobs, and Politics: The Story of FEPC.* New York, 1953.

2051 RUDWICK, Elliott M. "Fifty Years of Race Relations in East St. Louis: The Breaking Down of White Supremacy." *Midcon Am Stud J*, VI (Spring 1965), 3–15.

2052 SARRATT, Reed. *The Ordeal of Desegregation: The First Decade.* New York, 1966.

2053 SCHLUNDT, Ronald Alan. "Civil Rights Policies in the Eisenhower Years." Doctoral dissertation, Rice University, 1973.

2054 SCOTT, Alan. "Twenty-Five Years of Opinion on Integration in Texas." *S W Soc Sci Q*, XLVIII (1967), 155–163.

2055 SHOGAN, Robert, and Tom CRAIG. *The Detroit Race Riot.* Philadelphia, 1964.

2056 SHUMAN, Howard E. "Senate Rules and the Civil Rights Bill: A Case Study." *Am Pol Sci Rev*, LI (1957), 955–975.

2057 SILBERMAN, Charles E. *Crisis in Black and White.* New York, 1964.†

2058 SILVER, James W. *Mississippi: The Closed Society.* New York, 1966.†

2059 SITKOFF, Harvard. "The Detroit Race Riot of 1943." *Mich Hist*, LIII (1969), 183–194.

2060 SITKOFF, Harvard. "Harry Truman and the Election of 1948: The Coming of Age of Civil Rights in American Politics." *J S Hist*, XXXVII (1971), 597–616.

2061 SITKOFF, Harvard. "Racial Militancy and Interracial Violence in the Second World War." *J Am Hist*, LVIII (1971), 661–681.

2062 SMITH, Bob. *They Closed Their Schools: Prince Edward County, Virginia, 1951–1964.* Chapel Hill, N.C., 1965.†

2063 SMITH, Frank E. *Congressman from Mississippi.* New York, 1964.†

2064 SOSNA, Morton Philip. "In Search of the Silent South: White Southern Racial Liberalism 1920–1950." Doctoral dissertation, University of Wisconsin, 1972.

2065 SOUTHERN, David Wheaton. *"An American Dilemma* Revisited: Myrdal's Study through a Quarter Century." Doctoral dissertation, Emory University, 1971.

2066 STILLMAN, Richard J., II. *Integration of the Negro in the U.S. Armed Forces.* New York, 1968.

2067 STRONG, Donald S. *Negroes, Ballots, and Judges: National Voting Rights Legislation in the Federal Courts.* University, Ala., 1968.

2068 TOMBERLIN, Joseph A. "Florida Whites and the *Brown* Decision of 1954." *Fla Hist Q*, LI (1972), 22–36.

2069 ULMER, S. Sidney. "Earl Warren and the *Brown* Decision." *J Pol*, XXXIII (1971), 689–702.

2070 VANDEVER, Elizabeth Jane. "Brown v. Board of Education of Topeka: Anatomy of a Decision." Doctoral dissertation, University of Kansas, 1971.

2071 VAUGHAN, Philip H. "President Truman's Committee on Civil Rights: The Urban Implications." *Mo Hist Rev*, LXVI (1972), 413–430.

2072 VAUGHAN, Philip H., "Urban Aspects of Civil Rights and the Early Truman Administration, 1946–1948." Doctoral dissertation, University of Oklahoma, 1971.

2073 VOSE, Clement E. *Caucasions Only: The Supreme Court, the NAACP and the Restrictive Covenant Cases.* Berkeley, Cal., 1959.†

2074 WATTERS, Pat. *Down to Now: Reflections on the Southern Civil Rights Movement.* New York, 1971.

2075 WATTERS, Pat, and Reese CLEGHORN. *Climbing Jacob's Ladder.*[†] See 1457.

2076 WEISBORD, Robert G., and Arthur STEIN. *Bittersweet Encounter: The Afro-American and the American Jew.* Westport, Conn., 1970.[†]

2077 WIGGINS, Sam P. *The Desegregation Era in Higher Education.* Berkeley, Cal., 1966.[†]

2078 WILHOIT, Francis M. *The Politics of Massive Resistance.* New York, 1973.[†]

2079 WINKLER, Allan M. "The Philadelphia Transit Strike of 1944." See 1865.

2080 WOLK, Allan. *The Presidency and Black Civil Rights: Eisenhower to Nixon.* Rutherford, N.J., 1971.

2081 WOODWARD, C. Vann. *The Strange Career of Jim Crow.* New York, 1974.[†]

2082 WOOFTER, Thomas J. *Southern Race Progress: The Wavering Color Line.* Washington, 1957.

B. Black Life, Movements, Ideologies, and Leaders

2083 ANDERSON, Jervis. *A. Philip Randolph.*[†] See 1772.

2084 BARDOLPH, Richard. *The Negro Vanguard.* New York, 1959.

2085 BENNETT, Lerone, Jr. *Before the Mayflower: A History of the Negro in America, 1619–1969.* Chicago, 1969.[†]

2086 BENNETT, Lerone, Jr. *What Manner of Man: A Biography of Martin Luther King, Jr.* Chicago, 1964.[†]

2087 BISHOP, Jim. *The Days of Martin Luther King, Jr.* New York, 1971.

2088 BLAND, Randall W. *Private Pressure on Public Law.*[†] See 1543.

2089 BONE, ROBERT. *The Negro Novel in America.* New Haven, Conn., 1965.[†]

2090 BORDEN, Karen Wells. "Black Rhetoric in the 1960s." *J Black Stud,* III (1973), 423–431.

2091 BREITMAN, George. *The Last Year of Malcolm X: The Evolution of a Revolutionary.* New York, 1968.[†]

2092 BRISBANE, Robert H. *The Black Vanguard: Origins of the Negro Social Revolution 1900–1960.* Valley Forge, Pa., 1970.[†]

2093 BROWN, Claude. *Manchild in the Promised Land.* New York, 1965.[†] Growing up in Harlem.

2094 BULLOCK, Henry Allen. *A History of Negro Education in the South: From 1619 to the Present.* Cambridge, Mass., 1967.[†]

2095 BURNS, W. Haywood. *The Voices of Negro Protest in America.* New York, 1963.

2096 CHARNEY, Maurice. "James Baldwin's Quarrel with Richard Wright." *Am Q,* XV (1963), 65–75.

2097 CLARK, Kenneth. *Dark Ghetto: Dilemmas of Social Power.* New York, 1967.[†]

2098 COOK, Mercer, and Stephen E. HENDERSON. *The Militant Black Writer in Africa and the United States.* Madison, Wis., 1969.†

2099 CRUSE, Harold. *The Crisis of the Negro Intellectual.* New York, 1967.†

2100 DALFIUME, Richard M. " 'The Forgotten Years' of the Negro Revolution." *J Am Hist,* LV (1968), 90–106.

2101 DANIELS, Lee A. "The Political Career of Adam Clayton Powell: Paradigm and Paradox." *J Black Stud,* IV (1973), 115–138.

2102 DAVIS, Lenwood G. *I Have a Dream . . . The Life and Times of Martin Luther King, Jr.* Chicago, 1969.†

2103 DRAPER, Theodore. *The Rediscovery of Black Nationalism.* New York, 1970.†

2104 ECKMAN, Fern M. *The Furious Passage of James Baldwin.* New York, 1966.†

2105 ERSHKOWITZ, Miriam, and Joseph ZIKMUND, II. *Black Politics in Philadelphia.* See 1381.

2106 ESSIEN-UDOM, E. U. *Black Nationalism: A Search for an Identity in America.* Chicago, 1962.†

2107 FINKLE, Lee. "The Conservative Aims of Militant Rhetoric: Black Protest during World War II." *J Am Hist,* LX (1973), 692–713.

2108 FINKLE, Lee. "Forum for Protest: The Black Press during World War II." Doctoral dissertation, New York University, 1971.

2109 FRANKLIN, John Hope. *From Slavery to Freedom: A History of Negro Americans.* New York, 1974.†

2110 FRAZIER, E. Franklin. *The Negro Family in the United States.* New York, 1948.†

2111 FRAZIER, E. Franklin. *The Negro in the United States.* New York, 1957.

2112 FULLINWIDER, S. P. *The Mind and Mood of Black America: 20th Century Thought.* Homewood, Ill., 1969.†

2113 GARFINKEL, Herbert. *When Negroes March: The March on Washington Movement in the Organizational Politics for FEPC.* New York, 1959.†

2114 GLENN, Norval D. "Changes in the American Occupational Structure and Occupational Gains of Negroes during the 1940's." *Soc Forces,* XLI (1962), 188–195.

2115 GOLDMAN, Peter. *The Death and Life of Malcolm X.* New York, 1973.†

2116 HANDLIN, Oscar. *The Newcomers: Negroes and Puerto Ricans in a Changing Metropolis.* Cambridge, Mass., 1959.†

2117 HARPER, Frederick D. "The Influence of Malcolm X on Black Militancy." *J Black Stud,* I (1971), 387–402.

2118 HERO, Alfred O., Jr. "American Negroes and U.S. Foreign Policy: 1937–1967." See 251.

2119 HILL, Herbert, ed. *Anger, and Beyond: The Negro Writer in the United States.* New York, 1966.

2120 HIRSCH, Paul M. "An Analysis of *Ebony*: The Magazine and Its Readers." *Jour Q,* XLV (1968), 261–270, 292.

2121 ISAACS, Harold R. "The American Negro and Africa: Some Notes." *Phylon*, XX (1959), 219–233.

2122 ISAACS, Harold R. "Five Writers and Their Ancestors." *Phylon*, XXI (1960), 243–265, 317–336.

2123 JONES, Beau Fly. "James Baldwin: The Struggle for Identity." *Brit J Soc*, XVII (1966), 107–121.

2124 KAPLAN, Howard M. "The Black Muslims and the Negro American's Quest for Communion." *Brit J Soc*, XX (1969), 164–176.

2125 KEIL, Charles. *Urban Blues*. Chicago, 1966.† Black music.

2126 KILLIAN, Lewis M. *The Impossible Revolution? Black Power and the American Dream*. New York, 1968.†

2127 KING, Coretta Scott. *My Life with Martin Luther King, Jr*. New York, 1969.†

2128 KING, Martin Luther. *Stride toward Freedom: The Montgomery Story*. New York, 1958.

2129 LADD, Everett C. *Negro Political Leadership in the South.*† See 1413.

2130 LEONARD, Edward A. "Nonviolence and Violence in American Racial Protests, 1942–1967." *Rocky Mt Soc Sci J*, VI (April 1969), 10–22.

2131 LEWIS, David L. *King: A Critical Biography*. New York, 1970.†

2132 LINCOLN, C. Eric. *The Black Muslims in America*. Boston, 1973.†

2133 LITTLEJOHN, David. *Black on White: A Critical Survey of Writing by American Negroes*. New York, 1966.†

2134 LOMAX, Louis E. *The Negro Revolt*. New York, 1962.†

2135 MCCORMACK, Donald J. "Stokely Carmichael and Pan-Africanism: Back to Black Power." *J Pol*, XXXV (1973), 386–409.

2136 MALCOLM X. *The Autobiography of Malcolm X*. New York, 1965.†

2137 MARGOLIES, Edward. *Native Sons: A Critical Study of Twentieth-Century Negro American Authors*. Philadelphia, 1968.†

2138 MEIER, August, and Elliot RUDWICK. *CORE: A Study in the Civil Rights Movement, 1942–1968*. New York, 1973.

2139 MEIER, August, and Elliott RUDWICK. *From Plantation to Ghetto*. New York, 1970.†

2140 MILLER, William Robert. *Martin Luther King, Jr.: His Life, Martyrdom and Meaning for the World*. New York, 1968.†

2141 MOORE, Jesse Thomas. "The Urban League and the Black Revolution, 1941–1961: Its Philosophy and Its Policies." Doctoral dissertation, Pennsylvania State University, 1971.

2142 MUSE, Benjamin. *The American Negro Revolution: From Nonviolence to Black Power, 1963–1967*. Bloomington, Ind., 1968.†

2143 NEWBY, I. A. *Black Carolinians: A History of Blacks in South Carolina from 1895 to 1968*. Columbia, S.C., 1973.

2144 OHMANN, Carol. "*The Autobiography of Malcolm X*: A Revolutionary Use of the Franklin Tradition." *Am Q*, XXII (1970), 131–149.

2145 PARRIS, Guichard, and Lester BROOKS. *Blacks in the City: A History of the National Urban League.* Boston, 1971.

2146 PEAVY, Charles D. "The Black Art of Propaganda: The Cultural Arm of the Black Power Movement." *Rocky Mt Soc Sci J,* VII (April 1970), 9–16.

2147 POWELL, Adam Clayton, Jr. *Adam by Adam: The Autobiography of Adam Clayton Powell, Jr.* New York, 1971.

2148 PUTH, Robert C. "Supreme Life: The History of a Negro Life Insurance Company, 1919–1962." See 1743.

2149 RATHBUN, John W. "Martin Luther King: The Theology of Social Action." *Am Q,* XX (1968), 38–53.

2150 RECORD, Wilson. "American Racial Ideologies and Organizations in Transition." *Phylon,* XXVI (1965), 315–329.

2151 RECORD, Wilson. *Race and Radicalism: The NAACP and the Communist Party in Conflict.* Ithaca, N.Y., 1964.†

2152 REDDICK, L. D. *Crusader without Violence: A Biography of Martin Luther King, Jr.* New York, 1959.

2153 RELYEA, Harold C. "Black Power as an Urban Ideology." *Soc Stud,* LX (1969), 243–250.

2154 ROARK, James L. "American Black Leaders: The Response to Colonialism and the Cold War, 1943–1953." *Af Hist Stud,* IV (1971), 253–270.

2155 RUDWICK, Elliott, and August MEIER. "Organizational Structure and Goal Succession: A Comparative Analysis of the NAACP and CORE, 1964–1968." *Soc Sci Q,* LI (1970), 9–24.

2156 SALAMON, Lester M. "Leadership and Modernization: The Emerging Black Political Elite in the American South." See 1445.

2157 SEARS, David O. "Black Attitudes toward the Political System in the Aftermath of the Watts Insurrection." *M W J Pol Sci,* XIII (1969), 515–544.

2158 SHARMA, Mohan Lal. "Martin Luther King: Modern America's Greatest Theologian of Social Action." *J Neg Hist,* LIII (1968), 257–263.

2159 SMITH, Donald H. "An Exegesis of Martin Luther King, Jr.'s Social Philosophy." *Phylon,* XXXI (1970), 89–97.

2160 SMITH, T. Lynn. "The Redistribution of the Negro Population of the United States, 1910–1960." *J Neg Hist,* LI (1966), 155–173.

2161 SOLOMON, Mark. "Black Critics of Colonialism and the Cold War." *Cold War Critics: Alternatives to American Foreign Policy in the Truman Years.* Ed. Thomas G. Paterson. Chicago, 1971.†

2162 STEINKRAUS, Warren E. "Martin Luther King's Personalism and Non-Violence." *J Hist Ideas,* XXXIV (1973), 97–111.

2163 STEVENSON, Janet. "Rosa Parks Wouldn't Budge." *Am Her,* XXIII (February 1972), 56–64, 85.

2164 STRICKLAND, Arvarh E. *History of the Chicago Urban League.* Urbana, Ill., 1966.

2165 TYLER, Lawrence L. "The Protestant Ethic among the Black Muslims." *Phylon,* XXVII (1966), 5–14.

2166 VANDER ZANDEN, James W. "The Non-Violent Resistance Movement against Segregation." *Am J Soc,* LXVIII (1963), 544–550.

2167 WALTON, Hanes, Jr. *The Political Philosophy of Martin Luther King, Jr.* Westport, Conn., 1971.

2168 WASKOW, Arthur I. *From Race Riot to Sit-In, 1919 and the 1960s: A Study of the Connections between Conflict and Violence.* Garden City, N.Y., 1966.

2169 WEBB, Constance. *Richard Wright: A Biography.* New York, 1968.

2170 WEISBORD, Robert G. *Ebony Kinship: Africa, Africans, and the Afro-American.* Westport, Conn., 1973.

2171 WEISS, Samuel A. "The Ordeal of Malcolm X." *S Atl Q,* LXVII (1968), 53–63.

2172 WHITE, Walter. *A Man Called White: The Autobiography of Walter White.* New York, 1948.†

2173 WILSON, James Q. *Negro Politics: The Search for Leadership.* Glencoe, Ill., 1960.†

2174 WOLSELEY, Roland E. *The Black Press, U.S.A.* Ames, Ia., 1971.†

2175 YOUNG, Richard. "The Impact of Protest Leadership on Negro Politicians in San Francisco." *W Pol Q,* XXII (1969), 94–111.

2176 ZINN, Howard. *SNCC: The New Abolitionists.* Boston, 1964.†

C. Japanese Americans, Spanish Americans, American Indians, Jews, and Others

2177 ACUNA, Rodolfo. *Occupied America: The Chicano's Struggle toward Liberation.* San Francisco, 1972.†

2178 ANDERSON, William C. "Early Reaction in Arkansas to the Relocation of Japanese in the State." *Ark Hist Q,* XXIII (1964), 195–211.

2179 ARRINGTON, Leonard J. *The Price of Prejudice.* Logan, Utah, 1962.

2180 BARNHART, Edward N. "The Individual Exclusion of Japanese Americans in World War II." *Pac Hist Rev,* XXIX (1960), 113–130.

2181 BIERBRIER, Doreen. "The American Zionist Emergency Council: An Analysis of a Pressure Group." See 623.

2182 CARUSO, Samuel T. "After Pearl Harbor: Arizona's Response to the Gila River Relocation Center." *J Ariz Hist,* XIV (1973), 335–346.

2183 DANIELS, Roger. *Concentration Camps USA: Japanese Americans and World War II.* New York, 1971.†

2184 DEBO, Angie. *A History of the Indians of the United States.* Norman, Okla., 1970.

2185 DINNERSTEIN, Leonard, and Mary Dale PALSSON, eds. *Jews in the South.* See 1969.

2186 FUCHS, Lawrence H. "American Jews and the Presidential Vote." See 1168.

2187 FUCHS, Lawrence H. *The Political Behavior of American Jews.* See 1169.

2188 GERSON, Louis L. *The Hyphenate in Recent American Politics and Diplomacy.* See 234.

2189 GIRDNER, Audrie, and Anne LOFTIS. *The Great Betrayal: The Evacuation of the Japanese Americans during World War II.* New York, 1969.

2190 GLAZER, Nathan, and Daniel Patrick MOYNIHAN. *Beyond the Melting Pot: The Negroes, Puerto Ricans, Jews, Italians, and Irish of New York City.* Cambridge, Mass., 1963.

2191 GOTTLIEB, Moshe. "In the Shadow of War: The American Anti-Nazi Boycott Movement in 1939–1941." See 393.

2192 GREBLER, Leo, et al. *The Mexican-American People: The Nation's Second Largest Minority.* New York, 1970.

2193 GUTTMANN, Allen. *The Jewish Writer in America: Assimilation and the Crisis of Identity.* New York, 1971.

2194 HALPERIN, Samuel. *The Political World of American Zionism.* See 660.

2195 HANDLIN, Oscar. *The Newcomers.*† See 2116.

2196 HOSOKAWA, Bill. *Nisei: The Quiet Americans.* New York, 1969.†

2197 HUFF, Earl D. "A Study of a Successful Interest Group: The American Zionist Movement." See 668.

2198 IRONS, Peter H. " 'The Test Is Poland': Polish Americans and the Origins of the Cold War." See 547.

2199 JOSEPHY, Alvin M., Jr. "Toward Freedom: The American Indian in the Twentieth Century." *Indiana Historical Society Lectures, 1970–1971: American Indian Policy.* Indianapolis, Ind., 1971.

2200 LE DUC, Thomas. "The Work of the Indian Claims Commission under the Act of 1946." *Pac Hist Rev,* XXVI (1957), 1–16.

2201 LEVINE, Stuart, and Nancy O. LURIE, eds. *The American Indian Today.* Baltimore, 1968.†

2202 MARKER, Jeffrey M. "The Jewish Community and the Case of Julius and Ethel Rosenberg." See 1501.

2203 MATTHIESSEN, Peter. *Sal Si Puedes: Cesar Chavez and the New American Revolution.*† See 1824.

2204 MEIER, Matt S., and Feliciano RIVERA. *The Chicanos: A History of Mexican Americans.* New York, 1972.†

2205 MELENDY, H. Brett. *The Oriental Americans.* New York, 1972.†

2206 MOSTWIN, Danuta. "Post-World War II Polish Immigrants in the United States." *Pol Am Stud,* XXVI (1969), 5–14.

2207 MYER, Dillon S. *Uprooted Americans: The Japanese Americans and the War Relocation Authority during World War II.* Tucson, Ariz., 1971.†

2208 NEILS, Elaine. *Reservation to City: Indian Migration and Federal Relocation.* Chicago, 1971.

2209 RUTMAN, Herbert S. "Defense and Development: A History of Minneapolis Jewry, 1930–1950." Doctoral dissertation, University of Minnesota, 1970.

2210 SALOUTOS, Theodore. *The Greeks in the United States.* Cambridge, Mass., 1964.

2211 SCHLENKER, Gerald. "The Internment of the Japanese of San Diego County during the Second World War." *J San Diego Hist,* XVIII (Winter 1972), 1–9.

2212 SKLARE, Marshall. *America's Jews.* New York, 1971.[†]

2213 STEINER, Stan. *The New Indians.* New York, 1968.[†]

2214 STEMBER, Charles Herbert, *et al. Jews in the Mind of America.* New York, 1966.

2215 STEVENS, John D. "From behind Barbed Wire: Freedom of the Press in World War II Japanese Centers." *Jour Q,* XLVIII (1971), 279–287.

2216 SZASZ, Margaret Ann Connell. "American Indian Education, 1930–1970, from the Meriam Report to the Kennedy Report." Doctoral dissertation, University of New Mexico, 1972.

2217 TEN BROEK, Jacobus, *et al. Prejudice, War and the Constitution.*[†] See 1588.

2218 VORSPAN, Max, and Lloyd P. GARTNER. *History of the Jews of Los Angeles.* San Marino, Cal., 1970.

2219 WASHBURN, Wilcomb E. *Red Man's Land, White Man's Law: A Study of the Past and Present Status of the American Indian.* New York, 1971.[†]

2220 WYTRWAL, Joseph A. *Poles in American History and Tradition.* Detroit, Mich., 1969.

VIII. Society, Culture, Thought

A. Social Conditions and Policies

2221 ALLEN, James B. "Crisis on the Home Front: The Federal Government and Utah's Defense Housing Program in World War II." *Pac Hist Rev,* XXXVIII (1969), 409–428.

2222 ALTMEYER, Arthur J. *The Formative Years of Social Security.* Madison, Wis., 1966.[†]

2223 ANDERSON, Martin. *The Federal Bulldozer: A Critical Analysis of Urban Renewal, 1949–1962.* Cambridge, Mass., 1964.[†]

2224 BENNETT, Marion T. *American Immigration Policies: A History.* Washington, 1963.

2225 BENSMAN, Joseph, and Arthur J. VIDICH. *The New American Society: The Revolution of the Middle Class.* Chicago, 1971.[†]

2226 BERNSTEIN, Barton J. "Reluctance and Resistance: Wilson Wyatt and Veterans' Housing in the Truman Administration." *Reg Ky Hist Soc,* LXV (1967), 47–66.

2227 BERTHOFF, Rowland. *An Unsettled People: Social Order and Disorder in American History.* New York, 1971.

2228 BURKE, Vincent, and Vee BURKE. *Nixon's Good Deed: Welfare Reform.* New York, 1974.

2229 CHAFE, William H. *The American Woman: Her Changing Social, Economic, and Political Roles, 1920–1970.* New York, 1972.†

2230 CHAMBERS, Clarke A. *Paul U. Kellogg and the 'Survey': Voices for Social Welfare and Social Justice.* Minneapolis, Minn., 1971.

2231 CLARK, Kenneth B., and Jeannette HOPKINS. *A Relevant War against Poverty: A Study of Community Action Programs and Observable Social Change.* New York, 1969.

2232 CUTLIP, Scott M. *Fund Raising in the United States: Its Role in America's Philanthropy.* New Brunswick, N.J., 1965.

2233 DAVIES, Richard O. *Housing Reform during the Truman Administration.* Columbia, Mo., 1966.

2234 DAVIES, Richard O. " 'Mr. Republican' Turns 'Socialist': Robert A. Taft and Public Housing." *Ohio Hist,* LXXIII (1964), 135–143.

2235 DAVIES, Richard O. "Social Welfare Policies." *The Truman Period as a Research Field.* Ed. Richard S. Kirkendall. Columbia, Mo., 1967.

2236 DIMMITT, Marius Albert. "The Enactment of the McCarran-Walter Act of 1952." Doctoral dissertation, University of Kansas, 1970.

2237 DIVINE, Robert A. *American Immigration Policies, 1924–1952.* New Haven, Conn., 1957.

2238 DONOVAN, John C. *The Politics of Poverty.* New York, 1973.†

2239 FEINGOLD, Henry L. *The Politics of Rescue.* See 222.

2240 FLORER, John Harmon. "NOW: The Formative Years. The National Effort to Acquire Federal Action on Equal Employment Rights for Women in the 1960's." Doctoral dissertation, Syracuse University, 1972.

2241 FRIEDAN, Betty. *The Feminine Mystique.* New York, 1963.†

2242 FRIEDMAN, Saul S. *No Haven for the Oppressed.* See 226.

2243 FUNIGIELLO, Philip J. "City Planning in World War II: The Experience of the National Resources Planning Board." *Soc Sci Q,* LIII (1972), 91–104.

2244 GALLUP, George H., ed. *The Gallup Poll: Public Opinion, 1935–1971.* 3 Vols. New York, 1973.

2245 GANS, Herbert J. *The Levittowners: Ways of Life and Politics in a New Suburban Community.* New York, 1967.†

2246 GOODMAN, Jack, ed. *While You Were Gone.* New York, 1946. The home front in World War II.

2247 HARRINGTON, Michael. *The Other America: Poverty in the United States.* New York, 1962.†

2248 HAVIGHURST, Robert J., and H. Gerthon MORGAN. *The Social History of a War-Boom Community.* New York, 1951.

2249 HERTZLER, J. O. "Some Tendencies toward a Closed Class System in the United States." *Soc Forces,* XXX (1952), 313–323.

2250 HESS, Leland E. "The Coming of Urban Redevelopment and Urban Renewal to Oregon, 1949–1963." Doctoral dissertation, University of Chicago, 1968.

2251 JACKSON, Charles O., and Charles W. JOHNSON. "The Summer of '44: Observations on Life in the Oak Ridge Community." *Tenn Hist Q,* XXXII (1973), 233–248.

2252 JOSEPH, Peter. *Good Times: An Oral History of America in the Nineteen Sixties.* New York, 1973.

2253 KOLKO, Gabriel. *Wealth and Power in America: An Analysis of Social Class and Income Distribution.* New York, 1962.[†]

2254 LANKFORD, John. *Congress and the Foundations in the Twentieth Century.* River Falls, Wis., 1964.

2255 LINGEMAN, Richard R. *Don't You Know There's a War On? The American Home Front, 1941-1945.* New York, 1970.[†]

2256 LORIMER, M. Madeline. "America's Response to Europe's Displaced Persons, 1945-1952: A Preliminary Report." See 281.

2257 MCKELVEY, Blake. *The Emergence of Metropolitan America, 1915-1966.* New Brunswick, N.J., 1968.

2258 MADGWICK, P. J. "The Politics of Urban Renewal." *J Am Stud,* V (1971), 265-280.

2259 MARKOWITZ, Arthur A. "Humanitarianism vs. Restrictionism: The United States and the Hungarian Refugees." *Int Mig Rev,* VII (1973), 46-59.

2260 MERRILL, Francis E. *Social Problems on the Home Front.* New York, 1948.

2261 MILLS, C. Wright. *The Power Elite.* New York, 1956.[†]

2262 MINOTT, Rodney G. *Peerless Patriots: Organized Veterans and the Spirit of Americanism.* Washington, 1962.

2263 MORSE, Arthur D. *While Six Million Died.* See 288.

2264 MOYNIHAN, Daniel P. *Maximum Feasible Misunderstanding: Community Action in the War on Poverty.* New York, 1969.[†]

2265 MOYNIHAN, Daniel P. *The Politics of a Guaranteed Income: The Nixon Administration and the Family Assistance Plan.* New York, 1973.[†]

2266 NIELSEN, Waldemar. *The Big Foundations.* New York, 1972.[†]

2267 OLSON, Thomas Lyle. "Unfinished Business: American Social Work in Pursuit of Reform, Community, and World Peace, 1939-1950." Doctoral dissertation, University of Minnesota, 1972.

2268 O'Neill, William L., ed. *American Society since 1945.* Chicago, 1969.[†]

2269 PILISUK, Marc, and Thomas HAYDEN. "Is There a Military Industrial Complex Which Prevents Peace?: Consensus and Countervailing Power in Pluralistic Systems." *J Soc Issues,* XXI (July 1965), 67-117.

2270 PIOUS, Richard M. "Policy and Public Administration: The Legal Services Program in the War on Poverty." *Pol Soc,* I (1971), 365-391.

2271 RAE, John B. *The Road and the Car in American Life.* Cambridge, Mass., 1971.

2272 ROSS, Davis R. B. *Preparing for Ulysses: Politics and Veterans during World War II.* New York, 1969.

2273 SAGARIN, Edward, ed. "Sex and the Contemporary American Scene." *Ann Am Acad Pol Soc Sci,* CCCLXXVI (1968), 1-155.

2274 SCOTT, Mel. *American City Planning since 1890.* Berkeley, Cal., 1969.

2275 SIBLEY, M. Q., and P. E. JACOB. *Conscription of Conscience: The American State and the Conscientious Objector, 1940-1947.* Ithaca, N.Y., 1952.

2276 STOUFFER, Samuel A., *et al. The American Soldier.* See 1007.

2277 STRUNK, Mildred, and Hadley CANTRIL, eds. *Public Opinion, 1935–1946.* Princeton, N.J. 1951.

2278 SWEETSER, Frank L., and Paavo PIEPPONEN. "Postwar Fertility Trends and Their Consequences in Finland and the United States." *J Soc Hist,* I (1967), 101–118.

2279 TAEBER, Conrad. "Some Population Trends of the 1960's." *Soc Sci,* XLVII (1972), 145–152.

2280 THERNSTROM, Stephan. *The Other Bostonians: Poverty and Progress in the American Metropolis, 1880–1970.* Cambridge, Mass., 1973.

2281 THERNSTROM, Stephan. *Poverty, Planning, and Politics in the New Boston: The Origins of ABCD.* New York, 1969.

2282 WEAVER, Warren. *U.S. Philanthropic Foundations: Their History, Structure, Management, and Record.* New York, 1967.

2283 WHYTE, William H., Jr. *The Organization Man.* New York, 1956.†

2284 WILBURN, James Richard. "Social and Economic Aspects of the Aircraft Industry in Metropolitan Los Angeles during World War II." See 1765.

2285 WYMAN, David S. *Paper Walls.* See 365.

B. *Intellectual and Cultural Trends*

2286 ADLER, Leslie K. "The Red Image: American Attitudes toward Communism in the Cold War Era." Doctoral dissertation, University of California at Berkeley, 1970.

2287 ADLER, Les K., and Thomas G. PATERSON. "Red Fascism: The Merger of Nazi Germany and Soviet Russia in the American Image of Totalitarianism, 1930's–1950's." *Am Hist Rev,* LXXV (1970), 1046–1064.

2288 ALEXANDER, Charles C. *Nationalism in American Thought, 1930–1945.* Chicago, 1969.†

2289 ALTBACH, Philip G., and Robert S. LAUFER, eds. *The New Pilgrims: Youth Protest in Transition.* New York, 1972.†

2290 BAILEY, Margaret. "The Women's Magazine Short-Story Heroine in 1957 and 1967." *Jour Q,* XLVI (1969), 364–366.

2291 BAILYN, Bernard, and Donald FLEMING, eds. *The Intellectual Migration: Europe and America, 1930–1960.* Cambridge, Mass., 1968.

2292 BATCHELDER, Robert C. *The Irreversible Decision.* See 887.

2293 BELL, Daniel. *The End of Ideology: On the Exhaustion of Political Ideas in the Fifties.* New York, 1962.†

2294 BERLE, Beatrice Bishop, and Travis Beal JACOBS, eds. *Navigating the Rapids, 1918–1971: From the Papers of Adolf A. Berle.* New York, 1973.

2295 BERMAN, Ronald. *America in the Sixties: An Intellectual History.* New York, 1968.†

2296 BERNARD, Jessie, ed. "Teen Age Culture." *Ann Am Acad Pol Soc Sci,* CCCXXXVIII (1961), 1–136.

2297 BOSCH, William J. *Judgment on Nuremberg: American Attitudes toward the Major German War-Crime Trials.* Chapel Hill, N.C., 1970.

2298 BOTTOMORE, T. B. *Critics of Society: Radical Thought in North America.* New York, 1968.[†]

2299 CARLETON, William G. "American Intellectuals and American Democracy." *Ant Rev,* XIX (1959), 185–204.

2300 CHASE, Stuart. "American Values: A Generation of Change." *Pub Opin Q,* XXIX (1965), 357–367.

2301 COFFEY, John William. "Realist Social Thought in America: Reinhold Niebuhr and George F. Kennan." Doctoral dissertation, Stanford University, 1971.

2302 COZENS, Frederick W., and Florence Scovil STUMPF. *Sports in American Life.* Chicago, 1953.

2303 CURTI, Merle. *The Growth of American Thought.* New York, 1964.

2304 DIGGINS, John P. "The American Writer, Fascism and the Liberation of Italy." *Am Q,* XVIII (1966), 599–614.

2305 DIGGINS, John P. *Mussolini and Fascism: The View from America.* Princeton, N. J., 1972.

2306 ERISMAN, Fred. "The Environmental Crisis and Present-Day Romanticism: The Persistence of an Idea." *Rocky Mt Soc Sci J,* X (January 1973), 7–14.

2307 FERMI, Laura. *Illustrious Immigrants: The Intellectual Migration from Europe, 1930–1941.* Chicago, 1971.[†]

2308 FLINK, James J. "Three Stages of American Automobile Consciousness." *Am Q,* XXIV (1972), 451–473.

2309 GOOD, Robert C. "The National Interest and Political Realism: Neibuhr's 'Debate' with Morgenthau and Kennan." *J Pol,* XXII (1960), 597–619.

2310 HARTSHORNE, Thomas L. *The Distorted Image: Changing Conceptions of the American Character since Turner.* Cleveland, Ohio, 1968.

2311 HOPKINS, George E. "Bombing and the American Conscience during World War II." *Hist,* XXVIII (1966), 451–473.

2312 HOWELL, Robert Thomas. "The Writers' War Board: Writers and World War II." Doctoral dissertation, Louisiana State University, 1971.

2313 HUEBEL, Harry Russell, Jr. "The Beat Generation and the Bohemian-Left Tradition in America." Doctoral dissertation, Washington State University, 1970.

2314 JAY, Martin. "The Frankfurt School in Exile." *Pers Am Hist,* VI (1972), 339–385.

2315 KING, Richard. *The Party of Eros: Radical Social Thought and the Realm of Freedom.* Chapel Hill, N.C., 1972.[†]

2316 LASCH, Christopher. *The New Radicalism in America, 1889–1963: The Intellectual as a Social Type.* New York, 1965.[†]

2317 LEARY, William M., Jr. "Books, Soldiers and Censorship during the Second World War." *Am Q,* XX (1968), 237–245.

2318 LIPTON, Lawrence. *The Holy Barbarians.* New York, 1959. The Beat generation.

2319 MACDONALD, Dwight. *Memoirs of a Revolutionist: Essays in Political Criticism.* New York, 1957.[†]

SOCIETY, CULTURE, THOUGHT

2320 MCWILLIAMS, Wilson Carey. "Reinhold Neibuhr: New Orthodoxy for Old Liberalism." *Am Pol Sci Rev,* LVI (1962), 874–885.

2321 MORTON, Marian J. *The Terrors of Ideological Politics: Liberal Historians in a Conservative Mood.* Cleveland, Ohio, 1972.

2322 NEWMAN, William J. *The Futilitarian Society.* New York, 1961.

2323 NYE, Russel B. *The Unembarrassed Muse: The Popular Arts in America.* New York, 1970.†

2324 PURCELL, Edward A., Jr. *The Crisis of Democratic Theory: Scientific Naturalism and the Problem of Value.* Lexington, Ky., 1973.

2325 REMBAR, Charles. *The End of Obscenity: The Trials of 'Lady Chatterly,' 'Tropic of Cancer' and 'Fanny Hill.'* New York, 1968.†

2326 ROBERTS, Ron E. *The New Communes: Coming Together in America.* Englewood Cliffs, N.J., 1971.†

2327 ROSZAK, Theodore. *The Making of a Counter Culture.* New York, 1969.†

2328 SCOTT, James F. "Beat Literature and the American Teen Cult." *Am Q,* XIV (1962), 150–160.

2329 SIGLER, Jay A. "The Political Philosophy of C. Wright Mills." *Sci Soc,* XXX (1966), 32–49.

2330 SKOTHEIM, Robert Allen. *Totalitarianism and American Social Thought.* New York, 1971.

2331 TREVATHAN, Norman E. "The Toynbee Vogue in the United States, 1947–1957." Doctoral dissertation, George Peabody College for Teachers, 1968.

2332 UNGER, Irwin. "The 'New Left' and American History: Some Recent Trends in United States Historiography." *Am Hist Rev,* LXXXII (1967), 1237–1263.

2333 VOIGHT, David Quentin. *American Baseball: From the Commissioners to Continental Expansion.* Norman, Okla., 1970.

2334 WEINBERG, Sydney. "What to Tell America: The Writers Quarrel in the Office of War Information." *J Am Hist,* LV (1968), 73–89.

2335 WELLEK, Albert. "The Impact of German Immigration on the Development of American Psychology." *J Hist Behav Sci,* IV (1968), 207–229.

2336 WHITE, David Manning, ed. *Pop Culture in America.* Chicago, 1970.†

2337 WISH, Harvey. *Society and Thought in Modern America: A Social and Intellectual History of the American People from 1865.* New York, 1962.

2338 WITTNER, Lawrence S. *Rebels against War: The American Peace Movement, 1941–1960.* New York, 1969.†

2339 YAVENDITTI, Michael J. "The American People and the Use of Atomic Bombs on Japan: The 1940s." *Hist,* XXXVI (1974), 224–247.

2340 YAVENDITTI, Michael J. "American Reactions to the Use of Atomic Bombs on Japan, 1945–1947." Doctoral dissertation, University of California at Berkeley, 1970.

2341 YAVENDITTI, Michael J. "John Hersey and the American Conscience: The Reception of 'Hiroshima.'" *Pac Hist Rev,* XLIII (1974), 24–49.

C. Political Ideologies

2342 ALEXANDER, Robert J. "Schisms and Unifications in the American Old Left, 1953–1970." *Lab Hist,* XIV (1973), 536–561.

2343 ANNUNZIATA, Frank. "The Progressive as Conservative: George Creel's Quarrel with New Deal Liberalism." *Wis Mag Hist,* LVII (1974), 220–233.

2344 ANNUNZIATA, Frank A. "The Attack on the Welfare State: Patterns of Anti-Statism from the New Deal to the New Left." Doctoral dissertation, Ohio State University, 1968.

2345 AUERBACH, M. Morton. *The Conservative Illusion.* New York, 1959.

2346 BACCIOCCO, Edward J., Jr. *The New Left in America: Reform to Revolution, 1956–1970.* Stanford, Cal., 1974.

2347 BELL, Daniel, ed. *The Radical Right.* Garden City, N.Y., 1963.[†]

2348 CLECAK, Peter, *Radical Paradoxes: Dilemmas of the American Left, 1945–1970.* New York, 1973.

2349 DELEON, David. "The American as Anarchist: Social Criticism in the 1960's." *Am Q,* XXV (1973), 516–537.

2350 DIGGINS, John P. *The American Left in the Twentieth Century.* New York, 1973.[†]

2351 EGBERT, D. D., and Stow PERSONS, eds. *Socialism and American Life.* 2 Vols. Princeton, N.J., 1952.

2352 EKIRCH, Arthur A., Jr. *The Decline of American Liberalism.* New York, 1955.[†]

2353 EPSTEIN, Benjamin R., and Arnold FORSTER. *The Radical Right: Report on the John Birch Society and Its Allies.* New York, 1967.[†]

2354 EPSTEIN, Marc Joel. "The Third Force: Liberal Ideology in a Revolutionary Age, 1945–1950." Doctoral dissertation, University of North Carolina, 1971.

2355 FRANKLIN, Raymond S. "The Rise and Fall of Welfare-Liberalism." *Q Rev Econ Bus,* IV (Spring 1964), 43–50.

2356 GENTRY, Richard H. "Liberalism and the *New Republic:* 1914–1960." Doctoral dissertation, University of Illinois, 1961.

2357 GERBERDING, William P., and Duane E. SMITH, eds. *The Radical Left: The Abuse of Discontent.* Boston, 1970.[†]

2358 GILBERT, James Burkhart. *Writers and Partisans: A History of Literary Radicalism in America.* New York, 1968.

2359 GLAZER, Penina M. "A Decade of Transition: A Study of Radical Journals of the 1940's." Doctoral dissertation, Rutgers University, 1970.

2360 GLAZER, Penina M. "From the Old Left to the New: Radical Criticism in the 1940s." *Am Q,* XXIV (1972), 584–603.

2361 GOLDMAN, Eric F. *Rendezvous with Destiny.*[†] See 43.

2362 HALL, Chadwick. "America's Conservative Revolution." *Ant Rev,* XV (1955), 204–216.

2363 HAMBY, Alonzo L. *Beyond the New Deal.* See 1183.

2364 HAMBY, Alonzo L. "The Liberals, Truman, and FDR as Symbol and Myth." *J Am Hist,* LVI (1970), 859–867.

2365 HAMBY, Alonzo L. "Sixty Million Jobs and the People's Revolution: The Liberals, The New Deal, and World War II." *Hist,* XXX (1968), 578–598.

2366 HARRINGTON, Michael. *Fragments of the Century: A Social Autobiography.* New York, 1973.

2367 HERRESHOFF, David. "Transcendental Politics of the 1960's." *American Reform: The Ambiguous Legacy.* Ed. Daniel Walden. Yellow Springs, Ohio, 1967.

2368 HOFSTADTER, Richard. *The Paranoid Style in American Politics and Other Essays.* New York, 1965.†

2369 JACOBS, Paul, and Saul LANDAU. *The New Radicals: A Report with Documents.* New York, 1966.

2370 LASCH, Christopher. *The Agony of the American Left.* New York, 1969.†

2371 LEMMON, Sarah McCulloch. "The Ideology of the 'Dixiecrat' Movement." *Soc Forces,* XXX (1951), 162–171.

2372 LOWI, Theodore. "The Public Philosophy: Interest-Group Liberalism." *Am Pol Sci Rev,* LXI (1967), 5–24.

2373 MORGNER, Fred. "Ultraconservative Response to Supreme Court Judicial Behavior: A Study in Political Alienation, 1935–1965." Doctoral dissertation, University of Minnesota, 1970.

2374 O'BRIEN, James Putnam. "The Development of a New Left in the United States, 1960–1965." Doctoral dissertation, University of Wisconsin, 1971.

2375 ROSSITER, Clinton. *Conservatism in America: The Thankless Persuasion.* New York, 1962.†

2376 SALE, Kirkpatrick. *SDS.* New York, 1973.

2377 SELLEN, Robert W. "Patriotism or Paranoia: Right-Wing Extremism in America." *Dalhousie R,* XLIII (1963), 295–316.

2378 STERNSHER, Bernard. "Liberalism in the Fifties: The Travail of Redefinition." *Ant Rev,* XXII (1962), 315–331.

2379 THAYER, George. *The Farther Shores of Politics.* New York, 1967.†

2380 TOY, Eckard V., Jr. "Ideology and Conflict in American Ultraconservatism, 1945–1960." Doctoral dissertation, University of Oregon, 1965.

2381 TOY, Eckard V., Jr. "Spiritual Mobilization: The Failure of an Ultraconservative Ideal in the 1950's." *Pac N W Q,* LXI (1970), 77–86.

2382 TYLER, Robert L. "The American Veterans Committee: Out of a Hot War and into the Cold." *Am Q,* XVI (1966), 419–436.

2383 UNGER, Irwin. *The Movement: A History of the American New Left, 1959–1972.* New York, 1974.†

2384 VAUGHAN, Philip H. "The City and the American Creed: A Liberal Awakening during the Early Truman Period, 1946–1948." *Phylon,* XXXIV (1973), 51–62.

2385 VINZ, Warren L. "The Politics of Protestant Fundamentalism in the 1950s and 1960s." *J Ch State,* XIV (1972), 235–260.

2386 WHYATT, Nelson Thomas. "Planning for the Postwar World: Liberal Journalism during World War II." Doctoral dissertation, University of Minnesota, 1971.

2387 WILLS, Garry. *Nixon Agonistes.*[†] See 1354.

D. Domestic Disorder

2388 *Attica: The Official Report of the New York State Special Commission on Attica.* New York, 1972.[†]

2389 BOESEL, David, and Peter H. ROSSI, eds. *Cities under Siege.* See 1950.

2390 BOSKIN, Joseph. "Violence in the Ghettos: A Consensus of Attitudes." See 1952.

2391 BOSKIN, Joseph, and Robert A. ROSENSTONE, eds. "Protest in the Sixties." *Ann Am Acad Pol Soc Sci,* CCCLXXXII (1969), 1–144.

2392 *The Challenge of Crime in a Free Society: A Report by the President's Commission on Law Enforcement and Administration of Justice.* Washington, 1967.[†]

2393 CONNERY, Robert H., ed. "Urban Riots: Violence and Social Change." See 1961.

2394 CONOT, Robert. *Rivers of Blood, Years of Darkness.*[†] See 1962.

2395 COX, Archibald, *et al. Crisis at Columbia: Report of the Fact-Finding Commission Appointed to Investigate Disturbances at Columbia University in April and May 1968.* New York, 1968.

2396 DAVIES, Peter, *et al. The Truth about Kent State: A Challenge to the American Conscience.* New York, 1973.[†]

2397 EPSTEIN, Edward Jay. *Inquest: The Warren Commission and the Establishment of Truth.* New York, 1966.[†]

2398 EPSTEIN, Jason, *The Great Conspiracy Trial: An Essay on Law, Liberty and the Constitution.* New York, 1970.[†]

2399 FEAGIN, Joe R., and Harlan HAHN. *Ghetto Revolts.* See 1975.

2400 FOGELSON, Robert M. "From Resentment to Confrontation: The Police, the Negroes, and the Outbreak of the Nineteen-Sixties Riots." See 1978.

2401 Governor's Select Commission on Civil Disorder, State of New Jersey. *Report for Action.* See 1984.

2402 GRAHAM, Hugh Davis, and Ted GURR, eds. *Violence in America: Historical and Comparative Perspectives.* Vols. I & II. *A Report to the National Commission on the Causes and Prevention of Violence.* Washington, 1969.[†]

2403 GREENBERG, Bradley S., and Edwin B. PARKER, eds. *The Kennedy Assassination and the American Public: Social Communication in Crisis.* Stanford, Cal., 1965.

2404 HAYS, Samuel P. "Right Face, Left Face: The Columbia Strike." *Pol Sci Q,* LXXXIV (1969), 311–327.

2405 HEIRICH, Max. *The Spiral of Conflict: Berkeley, 1964.* New York, 1971.[†]

2406 HIGHAM, Robin D., ed. *Bayonets in the Streets: The Use of Troops in Civil Disturbances.* Lawrence, Kans., 1969.

2407 LANE, Mark. *Rush to Judgment.* New York, 1966. Re the assassination of John F. Kennedy.

2408 LEONARD, Edward A. "Nonviolence and Violence in American Racial Protests, 1942–1967." See 2130.

2409 LOCKE, Hubert G. *The Detroit Riot of 1967.* See 2010.

2410 LUSKY, Louis, and Mary H. LUSKY. "Columbia 1968: The Wound Unhealed." *Pol Sci Q,* LXXXIV (1969), 169–288.

2411 MANCHESTER, William. *The Death of a President.* New York, 1967. The Kennedy assassination.

2412 MOORE, William Howard. *The Kefauver Committee and the Politics of Crime.* See 1261.

2413 PROCTER, Ben H. "The Modern Texas Rangers: A Law-Enforcement Dilemma in the Rio Grande Valley." *Reflections of Western Historians.* Ed. John Alexander Carroll. Tucson, Ariz., 1969.

2414 *Report of the Warren Commission on the Assassination of President Kennedy.* New York, 1964.

2415 RUBENSTEIN, Richard E. *Rebels in Eden: Mass Political Violence in the United States.* Boston, 1970.†

2416 SCIMECCA, Joseph, and Roland DAMIANO. *Crisis at St. John's: Strike and Revolution on the Catholic Campus.* New York, 1967.

2417 SHANKMAN, Arnold. "A Temple Is Bombed—Atlanta, 1958." *Am Jew Arch,* XXIII (1971), 125–153.

2418 SHOGAN, Robert, and Tom CRAIG. *The Detroit Race Riot.* See 2055.

2419 SITKOFF, Harvard. "The Detroit Race Riot of 1943." See 2059.

2420 SITKOFF, Harvard. "Racial Militancy and Interracial Violence in the Second World War." See 2061.

2421 WALKER, Daniel. *Rights in Conflict: Convention Week in Chicago, August 25–29, 1968: A Report.* New York, 1968.

2422 WRONE, David R. "The Assassination of John Fitzgerald Kennedy: An Annotated Bibliography." See 31.

E. Religion

2423 AHLSTROM, Sydney E. *A Religious History of the American People.* New Haven, Conn., 1972.†

2424 BAILEY, Kenneth K. *Southern White Protestantism in the Twentieth Century.* New York, 1964.

2425 BELL, Daniel. "Religion in the Sixties." *Soc Res,* XXXVIII (1971), 447–497.

2426 BUETOW, Harold A. *Of Singular Benefit: The Story of Catholic Education in The United States.* New York, 1970.

2427 BURTON, William L. "Protestant America and the Rebirth of Israel." See 628.

2428 CAMPBELL, Ernest, and Thomas F. PETTIGREW. *Christians in Racial Crisis.* See 1956.

2429 CARTER, Paul A. "The Idea of Progress in Most Recent American Protestant Thought, 1930–1960." *Church Hist,* XXXII (1963), 75–89.

2430 CURRY, Lerond. *Protestant-Catholic Relations in America: World War I through Vatican II.* Lexington, Ky., 1972.

2431 DESANTIS, Vincent P. "American Catholics and McCarthyism." See 1481.

2432 EIGHMY, John Lee. *Churches in Cultural Captivity: A History of the Social Attitudes of Southern Baptists.* Knoxville, Tenn., 1972.

2433 ELLIS, John Tracy. *American Catholicism.* Chicago, 1969.[†]

2434 ELLIS, John Tracy, ed. *The Catholic Priest in the United States: Historical Investigations.* Collegeville, Minn., 1971.

2435 FUCHS, Lawrence H. *John F. Kennedy and American Catholicism.* New York, 1967.

2436 GASPER, Louis. *The Fundamentalist Movement.* The Hague, 1963.

2437 GLAZER, Nathan. *American Judaism.* Chicago, 1972.[†]

2438 GLEASON, Philip, ed. *Contemporary Catholicism in the United States.* Notre Dame, Ind., 1969.

2439 GUSTAFSON, James M., ed. "The Sixties: Radical Change in American Religion." *Ann Am Acad Pol Soc Sci,* CCCLXXXVII (1970), 1–140.

2440 GUSTAFSON, Merlin. "Church, State, and the Cold War, 1945–1952." *J Ch State,* VIII (1966), 49–63.

2441 GUSTAFSON, Merlin. "Religion and Politics in the Truman Administration." *Rocky Mt Soc Sci J,* III (October 1966), 125–134.

2442 GUSTAFSON, Merlin. "The Religion of a President." *J Ch State,* X (1968), 379–387.

2443 HARRELL, David Edwin, Jr. *White Sects and Black Men in the Recent South.* See 1991.

2444 HARVEY, Charles E. "Dr. Fifield of Los Angeles' First Congregational Church against the Ecumenical Movement." *S Calif Q,* LIII (1971), 67–82.

2445 HATTERY, John W. "The Presidential Election Campaigns of 1928 and 1960: A Comparison of *The Christian Century* and *America.*" See 1188.

2446 HERSHBERGER, Guy Franklin. *The Mennonite Church in the Second World War.* Scottsdale, Pa., 1951.

2447 HOSTETLER, John A. *Amish Society.* Baltimore, 1963.[†]

2448 HOUGH, Joseph C., Jr. *Black Power and White Protestants.*[†] See 1994.

2449 HUDSON, Winthrop S. *Religion in America: An Historical Account of the Development of American Religious Life.* New York, 1973.[†]

2450 KEIM, Albert N. "John Foster Dulles and the Federal Council of Churches, 1937–1949." See 266.

2451 KRAUSE, P. Allen. "Rabbis and Negro Rights in the South, 1954–1967." See 2004.

2452 LACHMAN, Seymour P. "Barry Goldwater and the 1964 Religious Issue." See 1212.

2453 LACHMAN, Seymour P. "The Cardinal, the Congressmen, and the First Lady." *J Ch State,* VII (1965), 35–66.

2454 LEBRUN, John Leo. "The Role of the Catholic Worker Movement in American Pacifism, 1933–1972." Doctoral dissertation, Case Western Reserve University, 1973.

2455 MCAVOY, Thomas T. *A History of the Catholic Church in the United States.* Notre Dame, Ind., 1969.

2456 MCAVOY, Thomas T., ed. *Roman Catholicism and the American Way of Life.* Notre Dame, Ind., 1960.

2457 MCBETH, Leon. "Southern Baptists and Race since 1947." See 2013.

2458 MCLOUGHLIN, William G. *Billy Graham: Revivalist in a Secular Age.* New York, 1960.

2459 MCLOUGHLIN, William G. *Modern Revivalism.* New York, 1959.

2460 MCLOUGHLIN, William G., and Robert N. BELLAH, eds. *Religion in America.* Boston, 1968.†

2461 MARTY, Martin E. *The New Shape of American Religion.* New York, 1959.

2462 MARTY, Myron A. *Lutherans and Roman Catholicism: The Changing Conflict: 1917–1963.* Notre Dame, Ind., 1968.

2463 MILLER, William D. *A Harsh and Dreadful Love: Dorothy Day and the Catholic Worker Movement.* New York, 1973.†

2464 MOUNGER, Dwyn M. "Racial Attitudes in the Presbyterian Church in the United States, 1944–1954." See 2027.

2465 MUELDER, Walter G. *Methodism and Society in the Twentieth Century.* New York, 1961.

2466 MULDER, John M. "The Moral World of John Foster Dulles: A Presbyterian Layman and International Affairs." See 289.

2467 NELSON, E. Clifford. *Lutheranism in North America,1914–1970.* Minneapolis, Minn., 1972.

2468 O'BRIEN, David J. *The Renewal of American Catholicism.* New York, 1972.

2469 O'BRIEN, F. William. "General Clark's Nomination to the Vatican: American Reaction." *Cath Hist Rev,* XLIV (1959), 421–439.

2470 OLMSTEAD, Clifton E. *History of Religion in the United States.* Englewood Cliffs, N.J., 1960.

2471 ORSER, W. Edward. "Racial Attitudes in Wartime." See 2036.

2472 ORSER, W. Edward. "World War II and the Pacifist Controversy in the Major Protestant Churches." *Am Stud,* XIV (Fall 1973), 5–24.

2473 OSBORNE, William A. *The Segregated Covenant.* See 2037.

2474 PARMELEE, K. Stephen. "The Presbyterian Letter against McCarthyism." See 1506.

2475 PRATT, Henry J. "The Growth of Political Activism in the National Council of Churches." *Rev Pol,* XXXIV (1972), 323–341.

2476 REIMERS, David M. *White Protestantism and the Negro.* See 2046.

2477 ROBB, Dennis Michael. "Specialized Catholic Action in the United States, 1936–1949: Ideology, Leadership, and Organization." Doctoral dissertation, University of Minnesota, 1972.

2478 ROY, Ralph Lord. *Communism and the Churches.* New York, 1960.

2479 SAPPINGTON, Roger E. *Brethren Social Policy, 1908–1958.* Elgin, Ill., 1961.

2480 SCHMIDT, William J. "Samuel McCrea Cavert: American Bridge to the German Church 1945–46." *J Presby Hist,* LI (1973), 3–23.

2481 SCHNEIDER, Herbert W. *Religion in Twentieth Century America.* New York, 1964.†

2482 SHANKMAN, Arnold. "A Temple Is Bombed—Atlanta, 1958." See 2417.

2483 SIEGEL, Lawrence. "Reflections on Neo-Reform in the Central Conference of American Rabbis." *Am Jew Arch,* XX (1968), 63–84.

2484 SMITH, James Ward, ed. *Religion in American Life.* 4 Vols. Princeton, N.J., 1961.†

2485 SMYLIE, James H. "American Religious Bodies, Just War, and Vietnam." See 715.

2486 SMYLIE, James H. "Mackay and McCarthyism, 1953–1954." See 1519.

2487 STRINGFELLOW, William, and Anthony TOWNE. *The Bishop Pike Affair: Scandals of Conscience and Heresy, Relevance and Solemnity in the Contemporary Church.* New York, 1967.

2488 SULLIVAN, Robert R. "The Politics of Altruism: The American Church-State Conflict in the Food-for-Peace Program." *J Ch State,* XI (1969), 47–61.

2489 TAYLOR, Rachel Jean. "The 'Return to Religion' in America after the Second World War: A Study of Religion in American Culture 1945–1955." Doctoral dissertation, University of Minnesota, 1961.

2490 TOY, E. V., Jr. "The National Lay Committee and the National Council of Churches: A Case Study of Protestants in Conflict." *Am Q,* XXI (1969), 190–209.

2491 VINZ, Warren L. "The Politics of Protestant Fundamentalism in the 1950s and 1960s." See 2385.

2492 WATSON, Richard A. "Religion and Politics in Mid-America: Presidential Voting in Missouri, 1928 and 1960." See 1342.

2493 WITTNER, Lawrence S. "MacArthur and the Missionaries: God and Man in Occupied Japan." See 727.

F. Science

2494 AMRINE, Michael. *The Great Decision.* See 881.

2495 BACHER, Robert F. "Robert Oppenheimer (1904–1967)." See 1461.

2496 BAILYN, Bernard, and Donald FLEMING, eds. *The Intellectual Migration.* See 2291.

2497 BATCHELDER, Robert C. *The Irreversible Decision.* See 887.

2498 BAXTER, James P., III. *Scientists against Time.*† See 888.

2499 BUSH, Vannevar. *Pieces of the Action.*† See 901.

2500 CONANT, James B. *My Several Lives.* See 802.

2501 FERMI, Laura. *Illustrious Immigrants.*† See 2307.

2502 GILPIN, Robert. *American Scientists and Nuclear Weapons Policy.*† See 817.

2503 GILPIN, Robert, and Christopher WRIGHT, eds. *Scientists and National Policy-Making.* New York, 1964.

2504 GREENBERG, Daniel S. *The Politics of Pure Science.* New York, 1967.

2505 GROUEFF, Stephane. *Manhattan Project.* See 934.

2506 GROVES, Leslie R. *Now It Can Be Told.* See 935.

2507 LAMONT, Lansing. *Day of Trinity.* See 953.

2508 LASBY, Clarence G. *Operation Paperclip: German Scientists and the Cold War.* New York, 1971.

2509 LAURENCE, William L. *Dawn over Zero.* See 955.

2510 LUDMERER, Kenneth M. *Genetics and American Society: A Historical Appraisal.* Baltimore, 1972.

2511 NIEBURG, H. L. *In the Name of Science.* Chicago, 1966.†

2512 PICCARD, Paul C. "Scientists and Public Policy: Los Alamos, August-November, 1945." *W Pol Q,* XVIII (1965), 251–262.

2513 PRICE, Don K. *Government and Science.* New York, 1954.

2514 PRICE, Don K. *The Scientific Estate.* Cambridge, Mass., 1965.

2515 SCHAFFTER, Dorothy. *The National Science Foundation.* New York, 1969.

2516 SCHOENBERGER, Walter Smith. *Decision of Destiny.* See 994.

2517 SEGRÉ, Emilio. *Enrico Fermi, Physicist.* Chicago, 1970.†

2518 SHERWOOD, Morgan. "Federal Policy for Basic Research: Presidential Staff and the National Science Foundation, 1950–1956." *J Am Hist,* LV (1968), 599–615.

2519 SKOLNIKOFF, Eugene B. *Science, Technology, and American Foreign Policy.*† See 329.

2520 SMITH, Alice Kimball. *A Peril and a Hope: The Scientists' Movement in America: 1945–47.* Cambridge, Mass., 1971.†

2521 STRICKLAND, Donald A. *Scientists in Politics: The Atomic Scientists Movement, 1945–46.* West Lafayette, Ind., 1968.

2522 VAN TASSEL, David D., and Michael G. HALL, eds. *Science and Society in the United States.* Homewood, Ill., 1966.

2523 VON KARMAN, Theodore, with Lee EDSON. *The Wind and Beyond: Theodore von Kármán, Pioneer in Aviation and Pathfinder in Space.* Boston, 1967.

G. Medicine and Health

2524 AUERBACK, Alfred. "The Anti-Mental Health Movement." *Am J Psychia,* CXX (1963), 105–111.

2525 BATEMAN, Herman E. "Observations on President Roosevelt's Health during World War II." *Miss Val Hist Rev,* XLIII (1956), 82–102.

2526 BENISON, Saul, ed. *Tom Rivers: Reflections on a Life in Medicine and Science.* Cambridge, Mass., 1967.

2527 BLAKE, John B., ed. *Safeguarding the Public: Historical Aspects of Medicinal Drug Control.* Baltimore, 1970.

2528 BLOOM, Lynn Z. *Doctor Spock.* See 1106.

2529 BRAND, Jeanne L. "The National Mental Health Act of 1946: A Retrospect." *Bull Hist Med,* XXXIX (1965), 231–245.

2530 BURROW, James G. *AMA: Voice of American Medicine.* Baltimore, 1963.

2531 CARTER, Richard. *Breakthrough: The Saga of Jonas Salk.* New York, 1966.

2532 CHRISTENSON, Cornelia V. *Kinsey: A Biography.* Bloomington, Ind., 1971.

2533 CORNER, George W. *A History of the Rockfeller Institute, 1901–1953: Origins and Growth.* New York, 1964.

2534 DAVIS, Kenneth S. "The Deadly Dust: The Unhappy History of DDT." *Am Her,* XXII (February 1971), 44–47, 92–93.

2535 DULLES, Foster Rhea. *The American Red Cross: A History.* New York, 1950.

2536 FAXON, Nathaniel W. *The Massachusetts General Hospital, 1935–1955.* Cambridge, Mass., 1959.

2537 FISHBEIN, Morris. *Morris Fishbein, M.D.: An Autobiography.* Garden City, N.Y., 1969.

2538 HARRIS, Richard. *The Real Voice.* New York, 1964. Re drug legislation.

2539 JONES, James Howard. "The Origins of the Institute for Sex Research: A History." Doctoral dissertation, Indiana University, 1973.

2540 LERNER, Monroe, and Odin W. ANDERSON. *Health Progress in the United States, 1900–1960.* Chicago, 1963.

2541 MCCLUGGAGE, Robert W. *A History of the American Dental Association: A Century of Health Service.* Chicago, 1959.

2542 MCNEIL, Donald R. *The Fight for Fluoridation.* New York, 1957.

2543 MORGAN, Daniel C., and Samuel E. ALLISON. "The Kefauver Drug Hearings in Perspective." *S W Soc Sci Q,* XLV (1964), 59–68.

2544 POEN, Monte M. "The Truman Administration and National Health Insurance." Doctoral dissertation, University of Missouri, 1967.

2545 POMEROY, Wardell B. *Dr. Kinsey and the Institute for Sex Research.* New York, 1972.†

2546 ROSEN, Samuel. *The Autobiography of Dr. Samuel Rosen.* New York, 1973.

2547 RUSK, Howard A. *A World to Care for: The Autobiography of Howard A. Rusk, M.D.,* New York, 1972.

2548 SIMONSON, David F. "The History of the Department of Health of Chicago, 1947–1956." Doctoral dissertation, University of Chicago, 1962.

2549 SKIDMORE, Max J. *Medicare and the American Rhetoric of Reconciliation.* University, Ala., 1970.

2550 STEELE, Henry. "The Fortunes of Economic Reform Legislation: The Case of the Drug Amendments of 1962." *Am J Econ Socio,* XXV (1966), 39–51.

2551 STEVENS, Rosemary. *American Medicine and the Public Interest.* New Haven, Conn., 1971.†

2552 STRICKLAND, Stephen P. *Politics, Science, and Dread Disease: A Short History of United States Medical Research Policy.* Cambridge, Mass., 1972.

2553 WHITE, Paul Dudley. *My Life and Medicine: An Autobiographical Memoir.* Boston, 1971.

2554 YOUNG, James Harvey. *The Medical Messiahs: A Social History of Health Quackery in Twentieth Century America.* Princeton, N.J., 1967.

H. Space

2555 ALEXANDER, Charles C. "Pathway to the Moon." *Aero Hist,* XIV (1967), 201–209, and XV (1968), 55–61.

2556 ARMSTRONG, Neil, et al. *First on the Moon: A Voyage with Neil Armstrong, Michael Collins, Edwin E. Aldrin, Jr.* Boston, 1970.

2557 EMME, Eugene M. "Historical Perspectives on 'Apollo'." *J Space Rock,* V (1968), 369–382.

2558 EMME, Eugene M., ed. *The History of Rocket Technology.* See 810.

2559 ERTEL, Ivan D. "Apollo." *S W Hist Q,* LXXIII (1969), 213–234.

2560 GREEN, Constance McLaughlin, and Milton LOMASK. *Vanguard: A History.* Washington, 1971.

2561 GRIMWOOD, James M., and Ivan D. ERTEL. "Project Gemini." *S W Hist Q,* LXXI (1968), 392–398.

2562 HALL, R. Cargill. "Origins and Development of the Vanguard and Explorer Satellite Programs." *Airpower Hist,* XI (1964), 101–112.

2563 HARTMAN, Edwin P. *Adventures in Research: A History of Ames Research Center, 1940–1965.* Washington, 1970.

2564 HAYES, E. Nelson. *Trackers of the Skies.* Cambridge, Mass., 1968.†

2565 KENNAN, Erland A., and Edmund H. HARVEY, Jr. *Mission to the Moon: A Critical Examination of NASA and the Space Program.* New York, 1969.

2566 LAPIDUS, Robert D. "Sputnik and Its Repercussions: A Historical Catalyst." *Aero Hist,* XVII (1970), 88–93.

2567 LEWIS, Richard S. *Appointment on the Moon: The Full Story of Americans in Space, from Explorer I to the Lunar Landing and Beyond.* New York, 1969.

2568 LOGSDON, John M. *The Decision to Go to the Moon: Project Apollo and the National Interest.* Cambridge, Mass., 1970.

2569 OATES, Stephen B. "NASA's Manned Spacecraft Center at Houston, Texas." *S W Hist Q,* LXVII (1964), 350–375.

2570 SCHWIEBERT, Ernest G., et al. *A History of the U.S. Air Force Ballistic Missiles.* See 862.

2571 SHELTON, William. *American Space Exploration: The First Decade.* Boston, 1967.

2572 SWENSON, Loyd S., Jr. "The Fertile Crescent: The South's Role in the National Space Program." *S W Hist Q,* LXXI (1968), 377–392.

2573 SWENSON, Loyd S., Jr. "The 'Megamachine' behind the Mercury Spacecraft." *Am Q,* XXI (1969), 210–227.

2574 SWENSON, Loyd S., Jr., et al. *The New Ocean: A History of Project Mercury.* Washington, 1966.

2575 VAN DYKE, Vernon. *Pride and Power: The Rationale of the Space Program.* Urbana, Ill., 1964.

2576 YOUNG, Hugo, et al. *Journey to Tranquility.* Garden City, N.Y., 1970.

I. Education

2577 BAILES, Sue. "Eugene Talmadge and the Board of Regents Controversy." *Ga Hist Q,* LIII (1969), 409–423.

2578 BERUBE, Maurice R., and Marilyn GITTELL, eds. *Confrontation at Ocean Hill-Brownsville: The New York School Strikes of 1968.* New York, 1969.[†]

2579 BOWERS, C. A. *The Progressive Educator and the Depression: The Radical Years.* New York, 1969.[†]

2580 BRUBACHER, John S., and Willis RUDY. *Higher Education in Transition: A History of American Colleges and Universities, 1636–1968.* New York, 1968.

2581 BUETOW, Harold A. *Of Singular Benefit.* See 2426.

2582 BULLOCK, Henry Allen. *A History of Negro Education in the South.*[†] See 2094.

2583 CONANT, James B. *My Several Lives.* See 802.

2584 CREMIN, Lawrence A. *The Transformation of the School: Progressivism in American Education, 1876–1957.* New York, 1961.[†]

2585 DISBROW, Donald W. *Schools for an Urban Society.* Vol. III. *A History of Education in Michigan.* Lansing, Mich., 1968.

2586 DUBERMAN, Martin. *Black Mountain: An Exploration in Community.* New York, 1972.[†]

2587 DUNBAR, Willis F. *The Michigan Record in Higher Education.* Vol. IV. *A History of Education in Michigan.* Detroit, Mich., 1963.

2588 EIDENBERG, Eugene, and Roy D. MOREY. *An Act of Congress: The Legislative Process and the Making of Education Policy.* New York, 1969.[†]

2589 GEIGER, Louis G. *Voluntary Accreditation: A History of the North Central Association, 1945–1970.* Menasha, Wis., 1970.

2590 GRAHAM, Patricia Albjerg. *Progressive Education: From Arcady to Academe. A History of the Progressive Education Association, 1919–1955.* New York, 1967.

2591 HANAWALT, Leslie K. *A Place of Light: The History of Wayne State University.* Detroit, Mich., 1968.

2592 HAZLETT, J. Stephen. "NEA and NCA Involvement in a School Controversy: Chicago, 1944–47." *School Rev,* LXXVIII (1970), 201–227.

2593 HENDRICK, Irving G. "Academic Revolution in California: A History of Events Leading to the Passage and Implementation of the 1961 Fisher Bill on Teacher Certification." *S Calif Q,* XLIX (1967), 127–166, 253–295, 359–406.

2594 HOFSTADTER, Richard, and C. De Witt HARDY. *The Development and Scope of Higher Education in the United States.* New York, 1952.

2595 IVERSON, Robert W. *The Communists and the Schools.* New York, 1959.

2596 JEFFREY, Julie Roy. "Education for Children of the Poor: A Study of the Origins and Implementation of the Elementary and Secondary Education Act of 1965." Doctoral dissertation, Rice University, 1972.

2597 KANDEL, Isaac. *The Impact of War upon American Education.* Chapel Hill, N.C., 1948.

2598 KIZER, George A. "Federal Aid to Education: 1945–1963." *Hist Edu Q*, X (1970), 84–102.

2599 MCCORMICK, Richard P. *Rutgers: A Bicentennial History.* New Brunswick, N.J., 1966.

2600 MACIVER, Robert M. *Academic Freedom in Our Time.* New York, 1955.

2601 MUNCIE, John G. "The Struggle to Obtain Federal Aid for Elementary and Secondary Schools, 1940–1965." Doctoral dissertation, Kent State University, 1969.

2602 OLSON, Keith W. "The G.I. Bill and Higher Education: Success and Surprise." *Am Q*, XXV (1973), 596–610.

2603 OLSON, Keith W. *The G.I. Bill, the Veterans and the Colleges.* Lexington, Ky., 1973.

2604 OLSON, Keith W. "World War II Veterans at the University of Wisconsin." *Wis Mag Hist,* LIII (1969–70), 82–97.

2605 PECKHAM, Howard H. *The Making of the University of Michigan, 1817–1967.* Ann Arbor, Mich., 1967.

2606 RIPPA, S. Alexander. *Education in a Free Society: An American History.* New York, 1971.†

2607 ROGERS, David. *110 Livingston Street: Politics and Bureaucracy in the New York City Schools.* New York, 1968.†

2608 RUDY, Willis. *Schools in an Age of Mass Culture: An Exploration of Selected Themes in the History of Twentieth-Century American Education.* Englewood Cliffs, N.J., 1965.

2609 SILBERMAN, Charles E. *Crisis in the Classroom: The Remaking of American Education.* New York, 1970.†

2610 STADTMAN, Verne A. *The University of California 1868–1968.* New York, 1970.

2611 SZASZ, Margaret Ann Connell. "American Indian Education, 1930–1970, From the Meriam Report to the Kennedy Report." See 2216.

2612 TUTTLE, William M., Jr. "Higher Education and the Federal Government: The Lean Years, 1940–1942." *Record,* LXXI (1969), 297–312.

2613 TUTTLE, William M., Jr. "Higher Education and the Federal Government: The Triumph, 1942–1945." *Record,* LXXI (1970), 485–499.

2614 WEAVER, Samuel Horton. "The Truman Administration and Federal Aid to Education." Doctoral dissertation, American University, 1972.

2615 WIGGINS, Sam P. *Higher Education in the South.* Berkeley, Cal., 1966.†

2616 ZITRON, Celia Lewis. *The New York City Teachers Union 1916–1964.* See 1866.

J. Journalism

2617 ABELL, Tyler, ed. *Drew Pearson: Diaries 1949–1959.* New York, 1974.

2618 ARONSON, James. *The Press and the Cold War.* Indianapolis, Ind., 1970.†

2619 BISHOP, Robert L., and La Mar S. MACKAY. "Mysterious Silence, Lyrical Scream: Government Information in World War II." *Jour M,* XIX (1971).

2620 BLIVEN, Bruce. *Five Million Words Later: An Autobiography.* New York, 1970.

2621 BURLINGAME, Roger. *Don't Let Them Scare You: The Life and Times of Elmer Davis.* Philadelphia, 1961.

2622 CATLEDGE, Turner. *My Life and The Times.* New York, 1971.

2623 CONRAD, Will C., *et al. The Milwaukee Journal: The First Eighty Years.* Madison, Wis., 1964.

2624 ELSON, Robert T. *The World of Time Inc.: The Intimate History of a Publishing Enterprise 1941–1960.* New York, 1973.

2625 EMERY, Edwin. *The Press and America: An Interpretive History of the Mass Media.* Englewood Cliffs, N.J., 1972.

2626 EPSTEIN, Edward Jay. *News from Nowhere: Television and the News.* New York, 1973.

2627 FARRAR, Ronald T. *Reluctant Servant: The Story of Charles G. Ross.* Columbia, Mo., 1969.

2628 FINKLE, Lee. "Forum for Protest: The Black Press during World War II." See 2108.

2629 FRIEDRICH, Otto. *Decline and Fall.* New York, 1970. The *Saturday Evening Post.*

2630 GLESSING, Robert J. *The Underground Press in America.* Bloomington, Ind., 1970.†

2631 HIRSCH, Paul M. "An Analysis of *Ebony*: The Magazine and Its Readers." See 2120.

2632 JOHNSON, Michael L. *The New Journalism: The Underground Press, the Artists of Nonfiction, and Changes in the Established Media.* Lawrence, Kans., 1971.†

2633 KENDRICK, Alexander. *Prime Time: The Life of Edward R. Murrow.* Boston, 1969.†

2634 KOBRE, Sidney. *Modern American Journalism.* Tallahassee, Fla., 1959.

2635 KROCK, Arthur. *Memoirs: Sixty Years on the Firing Line.* New York, 1968.†

2636 LAWRENCE, Bill. *Six Presidents, Too Many Wars.* New York, 1972.

2637 LEE, Richard W. *Politics and the Press.* Washington, 1970.

2638 LOGUE, Cal M. "Ralph McGill: Convictions of a Southern Editor." *Jour Q,* XLV (1968), 647–652.

2639 LORENZ, A. L., Jr. "Truman and the Press Conference." See 1233.

2640 LYONS, Louis M. *Newspaper Story: One Hundred Years of The Boston Globe.* Cambridge, Mass., 1971.

2641 MARTIN, Harold H. *Ralph McGill, Reporter.* Boston, 1973.

2642 MATTHEWS, Herbert L. *A World in Revolution: A Newspaperman's Memoir.* New York, 1971.

2643 MAULDIN, Bill. *The Brass Ring.* New York. 1971.† G.I. cartoonist of World War II.

2644 MOTT, Frank Luther. *American Journalism, A History: 1690–1960.* New York, 1962.

2645 PEMBER, Don R. "The Smith Act as a Restraint on the Press." *Jour M,* X (1969).

2646 PETERSON, Theodore. *Magazines in the Twentieth Century.* Urbana, Ill., 1964.

2647 PETERSON, Theodore. "The Role of the Minority Magazine." *Ant Rev,* XXIII (1963), 57–71.

2648 PILAT, Oliver. *Drew Pearson: An Unauthorized Biography.* New York, 1973.†

2649 POLLARD, James E. "The Kennedy Administration and the Press." See 1282.

2650 POLLARD, James E. *The Presidents and the Press.* See 1283.

2651 ROBERTS, Chalmers M. *First Rough Draft: A Journalist's Journal of Our Times.* New York, 1973.

2652 ROOT, Robert, and Christine V. ROOT. "Magazines in the United States: Dying or Thriving?" *Jour Q,* XLI (1964), 15–22.

2653 RUTLAND, Robert A. *The Newsmongers: Journalism in the Life of the Nation, 1690–1972.* New York, 1973.

2654 SCHAPSMEIER, Edward L., and Frederick H. SCHAPSMEIER. *Walter Lippmann: Philosopher-Journalist.* Washington,1969.

2655 SCHWARZLOSE, Richard A. "Trends in U.S. Newspapers' Wire Service Resources, 1934–66." *Jour Q,* XLIII (1966), 627–638.

2656 STEGNER, Wallace. *The Uneasy Chair: A Biography of Bernard De Voto.* Garden City, N.Y., 1974.

2657 STEVENS, John D. "From behind Barbed Wire: Freedom of the Press in World War II Japanese Centers." See 2215.

2658 SWANBERG, W. A. *Luce and His Empire.* New York, 1972.†

2659 TALESE, Gay. *The Kingdom and the Power.* New York, 1969.† Inside the *New York Times.*

2660 WOLSELEY, Roland E. *The Black Press, U.S.A.*† See 2174.

2661 WOOD, James Playsted. *Magazines in the United States.* New York, 1971.

K. Literature

2662 ALDRIDGE, John W. *After the Lost Generation: A Critical Study of the Writers of Two Wars.* New York, 1958.

2663 BAKER, Carlos. *Ernest Hemingway: A Life Story.* New York, 1969.†

2664 BLOTNER, Joseph. *Faulkner: A Biography.* 2 Vols. New York, 1974.

2665 BLOTNER, Joseph. *The Modern American Political Novel, 1900–1960.* Austin, Tex., 1966.

2666 BLUMBERG, Paul. "Sociology and Social Literature: Work Alienation in the Plays of Arthur Miller." *Am Q,* XXI (1969), 291–310.

2667 BONE, Robert. *The Negro Novel in America.*† See 2089.

2668 BRADBURY, John M. *Renaissance in the South: A Critical History of the Literature, 1920–1960.* Chapel Hill, N.C., 1963.

2669 CHARNEY, Maurice. "James Baldwin's Quarrel with Richard Wright." See 2096.

2670 CHARTERS, Ann. *Kerouac.* San Francisco, 1973.†

2671 COOK, Mercer, and Stephen E. HENDERSON. *The Militant Black Writer in Africa and the United States.*† See 2098.

2672 CORRIGAN, Robert A. "Ezra Pound and the Bollingen Prize Controversy." *Midcon Am Stud J,* VIII (Fall 1967), 43–57.

2673 CORRIGAN, Robert A. *"What's My Line:* Bennett Cerf, Ezra Pound and the American Poet." *Am Q,* XXIV (1972), 101–113.

2674 ECKMAN, Fern M. *The Furious Passage of James Baldwin.*† See 2104.

2675 EISINGER, Chester E. *Fiction of the Forties.* Chicago, 1963.†

2676 FRENCH, Michael R. "The American Novel in the Sixties." *Mid W Q,* IX (1968), 365–379.

2677 GALLOWAY, David D. *The Absurd Hero in American Fiction: Updike, Styron, Bellow, Salinger.* Austin, Tex., 1966.

2678 GUTTMANN, Allen. *The Jewish Writer in America.* See 2193.

2679 HARPER, Howard M., Jr. *Desperate Faith: A Study of Bellow, Salinger, Mailer, Baldwin, and Updike.* Chapel Hill, N.C., 1967.†

2680 HASSAN, Ihab. *Radical Innocence: Studies in the Contemporary American Novel.* Princeton, N.J., 1961.†

2681 HILL, Herbert, ed. *Anger, and Beyond.* See 2119.

2682 HOFFMAN, Frederick J. *The Art of Southern Fiction: A Study of Some Modern Novelists.* Carbondale, Ill., 1967.

2683 HOFFMAN, Frederick J. *The Modern Novel in America.* Chicago, 1963.†

2684 HOTCHNER, A. E. *Papa Hemingway: A Personal Memoir.* New York, 1966.†

2685 ISAACS, Harold R. "Five Writers and Their Ancestors." See 2122.

2686 KAZIN, Alfred. *Bright Book of Life: American Novelists and Storytellers from Hemingway to Mailer.* Boston, 1973.

2687 LINICK, Anthony. "A History of the American Literary *Avant-garde* since World War II." Doctoral dissertation, University of California at Los Angeles, 1965.

2688 LITTLEJOHN, David. *Black on White.*† See 2133.

2689 MARGOLIES, Edward. *Native Sons.*† See 2137.

2690 MILLER, Wayne Charles. *An Armed America: Its Face in Fiction: A History of the American Military Novel.* New York, 1970.

2691 MILNE, Gordon. *The American Political Novel.* Norman, Okla., 1966.†

2692 NELSON, Harland S. "Steinbeck's Politics Then and Now." *Ant Rev,* XXVII (1967), 118–133.

2693 RIDEOUT, Walter B. *The Radical Novel in the United States, 1900–1954.* Cambridge, Mass., 1956.†

2694 RUBIN, Louis D., Jr. *The Faraway Country: Writers of the Modern South.* Seattle, Wash., 1963.†

2695 SANDERS, Clinton R. "The Portrayal of War and the Fighting Man in Novels of the Vietnam War." *J Pop Cult,* III (1969), 553–564.

2696 SCHORER, Mark. *Sinclair Lewis: An American Life.* New York, 1961.

2697 WALDMEIR, Joseph J. *American Novels of the Second World War.* The Hague, 1969.

2698 WATKINS, Floyd C. *The Death of Art: Black and White in the Recent Southern Novel.* Athens, Ga., 1970.

2699 WAY, Brian. "Formal Experiment and Social Discontent: Joseph Heller's 'Catch-22.'" *J Am Stud,* II (1968), 253–270.

2700 WEBB, Constance. *Richard Wright.* See 2169.

L. Art and Architecture

2701 ACKERMAN, James S. "The Demise of the Avant Garde: Notes on the Sociology of Recent American Art." *Com Stud Soc Hist,* XI (1969), 371–384.

2702 BAIGELL, Matthew. "American Painting: On Space and Time in the Early 1960's." *Art J,* XXVIII (1969), 368–374, 387, 401.

2703 BAUR, John I. H. *Revolution and Tradition in Modern American Art.* Cambridge, Mass., 1958.

2704 BURCHARD, John, and Albert BUSH-BROWN. *The Architecture of America: A Social and Cultural History.* Boston, 1961.†

2705 BUSH, Martin H. *Doris Caesar.* Syracuse, N.Y., 1970.

2706 CONDIT, Carl W. *American Building Art: The Twentieth Century.* New York, 1961.

2707 CONDIT, Carl W. *American Building: Materials and Techniques from the First Colonial Settlements to the Present.* Chicago, 1968.†

2708 ECHOLS, Paul Clinton. "The Development of Shell Architecture in the United States, 1932–1962: An Examination of the Transfer of a Structural Idea." *S Atl Q,* LXVII (1968), 203–242.

2709 GREEN, Samuel M. *American Art: A Historical Survey.* New York, 1966.

2710 HUNTER, Sam. *Modern American Painting and Sculpture.* New York, 1959.

2711 LARKIN, Oliver. *Art and Life in America.* New York, 1960.

2712 MENDELOWITZ, Daniel M. *A History of American Art.* New York, 1970.

2713 ROSE, Barbara. *American Art since 1900: A Critical History.* New York, 1967.†

2714 ROSENBERG, Harold. *The Anxious Object: Art Today and Its Audience.* New York, 1964.†

2715 SCHULZE, Franz. "The New Chicago Architecture." *Art Am,* LVI (1968), 60–71.

2716 TOMKINS, Calvin. *Merchants and Masterpieces: The Story of the Metropolitan Museum of Art.* New York, 1970.

2717 TWOMBLY, Robert C. *Frank Lloyd Wright: An Interpretive Biography.* New York, 1973.†

2718 WHITEHILL, Walter Muir. *Museum of Fine Arts, Boston: A Centennial History.* 2 Vols. Cambridge, Mass., 1970.

M. Music

2719 BELZ, Carl I. "Popular Music and the Folk Tradition." *J Am Folk*, LXXX (1967), 130–142.

2720 BELZ, Carl. *The Story of Rock.* New York, 1969.†

2721 CHASE, Gilbert. *America's Music: From the Pilgrims to the Present.* New York, 1955.

2722 CHENOWETH, Lawrence. "The Rhetoric of Hope and Despair: A Study of the Jimi Hendrix Experience and The Jefferson Airplane." *Am Q*, XXIII (1971), 25–45.

2723 DENISOFF, R. Serge. "The Evolution of Pop Music Broadcasting: 1920–1972." *Pop Mus Soc*, II (1973), 202–226.

2724 DENISOFF, R. Serge. "Folk Music and the American Left: A Generational-Ideological Comparison." *Brit J Soc*, XX (1969), 427–442.

2725 DENISOFF, R. Serge. *Great Day Coming: Folk Music and the American Left.* Urbana, Ill., 1971.†

2726 DENISOFF, R. Serge. "Protest Songs: Those on the Top Forty and Those of the Streets." *Am Q*, XXII (1970), 805–823.

2727 FORD, Larry. "Geographical Factors in the Origin, Evolution, and Diffusion of Rock and Roll Music." *J Geog*, LXX (1971), 455–464.

2728 GILLETT, Charlie. *The Sound of the City: The Rise of Rock and Roll.* New York, 1970.†

2729 HASBANY, Richard. "Bromidic Parables: The American Musical Theatre during the Second World War." *J Pop Cult*, IV (1973), 642–665.

2730 HITCHCOCK, H. Wiley. *Music in the United States: A Historical Introduction.* Englewood Cliffs, N.J., 1969.†

2731 HOWARD, John Tasker. *Our American Music: A Comprehensive History from 1620 to the Present.* New York, 1965.

2732 HOWARD, John Tasker, and George Kent BELLOWS. *A Short History of Music in America.* New York, 1967.†

2733 KEIL, Charles. *Urban Blues.*† See 2125.

2734 LUND, Jens, and R. Serge DENISOFF. "The Folk Music Revival and the Counter Culture: Contributions and Contradictions." *J Am Folk*, LXXXIV (1971), 394–405.

2735 MACDONALD, J. Frederick. " 'Hot Jazz,' the Jitterbug, and Misunderstanding: The Generation Gap in Swing 1935–1945." *Pop Mus Soc*, II (1972), 43–55.

2736 MOONEY, H. F. "Popular Music since the 1920s: The Significance of Shifting Taste." *Am Q*, XX (1968), 67–85.

2737 PETERSON, Frank Ross. "Protest Songs for Peace and Freedom: People's Songs and the 1948 Progressives." *Rocky Mt Soc Sci J*, IX (January 1972), 1–10.

2738 RODNITZKY, Jerome L. "The New Revivalism: American Protest Songs, 1945–1968." *S Atl Q*, LXX (1971), 13–21.

2739 RODNITZKY, Jerome L. "Popular Music as a Radical Influence, 1945–1970." *Essays on Radicalism in Contemporary America.* Ed. Leon Borden Blair. Austin, Tex., 1972.

2740 ROSENBERG, Neil V. "From Sound to Style: The Emergence of Bluegrass." *J Am Folk,* LXXX (1967), 143–150.

2741 ROUT, Leslie B., Jr. "Some Post-War Developments in Jazz." *Midcon Am Stud J,* IX (Fall 1968), 27–50.

2742 SABLOSKY, Irving L. *American Music.* Chicago, 1969.†

2743 THOMSON, Virgil. *American Music since 1910.* New York, 1971.†

N. Film, Theater, Mass Media

2744 BARNOUW, Erik. *The Golden Web.* Vol. II. *A History of Broadcasting in the United States.* New York, 1968.

2745 BARNOUW, Erik. *The Image Empire.* Vol. III. *A History of Broadcasting in the United States.* New York, 1970.

2746 BENTLEY, Eric. *Are You Now or Have You Ever Been?*† See 1464.

2747 BOGART, Leo. *The Age of Television: A Study of Viewing Habits and the Impact of Television on American Life.* New York, 1958.

2748 CAPRA, Frank. *The Name above the Title: An Autobiography.* New York, 1971.

2749 CARMEN, Ira H. *Movies, Censorship, and the Law.* Ann Arbor, Mich., 1966.

2750 CHESTER, Edward W. *Radio, Television and American Politics.*† See 1123.

2751 COLLE, Royal D. "Negro Image in the Mass Media: A Case Study in Social Change." See 1960.

2752 CRIPPS, Thomas R. "The Death of Rastus: Negroes in American Films since 1945." See 1963.

2753 FRIENDLY, Fred W. *Due to Circumstances beyond Our Control . . .* New York, 1967.†

2754 GILBERT, Robert E. *Television and Presidential Politics.* See 1173.

2755 HIGHAM, Charles. *Hollywood at Sunset.* New York, 1972.

2756 HIGHAM, Charles, and Joel GREENBERG. *Hollywood in the Forties.* New York, 1968.†

2757 KANFER, Stefan. *A Journal of the Plague Years.* See 1495.

2758 LANG, Kurt, and Gladys Engel LANG. *Politics and Television.*† See 1214.

2759 LYONS, Eugene. *David Sarnoff: A Biography.* New York, 1966.

2760 MCCLURE, Arthur F. "Hollywood at War: The American Motion Picture and World War II." *J Pop Film,* I (1972), 123–135.

2761 MICKELSON, Sig. *The Electric Mirror.* See 1257.

2762 POGGI, Jack. *Theater in America: The Impact of Economic Forces, 1870–1967.* Ithaca, N.Y., 1968.

2763 RANDALL, Richard S. *Censorship of the Movies: The Social and Political Control of a Mass Medium.* Madison, Wis., 1968.†

SOCIETY, CULTURE, THOUGHT

2764 SCHICKEL, Richard. *The Disney Version: The Life, Times, Art and Commerce of Walt Disney.* New York, 1968.†

2765 SMALL, Melvin. "Buffoons and Brave Hearts: Hollywood Portrays the Russians, 1939–1944." *Calif Hist Soc Q,* LII (1973), 326–337.

2766 TAUBMAN, Howard. *The Making of the American Theatre.* New York, 1965.

2767 TYLER, Parker. "An American Theater Motif: The Psychodrama." *Am Q,* XV (1963), 140–151.

2768 VAUGHN, Robert. *Only Victims.* See 1530.

2769 WILSON, Garff B. *Three Hundred Years of American Drama and Theatre: From 'Ye Bear and Ye Cubb' to 'Hair.'* Englewood Cliffs, N.J., 1973.

INDEX

INDEX

INDEX

INDEX

INDEX

INDEX

INDEX

INDEX

INDEX

INDEX

INDEX

INDEX

INDEX

NOTES